A Reader's Guide to
Contemporary Feminist Literary Criticism

To Dan, as always

A Reader's Guide to Contemporary Feminist Literary Criticism

Maggie Humm
Co-ordinator of Women's Studies
University of East London

HARVESTER
WHEATSHEAF

New York   London   Toronto   Sydney   Tokyo   Singapore

First published 1994 by
Harvester Wheatsheaf
Campus 400, Maylands Avenue
Hemel Hempstead
Hertfordshire,
HP2 7EZ
A division of
Simon & Schuster International Group

Typeset in 10pt Palatino
by Photoprint, Torquay, Devon

Printed and bound in Great Britain by Biddles Ltd,
Guildford and King's Lynn

British Library Cataloguing in Publication Data

A catalogue record for this book is available from
the British Library

ISBN 0 7450 1194 2 (pbk)

2   3   4   5   98   97   96   95

Contents

Preface

During the last decades feminist criticism has transformed education, publishing, and the media as well as everyday language. Similarly, literary studies is shot through with feminist themes. Clearly no straight line can be drawn between feminist criticism and feminist literary criticism but neither can it simply be assumed that these are identical. In general, feminist criticism addresses social ideologies and practices while feminist *literary* criticism attends to how those ideologies and practices shape literary texts. Yet both focus on gender as a fundamental category of analysis. Both are preoccupied with theories and feminist praxis. It is impossible to write feminist literary criticism in the 1990s untouched by feminist thinking in other disciplines and feminist thinking outside the academy. So that while feminist literary criticism's attention is to literary topics – language/discourse, textuality, authors – feminist literary critics take the view that gendered readings necessitate a wider, cultural politics of race, sex and other differences.[1]

Throughout the world feminist literary criticism has changed the way we teach, write and think about literature. The history of this process in the West is now recorded but *international* feminist literary criticism in general is not. Given the ways in which feminists like to work – that is, collectively – it is odd that most accounts of feminist literary criticism describe Anglo-American and French feminisms and ignore exciting work in India, Africa and elsewhere.

Yet everyone who studies literature, whether in the East or the West, asks the same basic questions: what should I be looking for in a book? What can help me understand how literary representations and ideas function? In addition, feminist literary critics are concerned with the ways in which literary texts have the power to produce gender representations at odds with women's experiences. By showing how women can deconstruct, or pull apart, patriarchal writing and its conceptual frameworks, feminist literary criticism, like feminist politics, understands 'the *political* implications of *analytic* strategies and principles'.[2] Black critics rightly argue that by focusing mainly on white Anglo-American and French thought, Western feminist literary criticism to date often ignores the multiple and exciting ideas and techniques that critics elsewhere currently offer.

This book tries to portray part of that wider world which has sprung into life since the late 1960s. Although by no means a full portrait, this *Reader's Guide* is an overview of contemporary international feminist literary criticism. I hope to take the reader through the important critical work of the past decades, giving clear pointers to those ideas and techniques which can help readers create their own critical responses. In order to create a further dialogue with that diverse audience I include guides both to the basic texts and to further reading.

The *Reader's Guide* began surreptitiously. Jackie Jones of Harvester Wheatsheaf asked me to consider updating *Feminist Criticism: Women as Contemporary Critics*, perhaps to amalgamate the book with my *Annotated Critical Bibliography of Feminist Criticism*. Jackie cleverly eased me into the task by suggesting 'only an additional chapter'. In the mid-1980s the binary opposition between Anglo-American and French feminisms structured a number of feminist critiques, not just my own. In the rear mirror of the mid-1990s this opposition looks very ethnocentric. By 1994 new debates, new creations and most importantly a new international politics mean that feminist literary criticism has radically changed. The 'additional chapter' soon became a new book.

Running throughout the *Reader's Guide* then are two concerns: to acknowledge as far as I can the multiple differences within feminist literary criticism; and to show how this criticism continually changes our and its own ways of reading.

NOTES

1. I shall, however, have to interchange the term 'feminist literary criticism' with 'feminist criticism' to avoid repetition.
2. Mohanty, C.T. (1984) 'Under Western Eyes: Feminist Scholarship and Colonial Discourses', *Boundary* 2 (12:3/13:1) Spring/Fall.

Acknowledgements

A Reader's Guide draws on some material first presented in *Feminist Criticism* while hopefully it reaches out much further. The *Guide* owes a great deal to the expert and feminist thinking of Jackie Jones; to inspiring conversations with Cheris Kramarae and Dale Spender, Jennifer FitzGerald and other feminist critics too numerous to list; to my son's less patient but always stimulating criticism; to my knowledgeable feminist colleagues and students at the University of East London; to my careful Harvester Wheatsheaf readers; and, as always, to the immaculate work of Joyce Lock.

Introduction
Feminist criticism: the 1960s to the 1990s

Once upon a time, and a very sad time it was, though it wasn't in my time, nor in your time, nor in any real time, there was a man who told secrets to other men. And the man was a Critic King and the other men were his vassals. And no woman ever heard the secrets. And no woman ever read the books which the secrets were about. But the king had a daughter. And, one day, the daughter read the books and heard the secrets. And the daughter saw that the secrets were not real secrets and the books were not real books. And she was very angry. So she talked to other women. Through nights and days and dreams and waking the women talked together. And the king and his vassals grew old and died. The women looked at each other's golden faces and heard each other's golden voices. And they lived long together in the land, whole again, which they called Feminist Criticism.

The actual history of feminist criticism has fortunately been of a much quicker gestation. In 'Defining Feminism' Karen Offen (1988) states that 'feminism' began to be used widely in Europe as a synonym for women's emancipation only in the 1880s. For example, the women's suffrage advocate Hubertine Auclert first described herself as feminist in her periodical *La Citoyenne* from 1882 and the first self-proclaimed 'feminist' congress in Paris was sponsored in May 1892 by Eugenie Potonie-Pierre and the women's group Solidarité. By 1894/95 the term had crossed the Channel to Britain.

1

Feminist literary criticism has developed in tandem with the women's movement. Although feminist criticism, like women's writing, might be said to begin with *Inanna*, a text written 2,000 years before the Bible, before Homer – about the first hanged goddess who attacked sexual 'discourse' – feminist criticism did not become recognised as representative of intellectual endeavour in the academy until second-wave feminism. Indeed, Jane Gallop dates this moment of visibility much later as the title of her book, *Around 1981*, implies. Yet Virginia Woolf's *A Room of One's Own* could be said to be the first modern work of feminist criticism both in its form – its liberating, fluid autobiographical openness – and in its content: it is a serious address to the social, literary and cultural aspects of female difference.

CRITICAL HISTORY

Twentieth-century feminist criticism, from the first, developed in a double if not multiple mode. One of the main achievements of Virginia Woolf was to show that literature read with a feminist eye involves a double perspective. First, she showed that since women's social reality, like men's social reality, is shaped by gender, the representation of female experience in literary form is gendered. Second, she showed that representations of women in literature, while not depicting innate characteristics of actual women, might disrupt the traditional symbolic order or language system of patriarchy. Here I am thinking of the famous disagreement between Woolf and her father, the literary critic Leslie Stephen, about Charlotte Brontë's 'hysteria'. Woolf argues that Brontë's subversion of syntactical order, her incomplete sentences and emotional outpourings are a sign of the isolation of writing women and a lack of cultural space, while her father in his essays rounded on Brontë's 'hysteria' as a sign of feminine instability (see Humm, 1986).

It is not surprising, therefore, that in that pioneering text of contemporary feminism, *Sexual Politics* (1970), Kate Millett chose to attack patriarchy through literary criticism. To question the representation of a raped woman in literature is to demystify patriarchal representations and hence subvert the role played by rape, and the fear of rape, in the power that men have over women. The growth of the feminist movement itself is inseparable from feminist criticism. Women become feminists by becoming conscious of, and criticising, the power of symbolic misrepresentations of women. To understand the ways in which we acquire a gender *through* language, and to perceive the role played by language in creating our subjectivities and our oppressions give feminist literary criticism an important task.

A long-term trajectory would trace the exaggerated role that literature, and hence literary criticism, have in national cultures. Criticism has always been part of the public expression of cultural power, whether in education or in periodicals. In England the teaching of criticism provided a viable alternative to the decline of theology in the nineteenth century. The opportunities for professional writers were greatly increased by the expansion of Victorian periodicals in the mid-nineteenth century. Yet that very expansion, by securing for periodicals the role of interpreting contemporary thought, forced academic criticism into becoming a specialism. Critical essays satisfied the ideological needs of Victorian capitalism. Their imagery provided the decorative outlines of patriarchal ideology. Matthew Arnold gave criticism an institutional base by advocating its incorporation into the curricula of universities and schools.

The construction of 'English' in higher education and in government reports became in the twentieth century a form of professional certification, with state schools using English as the compulsory hoop through which students had to jump. Criticism or 'English', did not deviate, in other words, from the original Greek meaning of *krino*, 'to judge'. The Victorian practice of Matthew Arnold continued in the twentieth century through the writings of T. S. Eliot, Cleanth Brooks and others, keeping intact the concept of criticism as judicial.

English as a compulsory subject will always be associated with power; and criticism, its 'weapon', will always involve the power to name, what to choose and who to exclude. The critical academy is both an institution controlling employment and regulating cultural productions as well as a place where productions are studied with special languages. Since what has been excluded, along with dissenters, is any concept of woman as an independent professional, then clearly feminists, in order to appropriate the land and the weapons, had to make literary criticism an integral part of feminist struggle.

ISSUES AND DEFINITIONS

The questions which feminist criticism addresses are of major importance: do we have the power to define a feminist agenda and aesthetic? Is it possible to analyse and deconstruct gendered representations, which are themselves problematic, without setting up an alternative canon of women writers? Or do we need both activities? How can we avoid hierarchies of 'high' and 'low' writing which are part of patriarchal literary practice? Crucially, how can we avoid binaries of First and Third Worlds, and avoid being ethnocentric? In traditional criticism there is too often a systematic and pervasive denigration of women as a critical trope: for example, David Lodge in the *Language of Fiction* claims that the novelist's medium, language, is never virgin: words come to the writer already violated by other men.

So what is, or could be, feminist criticism? Many critics writing what they call 'feminist criticism' seem to share three basic assumptions. The first is that gender is constructed through language and is visible in writing style; and style, therefore, must represent the articulation of ideologies of gender. But the definition of ideology contains the notion of contradiction. This is because ideology is what we construct to explain to ourselves our experience and the experience of others. Ideology is our way of coping with the contradictions of experience. Inevitably the ideologies of women are likely to encompass more contradictions than the ideologies of men since women are provided with many more confusing images of themselves than are men. But when one turns to feminist psychoanalysis one learns that the instability of the feminine, which Freud reveals as his great fear in 'Female Sexuality', can be a source of woman's power. By giving a systematic account of the interaction between gender and literary form, feminist criticism opens up questions about language to include general issues of power and sexual divisions.

The second major assumption is that there are sex-related writing strategies. Virginia Woolf's now famous comment about

Dorothy Richardson was that Richardson had invented or developed 'a sentence which we might call the psychological sentence of the feminine gender'. Of course, how women wrote is how they were allowed to write. In the nineteenth century the socialisation and subordination of middle-class women limited their access to, and means of, expression, as much as did the exclusion of working-class women from shipbuilding or public utilities as a means of employment. But researchers in linguistics, from Robin Lakoff (1975) onwards, have pointed out that men and women do *use* language in different ways. They often have different vocabularies and use their vocabularies in different kinds of sentences.

The last assumption of feminist criticism is that the tradition of literary criticism, like the economic and social traditions of which it is a part, uses masculine norms to exclude or undervalue women's writing and scholarship. In 1929 Virginia Woolf found when she went to the British Museum that professors and sociologists, journalists and novelists, 'men who had no qualification save that they were not women' had written hundreds of books describing women. The page was headed quite simply, WOMEN AND POVERTY, in block letters; but what followed was something like this:

Condition in Middle Ages of,
Habits in the Fiji Islands of,
Worshipped as goddesses by,
Weaker in moral sense than,

Woolf (1929) p. 25

Contemporary criticism also betrays a masculine frame of reference. Feminist critics question the appropriateness of applying to women's modes the traditional generic classifications based on texts written by men. Terms like 'intuitive' are applied to devalue women's judgements; and aesthetic criteria which overvalue the 'alienation', say, or the 'existentialism' of the bourgeois artist give preference to a masculine view of the world.

Present-day feminists have learned a good deal about literary meaning from masculine critiques and from alternative critical approaches proposed by male critics. For example, the post-war American critics Wayne C. Booth and Walter Gibson wrote within the confines of a formalist position, one which assumes the uniqueness of the literary work. Semiotic and structuralist approaches in the work of the French critics Genette and Riffaterre developed the idea of the reader in the text and took the literary activity to be not about assigning meaning as such but about codes that make the text readable. Their analysis remains, however, firmly committed to the notion of textual objectivity. The more phenomenological approach of Wolfgang Iser paid attention to the reader actively producing textual meaning.

Yet, although Continental theories have been of use to both feminist and non-feminist critics, in 'The Interpreter's Self' Walter Michaels makes a revealing suggestion. American males, Michaels argues, from the American pragmatist C. S. Peirce on, are frightened by the notion of an anarchist self. Women, on the other hand, as Hélène Cixous claims in 'The Laugh of the Medusa', are anarchic. Feminine texts pulsate with a rhetoric of rebellion and rupture.

Clearly it would be wrong to ignore the influences on feminist criticism of particular critics, such as Ricoeur, particular texts, such as Barthes' *S/Z*, and particular stances, such as Geoffrey Hartman's definition of reading as a 'dialogic' and creative act. But there is a way in which the reader who emerges from those texts has (for Booth and Gibson) no privileged status. He (and it is a 'he') takes a very abstract approach to reading (for Iser and Ricoeur). And, for psychoanalytic critics such as Holland, he is the totally unified self dear to American ego psychology.

Again, recent theories of reading by critics like David Bleich and Stanley Fish seem close to feminist criticism with their attractive descriptions of communities of interpreters engaged in a conscious process of negotiation. Bleich and Fish argue, in other words, that the art of criticism or reading is a direct result of the interpretative strategies we possess, not something necessarily in the text itself. This is attractive because it gets us away from a fixed hierarchy of texts – James Joyce 'good'/ Georgette Heyer 'bad' – but can become more paternal by replacing a hierarchy of texts with a hierarchy of readers.

Most reader-response criticism carries with it the implicit assumption of a 'free' reader set apart from external realities engaged in individualistic self-development. Clearly this is a reader without children or supermarket shopping. In 'Is There a Text in This Class?' Stanley Fish is horrifically paternalistic in the way in which he deliberately plays with, and puns on, the insecurity of a young female student. Fish prefers the kind of literature which can render readers insecure. Students in Fish's classes have to discover what is idiosyncratic in their own responses.

In Britain, Terry Eagleton, more than most critics, has addressed feminist criticism. It is the 'second' of his three approaches to the rape of Clarissa. Richardson's *Clarissa*, Eagleton argues, both represents and describes sexual politics since its epistolary form matches the sexual relations between Lovelace and Clarissa. But Eagleton does not *centralise* gender in his critique. *Clarissa*, it seems to me, is not only about a woman raped and excluded from speech but also about a woman who, like many women, excludes *herself* from speech. Eagleton ignores features like the ways in which Clarissa mutilates her own discourse as she 'mutilates' her own body in an anorexic refusal to eat. These are features crucial to a feminist critique. In *Feminist Literary Studies* K. K. Ruthven claims to take feminism seriously as a critical practice. Along with some contemporary feminists, Ruthven ignores Black and lesbian writing, but he was unusual in depoliticising feminist criticism by turning it simply into another pedagogical skill.

AIMS OF FEMINIST CRITICISM

Feminist criticism addresses four issues in literary criticism. First, the issue of a masculine literary history is addressed by re-examining male texts, noting their patriarchal assumptions and showing the way women in these texts are often represented according to prevailing social, cultural and ideological norms. This criticism is thematic, focusing on women's oppression as a theme in literature and assuming a woman reader to be a consumer of male-produced works. Second, the invisibility of women writers has been addressed. Feminist critics have charted a new literary history which gives full weight to the texts of neglected women, and women's oral culture, previously regarded as extra-literary.

Third, feminist criticism confronts the problem of the 'feminist reader' by offering readers new methods and a fresh critical practice. Such practice focuses on those techniques of significa-tion, such as the mirroring of mothers and daughters or textual moments of mother/daughter empathy, which are undervalued in traditional criticism. Fourth, feminist criticism aims to make us *act* as feminist readers by creating new writing and reading collectives.

FEMINIST CRITICISM: THE 1960s AND 1970s

In the late 1960s the notion of origin – of the significance of male or female authorship – provided the central feature of a feminist aesthetic, as exemplified in *The Authority of Experience* (1977) by Arlyn Diamond and Lee Edwards. Similarly Kate Millett in *Sexual Politics* (1970) undertook a content analysis of literature describing sexual stereotypes and archetypes in the fiction of D. H. Lawrence, Norman Mailer, Henry Miller and other male writers. One measure of the speed of critical development is visible in the way in which Millett's content – an intensive catalogue of misogynist imagery – flows far ahead of its own language. The first and major achievement of feminist criticism was thus to highlight gender stereotyping as an important feature of literary form. The second and equally major achieve-ment of feminist criticism was to give reasons for the persistent reproduction of such stereotypes. A third and triumphant success was the discovery of lost or ignored examples of women's literature and a hitherto unnumbered body of women's texts. In addition, feminist criticism was part of the women's movement in the late 1960s and 1970s. For example, an early and key political text edited by V. Gornick and B. K. Moran, *Woman in Sexist Society: Studies in Power and Powerlessness* (1971), contained articles by the major feminist critics Elaine Showalter, Catharine Stimpson and Kate Millett. American feminist criticism was also shaped by the general discounting of political and cultural authority in the de-schooling, free universities, and anti-Vietnam campaigns. Multiple approaches have marked feminist criticism from its beginnings and the construction of feminist criticism necessarily involved a specific dismantling or displacement of the notion that the majority culture represents the majority of people.

One of the first and now unjustly ignored works of feminist criticism to challenge the female stereotyping that shored up the institution of literature was Mary Ellmann's *Thinking About Women* (1968). Written, like much subsequent feminist criticism, from outside an institution, the book offers an exemplary interdisciplinary review of the politics of gendered image-making in the work of authors ranging from Matthew Arnold, Joyce and Freud to Norman Mailer. These writers, Ellmann shows, commonly ascribe images of instability, spirituality and passivity only to women. Ellmann's views were backed by contemporary feminist theory. Phyllis Chesler's *Women and Madness* (1971) delivers a similar broadside to psychotherapy and the practice of ascribing feminine attributes to mental disorders and labelling as hysterics those women who *were* challenging the dominant ideology.

But it was the Modern Language Association (MLA) Commission on the Status of Women in 1970 which marks the beginning of feminist criticism in the West if only because the poet Adrienne Rich was commissioned to write her classic essay 'When We Dead Awaken: Writing as Re-Vision' (1971) for that forum. As she argues in the essay: 'Re-vision – the act of looking back, of seeing with fresh eyes, of entering an old text from a new critical direction – is for women more than a chapter in cultural history: it is an act of survival.' Rich's essay describes the basic aim of feminist criticism: that feminist criticism should undermine the misogynist organisation of knowledge by exposing the political construction of that knowledge in the academy, in the media and in everyday society.

This first stage, often characterised as the break with the fathers, is a series of revisionary readings of what Ellmann calls 'phallic' writing. Notable critics were Carolyn Heilbrun, Judith Fetterley, Eva Figes; and notable texts were Alice Walker's 'In Search of Our Mothers' Gardens' (1974), and Annette Kolodny's *The Lay of the Land* (1975). Critics aimed, not simply to praise women's *essential difference* from patriarchal stereotypes of women, but to give a *material* shape to, and revalue, women's culture and writing. In many ways these critics undertook a materialist analysis of literature, or an analysis of social context, rather than an essentialist account of women's experience based on a belief in women's 'essential' difference from men. Judith Fetterley's influential *The Resisting Reader* (1978) symbolises this new, politically informed, approach to literary criticism. In her book Fetterley attacks the writers whose works were 'canonised' in literary departments throughout America – Henry James, Hemingway, Fitzgerald and Faulkner.

By the middle of the decade feminist critics were elaborating a poetics of gender difference as extensive in its catalogue of women writers as their catalogue of male misogyny five years earlier. In the 1970s feminist criticism moved into a new phase – gynocriticism, or the study of women writers – with the first anthology of feminist literary criticism: *Images of Women in Fiction* (Cornillon, 1972). Annis Pratt, Elaine Showalter, Sandra Gilbert and Susan Gubar and Alice Walker were rediscovering many neglected women writers while Ellen Moers's *Literary Women* (1977) gave shape to a tradition of women's literature. Although it was attacked in the 1980s for its partial racism, homophobia and idiosyncratic choices, *Literary Women* was one of the first texts of feminist criticism to give women writers a history, describe women's choices of literary expression, and to make an identificatory celebration of the power of women writers: 'There is no point saying what women cannot do in literature, for history shows they have done it all' (Moers, 1977, p. xiii).

The need to replace masculinist values with a new form of feminist criticism was the task of Josephine Donovan's *Feminist Literary Criticism* (1975). The volume is a good example of the diversity of feminist approaches at that time, ranging as it does across bibliographies, linguistic research, and the retrieval of feminist literary mothers (Woolf). While *Feminist Literary Criticism* remains time bound in its focus on androgyny or integrated sex-roles (although Donovan herself preferred the term 'cultural' feminism) the book prophetically included a vivid *femmes de lettres*, or dialogue, between Carolyn Heilbrun and Catharine Stimpson – a form which has come to revolutionise feminist criticism, as in Audre Lorde's 'An Open Letter to Mary Daly'.

A constant theme in feminist writing in this period is the issue of communication, as the titles of feminist books make clear: Tillie Olsen's *Silences* and Adrienne Rich's *The Dream of a Common*

Language. The need to explore a separate, distinctive woman's language and to establish a body of literary criticism were the vital work of this decade. 1975 was also the year in which *Signs* was founded with a review of literary criticism by Elaine Showalter. A similar debate developed outside the English-speaking world: the first programmatic discussion about 'Frauern Literature' took place in Germany in 1975/6; and the founding of the 'Frauenoffensive' publishing house and journal represented a common concern among German feminists to explore women's 'different' language and culture.

Dale Spender's *Man Made Language* (1980) described the ways in which the growing body of research on women and language had broadened knowledge about women's literary representation. Spender identified two key areas of research: first, the study of sex differences – do women and men use language differently and if so, what does this mean? And second, the study of sexism in language, its effects and the implications for feminism. Spender recognised that the best efforts to establish a feminist literary tradition could not succeed without a corresponding understanding about the way in which sexual power shapes language. Instead of simply *celebrating* women's writing, Spender asked probing questions about the power of language: should we be speaking about separate languages for men and women or dialects (genderlects)? In other words are there sex-preferential or sex-exclusive ways of speaking? Is linguistic sexism the cause or effect of women's oppression? When does it appear? What are its boundaries and how do men control language? Spender argued that these binaries are not innate in language patterns but are cultural discourses which are inscribed within the media and in popular and traditional literature. The challenge then to feminist criticism was to investigate and to re-figure gender differences, and to describe potentially new relationships between gender, language and literature.

A major problem for feminist criticism in the 1970s, indeed for feminist criticism today, is that feminist work lacks institutional power. The feminist critique of language needed to be linked to a critique of the construction and dissemination of knowledge in the academy. For feminist criticism to have a space, academic respect must be granted to its views. The feminist project of literary discovery was intimately linked therefore to a feminist pedagogical project – to the teaching and the interpretation of literature. It is not surprising that new pedagogical strategies were simultaneously pursued by leading feminist critics. Early examples include Elaine Showalter's essay 'Women and the Literary Curriculum' which appeared in *College English* in 1970; essays on women writers by Showalter, Rapone and Snitow which appeared, not in literary journals, but in the first anthology of the American women's movement – *Radical Feminism* (1973); and Adrienne Rich's 'Writing as Re-vision' which also appeared in *College English* (1972).

Elaine Showalter's *A Literature of Their Own* (1977) was an important contribution to this agenda. Reflecting on Woolf's *A Room of One's Own*, Showalter faced the similar issue of women's exclusion from the academy. Charting a long history of literary women, she brought attention to undervalued nineteenth-century writers such as Sarah Grand and George Egerton. Rather than defining a 'universal' woman's text, Showalter preferred to identify a female 'subculture' which created those texts. She replaced the traditional periods of literary history with an alternative three-stage process which she couched as a growth into consciousness – feminine, feminist and female. Cautioned by later critics for adopting a literary standard more applicable to the late twentieth century and for her resistance to theory, Showalter went on to develop her ideas in 'Toward a Feminist Poetics' (1979), 'Feminist Criticism in the Wilderness' (1981) and subsequent writings. In these essays Showalter divided criticism into two distinct categories: the first type focused on the woman reader, a consumer of literature, and the second focused on the woman writer, a producer of textual meaning. Showalter described four models of gender difference – biological, linguistic, psychoanalytic and cultural – and claimed that these would be best addressed by a gynocentric model of feminist criticism. Following the publication of *New French Feminisms* (1980), Showalter brought French feminists into her 1981 essay. Her quadruple focuses closely resemble those of Simone de Beauvoir's *The Second Sex* but, interestingly, Showalter ignores de Beauvoir's attention to politics in favour of a woman-centred history drawn from anthropology.

From the hindsight of the 1990s this description of difference seems implicitly binary and is caught up in the notion that women's literature is in one category, the 'Other' in relation to the masculine tradition. Yet Showalter's work in this decade did offer a firm agenda for feminist criticism by describing a panoply of women's writing as a continuous and progressive narrative.

FEMINIST CRITICISM: THE 1980s TO THE PRESENT

For the 1980s and 1990s feminist criticism needed to cultivate more multivoiced critiques of literature which the formulation of a single women's tradition could not address. Marxist feminism took up that challenge. Cora Kaplan's 'Pandora's Box' (1986) argued for a more problematic notion of feminist criticism, one which neither took women's repression and exclusion from literary institutions as its key nor relied on the authority of women's psychosexual experience. Pairing two different models of feminist criticism in relation to Charlotte Brontë's *Villette*, Kaplan describes how the psychoanalytic model – and her example is the work of Mary Jacobus – decodes the literary psyches as emblems of oppressed Victorian femininity while a sociofeminist model – for example, that of Judith Newton – makes the psychic merely a repository of social values. Kaplan offers a third reading which could integrate these approaches, one where women's literary sexuality *is* a displaced representation of experience but can stand for instabilities both of class and gender.

But it was gynocriticism's stress on the significance of women's literary friendships which held sway during the early 1980s, evident in the continuing popularity of Adrienne Rich's *Of Woman Born* and cultural feminism (for example, feminists writing about the mother/daughter nexus, in *The Lost Tradition*). This feminist fascination with reproductive imagery in literature continues still (for example, in Marianne Hirsch's *The Mother-Daughter Plot* (1989)) but it is the work of Sandra Gilbert and Susan Gubar above all in the 1980s which created a feminist aesthetic from within the female literary tradition itself.

The Madwoman in the Attic (1979) and their subsequent series of texts, *No Man's Land*, 3 vols (1988), focus on some of traditional criticism's most serious exclusions: the material and psychological controls over women; women's secret lives and culture; and anxieties of masculinity and femininity represented in literary metaphors of the frontier, the visual, the domestic and cross-dressing. Gilbert and Gubar built on Moers and Showalter's acts of retrieval and, like those critics, are passionate about the oppositional function of women's writing. *The Madwoman in the Attic*, appearing nine years after Millett's *Sexual Politics*, is a compelling display of interwoven discourses. It includes a close textual analysis of the work of Jane Austen, the Brontës, Emily Dickinson and George Eliot, combined with psychohistory and medical and historical analyses. Like *Sexual Politics*, *Madwoman* is basically a revisionist history taking an existing model – the androcentric paradigm described by Harold Bloom that literary sons suffer an anxiety of authorship and Oedipal struggle with male precursors – to show that women write in confrontation with culture and with themselves by creating an author's double, the madwoman in the attic.

In *No Man's Land*, Gilbert and Gubar moved on from *Madwoman*'s gynocritical focus which was in part shaped by a notion of patriarchal culture as a homogenous and uniformly repressive entity. Volume 1, *The War of the Words*, is also a revisionist literary history but provides a fresh history and theory of modernism by giving equal attention to the texts of female as well as of male modernists. As the title suggests, all three volumes argue that twentieth-century literary history is a history of sexual conflict, and Gilbert and Gubar's great achievement is to catalogue in full the repetitive sexual imagery (of rape and impotence) which dominate modernist writing by men. *No Man's Land* fosters a more pluralist feminist criticism than the singular psychoanalytic model of *Madwoman*. Gilbert and Gubar discuss how lesbian expatriates in Paris 'reinvented gender'; they explore the consumerism of the Gilded Age in an informed materialist analysis and describe the sexual imagery of imperialism. *No Man's Land* is sustained by a postmodern conviction that 'male' and 'female' are fictive constructs variously shaped by cultures.

The feminist criticism which emerged in the late 1980s was strongly influenced by *Madwoman*: Elizabeth Abel in *Writing and Sexual Difference* (1982) and *The Voyage In* (1983) also offers an informed psychoanalytic reading of women's writing. One of the great achievements of Anglo-American feminist criticism in the 1980s was its ability to identify and conduct a very diverse gendered literary criticism. Feminist criticism proved firstly that literature was not simply a collection of great texts but was deeply structured by social/sexual ideologies, and secondly that certain preoccupations and techniques predominate in women's writing in relation to those social structures. Of course there were problems with the politics of pluralism. The vigorous debate in the pages of *Feminist Studies* about Annette Kolodny's prize-winning essay, 'Dancing Through the Minefield' (1980), revealed how lesbian, Third World and working-class feminists could see the heterosexist and racist assumptions which pluralism covered over. Yet what is also clear now about that decade is the innovative and self-conscious rapprochement that was taking place between feminist criticism and feminist writing in the work of Audre Lorde, Alice Walker and Adrienne Rich. Feminist criticism was now married to feminist creative writing in a rich terrain of autobiographies, fictional narratives and poetic histories. And it is not insignificant for the future direction of feminist criticism in the late 1980s into theories of poststructuralism and postmodernism that Sandra Gilbert was the American editor of Hélène Cixous' and Catherine Clément's *The Newly Born Woman*.

In the 1980s Gilbert and Gubar's theme of a woman's anxiety of authorship is given shape in the first deconstructive text of feminist criticism, Toril Moi's *Sexual/Textual Politics* (1985). In her role as a hostile daughter, Moi made an extensive critique of Gilbert and Gubar's *Madwoman*, arguing that the book assumed that women's writing had a monolithic identity. Only six years separate the publication of these works by Gilbert and Gubar and Moi but during that period the writings of the French feminists, the linguistic philosopher Jacques Derrida and poststructuralists had begun to inform Western feminist criticism. *Sexual/Textual Politics* claimed for itself the status of the first 'full' English language introduction to the principles of feminist literary theory, and Moi gives a summary and analysis of the main kinds of Anglo-American and French criticism. As the reflecting title indicates, Moi saw herself as the key feminist critic of the 1980s just as Millett had inspired feminist criticism in the 1970s. She argues that Anglo-American feminist criticism was too empiricist, too essentialist and hostile to change. Moi's allegiance is to poststructuralism. Her accounts of Julia Kristeva, Luce Irigaray and Hélène Cixous are persuasive in presenting an argument that all three critics are profoundly important for feminist criticism (although Kristeva denies she is a feminist), because all three envisage a linguistic space where gender divisions might disappear. Moi's uncompromising attack on essentialism provided a solid theoretical base for later feminist criticism.

Moi's defence of theory as an identifiable part of feminist literary criticism takes shape in the work of other feminists engaging with the French intellectual tradition such as Mary Jacobus, Alice Jardine, Jane Gallop and Nancy Miller. The key feminist focus in this work of the late 1980s was on language. The challenge was, by interrogating the relation between gender identity and language, to refigure the powerful and sexually expressive relationships between language, literary forms and women's and men's psyches. French feminist critics adopted the term *écriture féminine* to describe a feminine style (which was equally available to both men and women). They discovered this 'style' in absences, ruptures and 'jouissances' in modernist writing. Cixous, in particular, argues that *écriture féminine* is to be found in metaphors of female sexuality and women's genital and libidinal differences. These writers suggest that developing a literary identity is extraordinarily difficult for women, when literature, like any other institution, privileges a system of masculine meanings. As I describe French feminism elsewhere in detail, I shall confine myself here simply to highlighting the significance of these ideas for the history of feminist literary . criticism.

French feminists' determination to break through patriarchal critical practices – by creating new forms of writing/thinking which could not be described as the 'other' half of male-defined rationality – inspired excitement and debate. Cixous and Irigaray laid claim to a repressed sexuality which created ways of thinking lying mute in patriarchy. Julia Kristeva identified this new feminine language as 'the semiotic' which she defines as the pre-Oedipal language of the mother and infants. In this way French feminism could make an explicit connection between a woman's body and language. Hélène Cixous in particular was able to suggest a very direct link between women's desires and language in opposition to the negative accounts of women's repression offered by the psychoanalytic theories of Jacques Lacan.

French feminist theory played a crucial role in feminist criticism of the late 1980s by offering critics a new conceptualisation of the relationship between women, psychoanalysis and language. While some Third World critics, (for example, Gayatri Spivak) and American critics (for example, Nina Auerbach and Nina Baym) were disturbed by the gender determinations implied by French theory and its disregard of other differences such as race, class and the separation of the public social world from the private, French feminism has undoubtedly enriched Anglo-American feminist criticism. For example, Mary Jacobus's essays (collected in *Reading Woman*, 1986) display a dazzling utilisation of Freudian psychoanalytic theory together with the ideas of Kristeva and Irigaray. Jacobus traces how texts such as *Villette*, *Middlemarch* and *The Mill on the Floss* reproduce gender in psychoanalytic categories. A sister text, *Gynesis* (1985) by Alice Jardine, also takes up the challenge of French feminism. Warmly welcoming deconstruction, Jardine analyses how female images are deployed to represent powerlessness and absence in the work of Freud, Lacan, Derrida and other modern philosophers. The term gynesis means 'putting into discourse of "woman" ' (Jardine, 1985, p. 25) which Jardine claims is an intrinsic feature of modernism. Jardine's call to feminist criticism to engage with the works of modernism was subsequently and eagerly undertaken by Gilbert and Gubar in *No Man's Land*, and Scott in *The Gender of Modernism*, among others.

Grounding feminist criticism in a modernist poetics was not without its problems. Simply to celebrate the modernist women writers, Gertrude Stein, Djuna Barnes and Natalie Barney, as models of subversive sexual politics often did not engage with the social construction of modernist writing. To argue that experimental techniques and deconstructive practices could in themselves be a literary politics was to fall into the fallacy expounded by traditional supporters of modernism. Arguments about language and gender, combined with a poststructuralist focus on how literature works in particular cultural contexts, questioned how language can ever represent the 'reality' of women, and went some way to transform feminist criticism in the 1980s. It seemed possible that deconstruction or the attack on naturalised oppositions in language (black/white), psychoanalysis (particularly the study of how gender relations are created and expressed) and postmodernism's mixtures of histories and genres could point the way out of a circular – reality/author/representation – paradigm. These theories called into question the identification between female author and feminine text. It is easy to see why poststructuralism was so attractive to feminist critics. Feminists have always argued that women *become* women, as Simone de Beauvoir astutely suggested; hence, theories which unpick the connections between gender construction and language construction are enormously important. For example, Margaret Homans in *Women Writers and Poetic Identity* (1980) and *Bearing the Word: Language and Female Experience in Nineteenth-Century Women's Writing* (1986) responded to the ideas of Derrida and Irigaray, applying these to texts by the Brontës, Mary Shelley and George Eliot in order to show how women's writing struggles to gain a separate identity but also to be recognised by the paternal.

Critical theory and deconstruction, in particular, appears sophisticated and potentially revolutionary because it attacks linguistic binary oppositions between men and women. However, deconstruction can also evade the real practical and theoretical differences between white and Black feminists and white and Black lesbian feminists. Barbara Christian exposed the reactionary assumptions underlying the American academy's wholesale embrace of critical theory in the 1980s (see chapter 7). The 'race for theory', she argued, further marginalised feminists outside the academy, frequently Black and/or lesbian women.

From the mid-1980s racial difference became a key focus for feminist criticism as white feminists at last addressed the absences in their own processes of critical selection and commentary, an address prefigured in Adrienne Rich's 'Notes Towards a Politics of Location' (1984). This was the challenge of feminist criticism in the 1980s: how to name Black women writers and understand and apply Black principles of criticism. It was Audre Lorde who posed the provocative question: can we create a useful feminist criticism with the methods and forms of language we inherit from 'the masters'? As Lorde argues, 'the master's tools will never dismantle the master's house'.

In addition, as Barbara Christian complained, Black women are 'tired of being asked to produce a Black feminist literary theory as if I were a mechanical man'. Christian pushed the theoretical debate further by pointing out that 'peoples of color have always theorized – but in forms quite different from our Western form of abstract logic . . . in the stories we create, in riddles and proverbs' (1987, p. 53). The Black critical tradition that Christian describes began with Alice Walker's work in *Ms* (1974) and with Barbara Smith's groundbreaking essay 'Toward a Black Feminist Criticism' (1977); and it continued in the first American anthology about Black women writers, *Sturdy Black Bridges* (1979), as well as in collections co-edited by Smith, *But Some of Us Are Brave* (Hull, 1982) (the first anthology of Black women's studies) and *Home Girls* (1983) which focuses on Black lesbian writing. Several themes emerged in these texts: the ways in which extra-literary folk traditions and spirituality influence Black writing; the significance of mother/daughter relationships and varieties of female bonding in Black writing which are replicated in the close relationships between Black readers/ critics/writers. Building on this work Black feminist criticism of the late 1980s and 1990s (for example, Marjorie Pryse and Hortense Spillers (eds) *Conjuring: Black Women, Fiction and the Literary Tradition* (1985) and Joanne Braxton and Andrée McLaughlin (eds) *Wild Women in the Whirlwind* (1990)) began to create a Black aesthetic. These works and many others retrieved Black women's lost texts, placed these in history, described myths and women's traditions which proved that Black narratives, while not necessarily wanting to be *like* poststructuralism, could be said to be more akin to poststructuralism than many white critical texts. In other words, Black criticism was not simply a self-naming distinctive or essentially 'other' school or method *alongside* white criticism but was transforming the whole agenda of feminist criticism.

Similar crucial and valuable feminist critiques at the end of the decade were the projects and explorations of lesbian critics, white and Black. The critique of heterosexism in literary criticism, the recovery of lost lesbian writing and the search for a lesbian aesthetic, or queer theory, are the extensive work of critics Bonnie Zimmerman, Audre Lorde, Teresa de Lauretis and Adrienne Rich, among others. Lesbian feminist criticism opened up the field of feminist criticism as a whole (see chapter 8).

The next step into the 1990s was perhaps predictable. The questions raised by the theoretical ferment of the 1980s and by the revelations of Black and lesbian critics led to a reshaping of critical identity which emerged as gender theory. This more recent development on the critical horizon presents feminist criticism both with new possibilities and new problems. Elaine Showalter's career is a good example here. Showalter moved on from forceful accounts of a women's literary tradition at the end of the 1980s to a focus on gender studies with the publication of *Speaking of Gender* (1989). In that volume, Showalter claimed that feminist criticism had finished with her own gynocriticism and needed to focus on gender and sexual difference in texts by men as much as by women. *Speaking of Gender* represents a significant shift from the focus on women's writing in earlier feminist criticism and the focus on significations of the feminine in the work of Irigaray, Jardine and others.

Gender studies opened up the possibility that feminist literary criticism could respond to gender theories in other disciplines (for example, in science (Evelyn Fox Keller) or history (Joan Scott)), and could also retrieve homosexual literature from the margins of literary analysis. Eve Kosofsky Sedgwick's *Between Men* argued convincingly that representations of homosexuality could not be understood outside of their relation to women and to the gender system itself. Drawing on feminist theory of the 1980s, Sedgwick asked what theoretical framework could link sexual relations and power relations. Her answer was to recruit 'the representational finesse of deconstructive feminism' (Sedgwick, 1985, p. 12). For example, in her reading of James Hogg's *Confessions of a Justified Sinner* Sedgwick treats representations of homophobia as tools for understanding the gender system as a whole. While Sedgwick's work challenged feminist criticism to explore how constructions of homosexuality are conjoined with misogynist constructions in general, gender studies as a practice, separated itself from what has to be a fundamental aim of any feminist cultural work: what contribution can literary criticism make to *feminist* projects?

The diffusion of feminist criticism in the 1990s continued apace with the founding of journals with titles *Genders* and *Differences* and in dialogues between feminist critics and men hostile in the main to feminism. Examples of the latter are the double volumes edited by Linda Kauffman, *Gender and Theory* (1989) and *Feminism and Institutions* (1989). As Tania Modleski incisively argues, such work is based on two fundamental and totally fallacious assumptions: one a heterosexual 'presumption' and the second an assumption of the 'equality between men and women' (Modleski, 1991, p. 6). In this respect the appropriations of gender theory seem a retrograde entrée into the 1990s. Yet, as Joan Kelly Gadol pointed out long ago, women cannot unproblematically adopt the decade constructs of a linear 'masculine' history. For example, currently Italian feminist semioticians are engaged in a highly complex theoretical debate about women's language. The Milanese group, *Libreria delle donne* (Women's Bookshop), devotes itself to a systematic analysis of mothering discourses.

Feminist shifts seem often breathtakingly speedy to outsiders, but the most significant lesson from this history is the recognition that literary criticism must continually address gender and class and race and sexual preference.

OVERVIEW

Chapter 1: Second wave

This sets out the questions and provides some historical context to the answers that later feminists would provide. A starting point in post-war feminist criticism is the assumption that culture is emblematic of patriarchal social attitudes. In the work of Kate Millett, Simone de Beauvoir, Betty Friedan and Germaine Greer there are major and encompassing questions about literature and culture. All four address the sex caste system as represented in literature and culture, and their writings balance critical analysis with moral debates. All four are fundamentalists because they try to find fundamental and universal explanations for the subordination of women in literary representations. Millett, de Beauvoir, Friedan and Greer created a major agenda for post-war feminist criticism. It was the first time since Woolf that the interrelation of sexual ideology and culture was addressed as a fundamental condition of literary form. Such fundamentalism has lost much of its appeal in recent critical theory since it depends on a static conception of patriarchy. Paradoxically, none of the four really tackled the institutional nature of literature itself. Perhaps because Millett and de Beauvoir, in particular, see education and the humanities as the vehicle of social change, they left to later feminist critics the additional task of making a fuller account of 'experience' and the subconscious.

Chapter 2: Myth criticism

The core of feminist myth criticism is a refusal of traditional criticism's account of myth and gender representations and an attempt to find new literary vocabularies, often drawn from psychoanalysis.

Black writers frequently focus on myths in Black culture and history. Feminist critics argue that Graeco-Roman myths are masculine constructs whose narratives reflect, ontogenetically, only the male psyche. There is a greater power and resonance, they argue, in earlier, specifically female, mythologies. Virginia Woolf, for example, intensively reworked Isis myths and iconography. Mary Daly claims that myth criticism is a crucial tool in decoding the masculine biases of literature and culture.

Chapter 3: Marxist/socialist-feminist criticism

The relation between literary and social experience is the topic of the critics Lillian Robinson, Michèle Barrett, and British cultural critics. Their concern is the conjunction of the subject and her history as part of discourse. Those whom I term 'Marxist-feminists' are not necessarily committed to orthodox Marxism. I use the term mainly to indicate that the themes and techniques such critics use are derived in some way from their political theories, which may be anywhere on a continuum from socialism to Marxism.

Contemporary Marxist critics have turned from a determinist model of culture – one in which literature is primarily shaped by institutions and historical divisions of labour – to a focus on cultural and gendered *agencies*.

Chapter 4: French feminist criticism

The writings of Julia Kristeva, Hélène Cixous and Luce Irigaray among others, build on Simone de Beauvoir's concept of 'woman as Other to man' and examine the opposites (or binaries) – men/women, mind/nature – which are the dominant literary representations of sexual difference. French feminists aim to create positive representations of the feminine in a new language which is often referred to as *écriture féminine*, or women's writing.

Chapter 5: Psychoanalytic criticism

The dialogue between feminist criticism and psychoanalysis is invaluable for several reasons. Both address common themes: the psychic relationship of mothers, fathers and children; the relation between sexuality and its expression; the instability of identity shared by authors and readers. Both share similar methods: treating texts as codes and as representing the 'unsaid' in everyday life. Both examine dreams, displacement and transference to explain motivations and hidden 'truths'. For example, Juliet Mitchell, Sandra Gilbert and Susan Gubar and Mary Jacobus focus on representations of sexual difference syntactically as well as thematically.

Chapter 6: Poststructuralism/deconstruction/postmodernism

From the 1970s on feminist poststructuralists and postmodernists have made radical breaks with humanism. They respond to canonical works with challenging and interrogative critiques. All highlight the *processes of literary production* as much as the content of literary products. The single most important contribution of deconstructionists (see, for example, the work of Gayatri Spivak) is to make us think deeply about the racism and sexism embedded in literary structures. In contrast to modernism and humanism, poststructuralists and postmodernists (for

)le, the writer Rachel Blau DuPlessis) favour open,
tred texts where theory can mix with fiction, and high
culture mix with low. Most critics accepting the labels poststructuralist, deconstructionist and postmodernist agree that
literature and language are controlled by social power and that
by pluralising meanings we can open up fixed literary terms
(man = civilisation), understand the political determinants of
these terms and move beyond them.

Chapter 7: Black feminisms: the African diaspora

Black feminist criticism intensively explores the traditions,
history and culture of Africa, African America and the Caribbean,
focusing, for example, on the spiritual energy of oral history, of
songs, crafts and gardens and representations of mothering.
From a Black standpoint, literature is integral with other social
activities, not isolated 'high art'. Writing often provides a safe
space where these standpoints can be defined and also offers
new categories of thought, as exemplified in Alice Walker's term
'familiars' for her spiritual foremothers.

Barbara Smith, Audre Lorde, Alice Walker, Barbara Christian
and African and Caribbean feminist critics are preoccupied by
two closely related questions. First, what is the relationship
between Black critics and writers and the majority of Black
people and readers? Second, what is the relationship between
Black feminist criticism and poststructuralism, postmodernism
and academic theory in general? Both of these questions refer to
issues of essentialism and difference.

Chapter 8: Lesbian feminist criticism

In the 1980s a reconfiguration of feminist criticism took place
which insisted on the important contributions made by lesbian
literary women. One of the first, and most influential, lesbian
feminist essays was Adrienne Rich's 'When We Dead Awaken:
Writing as Re-Vision' which forcefully addresses key issues of
visibility and invisibility and the need for a new literary
tradition. A major theme in lesbian criticism is the tension
between identifying the 'real' nature of lesbian writing which is
bound up with identifying a history of 'real' lesbian women.

Together with Rich, Jane Rule, Bonnie Zimmerman and other lesbian critics make a strong case for a tradition of lesbian writing with its own patterns of images, preferred genres and themes from which feminist criticism can challenge the heterosexist and homophobic assumptions of literary studies.

Chapter 9: Third World feminist criticism: third wave and fifth gear

Literary criticism is crucial to Third World feminists asking complex questions about the subjective and symbolic nature of imperial texts and the social and ethnic discriminations such texts entail. The critics Rosario Castellanos, Chandra Mohanty, Gloria Anzaldúa, Rey Chow, among others, seek to create new representations in a dynamic new critical language. They focus on the significance of memory and autobiography and on place and displacement. Their writings are hybrid and multigeneric and rewrite history in tension with European theory. Third World critics lay great stress on the political power of remembering and writing, whilst many writers (for example, Anzaldúa) stress the power of a matriarchal consciousness.

Chapter 10: Feminist futures

The possible future of feminist criticism seems to me to involve a complex relation between creative writing and ways of thinking about writing. The work of several Black women writers in Britain marks very powerful shifts in contemporary criticism as writers create alternative myths in order to counter the destructive impact of white myths on the Black psyche. In addition, there are texts whose entire energy comes from feminist criticism; for example, Shoshana Felman's *Testimony* where issues of textuality and history, memory and context are inevitably gendered. Feminist criticism seems likely to leap the gap between theory and practice, between creation and criticism: Ailbhe Smyth's essays mix poems, quotations, history and academic writing in order to disrupt the norms of traditional literary criticism and disrupt a traditional Irish history. As a result, literary criticism – the activity of textual *analysis* – and literary creativity – the *expression* of female experience – are now interwoven.

SUMMARY

A number of problems arise when I try to sketch out feminist criticism in this way. First, as one might expect, it is very difficult to contain a writer like Mary Daly within one kind of criticism. Second, by describing different critical positions and projecting these in part as differences between critical methods, my approach might appear to assume an artificial homogeneity within critical 'schools'. Clearly French feminism *is* psychological; some Black theorists are also 'Third World' and Marxist (see chapters 5, 7 and 9 for further discussion). It might be more realistic to note down our own reading experiences, which can range from historical awareness to ethnic awareness, occurring not as types or levels but more as moments in a single reading.

Clearly any notion that criticism must originate in the critic's experience and that the function of critical writing is to recreate or relive this experience makes literary criticism very reductive. It assumes that the function of criticism is basically therapeutic. The project of feminist criticism is precisely to relate reading to social activity. The strength of feminist criticism lies in its refusal to accept the dislocation of literature from social practices, and this has far-reaching institutional implications. The very difficulty of reconciling feminism's 'isms' suggests that feminist criticism has undercut traditional assumptions about literature and criticism.

The key issue in feminist criticism, and I hope a continual tension running throughout *A Reader's Guide*, is the relationship between feminism as political *action* and feminism as political or critical *thinking*. The *Guide* focuses on the *critical consequences* of that issue. I conclude in the final chapter 'Feminist futures' that the binary 'women's movement/the academy' is a false division. What attracts many students to women's studies and many readers to women's books and feminist criticism is the 'woman-centred perspective' and a deepening political commitment to women's issues, even to positive role models. Yet it might appear that feminist thinking has fractured into a poststructuralist rejection of the 'essentialism' in such a perspective (Riley, 1988); attacks on the ethnocentrism implied by its exclusions (Spelman, 1988; Spivak, 1987); psychoanalytic attacks on a unified subjectivity (Mitchell and Rose, 1982); and anxieties about the heterosexism of a singular perspective (Fuss, 1991). However, the *Guide* aims to show (explicit in 'Third World feminist criticism' and in 'Black feminisms: the African diaspora', but also continually throughout) that the overlap and interaction between political and academic thinking have been part of feminism's project from the beginning, if more visible in recent years. It also argues that this very overlap gives feminist literary criticism and feminist politics a wonderful capacity for change *and* inclusiveness; indeed, a feminist future.

Contemporary feminist criticism has addressed the major problem confronting all cultural theory; that is, in its symbiotic relation to the Women's Movement, feminist criticism can help support a viable counter-culture. Throughout the 1970s and 1980s feminists built a series of feminist institutions. They equipped feminism with its own bookshops, libraries, theatre groups, book clubs, magazines and newspapers, arts centres, community centres, local authority women's committees, women's transport and social facilities, nightclubs and women's film and video in a whole range of cultural spaces. The audience who fill these spaces, supported by consciousness-raising and education groups, enables feminist criticism to be part of a broader movement. Feminist criticism is engaged in one of the most potentially important jobs in any intellectual activity – that of the critical interrogation of ideology for readers who can seize on images and ideas for feminist action. Within the space of feminist criticism, feminists can explore a huge variety of cultural symbols and motifs. Feminist criticism could be a land of golden voices.

SELECTED READING

Basic texts

Abel, E. (ed.) (1982) *Writing and Sexual Difference*, Chicago: University of Chicago Press

Abel, E. *et al.* (eds) (1983) *The Voyage In: Fictions of female development*, Dartmouth College, Hanover: University Press of New England

Bell, P. R., Parker, B. J. and Guy-Sheftall, B. (eds) (1979) *Sturdy Black Bridges: Visions of black women in literature*, Garden City, NY: Anchor Books

Braxton, J. M. and McLaughlin, A. N. (eds) (1990) *Wild Women in the Whirlwind: Afra-American culture and the contemporary literary renaissance*, London: Serpents Tail

Christian, B. (1987) 'The race for theory', *Cultural Critique*, 6 (Spring) pp. 51–63

Cixous, H. (1976) 'The laugh of the Medusa', *Signs*, 1:4 (Summer) pp. 875–93

Cornillon, S. K. (ed.) (1972) *Images of Women in Fiction: Feminist perspectives*, Bowling Green, Ohio: Bowling Green University Popular Press

Diamond, A. and Edwards, L. (eds) (1977) *The Authority of Experience: Essays in feminist criticism*, Amherst: University of Massachusetts Press

Donovan, J. (ed.) (1975) *Feminist Literary Criticism: Explorations in theory*, Lexington: University Press of Kentucky

Ellmann, M. (1968) *Thinking About Women*, New York: Harcourt Brace Jovanovich

Fetterley, J. (1978) *The Resisting Reader: A feminist approach to American fiction*, Bloomington: Indiana University Press

Gilbert, S. and Gubar, S. (1979) *The Madwoman in the Attic: The woman writer and the nineteenth-century literary imagination*, New Haven: Yale University Press

Gilbert, S. and Gubar, S. (1988) *No Man's Land: The place of the woman writer in the twentieth century*, 3 vols, New Haven: Yale University Press

Greene, G. and Kahn, C. (eds) (1985) *Making A Difference: Feminist literary criticism*, London: Methuen

Hirsch, M. (1989) *The Mother-Daughter Plot: Narrative, psycho-analysis, feminism*, Bloomington: Indiana University Press

Homans, M. (1980) *Women Writers and Poetic Identity*, Princeton: Princeton University Press

Homans, M. (1983) ' "Her Very Own Howl": the ambiguities of representation in recent women's fiction', *Signs*, 9:2 (Winter) pp. 186–205

Homans, M. (1986) *Bearing the Word: Language and female experience in nineteenth-century women's writing*, Chicago: University of Chicago Press

Hull, G. T., Scott, P. B. and Smith, B. (eds) (1982) *All the Women Are White, All the Blacks Are Men, But Some of Us Are Brave: Black women's studies*, New York: The Feminist Press

Irigaray, L. (1985) *This Sex Which Is Not One*, Ithaca: Cornell University Press

Jacobus, M. (ed.) (1979) *Women Writing and Writing About Women*, London: Croom Helm

Jacobus, M. (1986) *Reading Woman: Essays in feminist criticism*, London: Methuen

Jardine, A. A. (1985) *Gynesis: Configurations of women in modernity*, Ithaca: Cornell University Press

Kaplan, C. (1986) 'Pandora's Box' in *Sea Changes: Culture and feminisms*, London: Verso

Kauffman, L. (1989a) *Gender and Theory*, Oxford: Basil Blackwell

Kauffman, L. (1989b) *Feminism and Institutions*, Oxford: Basil Blackwell

Kolodny, A. (1980) 'Dancing through the minefield: some observations on the theory, practice and politics of a feminist literary criticism', *Feminist Studies*, 6:1 (Spring) pp. 1–25

Kristeva, J. (1980) *Desire in Language: A semiotic approach to literature and art*, Oxford: Blackwell

Millett, K. (1970) *Sexual Politics*, New York: Doubleday

Moers, E. (1977) *Literary Women*, Garden City, NY: Anchor Books

Moi, T. (1985) *Sexual/Textual Politics: Feminist literary theory*, London: Methuen

Newton, J. and Rosenfelt, D. (eds) (1985) *Feminist Criticism and Social Change: Sex, class and race in literature*, London: Methuen

Olsen, T. (1978) *Silences*, New York: Delacorte Press

Pryse, M. and Spillers, H. (eds) (1985) *Conjuring: Black women, fiction and literary tradition*, Bloomington: Indiana University Press

Rich, A. (1979) 'When we dead awaken: writing as re-vision', in *On Lies, Secrets, Silence: Selected prose 1966–1978*, New York: Norton

Robinson, L. (1978) *Sex, Class and Culture*, Bloomington: Indiana University Press

Russ, J. (1983) *How to Suppress Women's Writing*, Austin: University of Texas Press

Scott, B. K. (1990) *The Gender of Modernism*, Bloomington: Indiana University Press
Sedgwick, E. K. (1985) *Between Men: English literature and male homosocial desire*, New York: Columbia University Press
Showalter, E. (1977) *A Literature of Their Own*, Princeton: Princeton University Press
Showalter, E. (ed.) (1985) *The New Feminist Criticism: Essays on women, literature and theory*, New York: Pantheon
Showalter, E. (ed.) (1989) *Speaking of Gender*, London: Routledge
Smith, B. (1977) *Toward A Black Feminist Criticism*, New York: Out & Out Press
Smith, B. (ed.) (1983) *Home Girls: A black feminist anthology*, New York: Kitchen Table Press
Spender, D. (1980) *Man Made Language*, London: Routledge & Kegan Paul
Spivak, G. (1987) *In Other Worlds: Essays in cultural politics*, London: Methuen
Walker, A. (1983) *In Search of Our Mothers' Gardens*, New York: Harcourt Brace Jovanovich
Woolf, V. (1929) *A Room of One's Own*, London: Hogarth Press
Woolf, V. (1938) *Three Guineas*, London: Hogarth Press

Introductions

Anzaldúa, G. (ed.) (1990) *Making Face, Making Soul: Haciendo Caras: Creative and critical perspectives of women of color*, San Francisco: Aunt Lute Foundation Books
Ashcroft, B., Griffiths, G. and Tiffin, H. (eds) (1989) *The Empire Writes Back: Theory and practice in post-colonial literatures*, London: Routledge
Benstock, S. (ed.) (1987) *Feminist Issues in Literary Scholarship*, Bloomington: Indiana University Press
Donovan, J. (1989) 'Introduction to the Second Edition' in J. Donovan (ed.) *Feminist Literary Criticism: Explorations in theory*, 2nd edition, Lexington: University Press of Kentucky
Gallop, J. (1992) *Around 1981: Academic feminist literary theory*, London: Routledge
Gates, H. L. Jr. (ed.) (1990) *Reading Black: Reading Feminist: A critical anthology*, New York: Meridian

Humm, M. (1986) *Feminist Criticism: Women as contemporary critics*, Hemel Hempstead: Harvester Wheatsheaf

Jay, K. and Glasgow, J. (eds) (1990) *Lesbian Texts and Contexts: Radical revisions*, New York: New York University Press

Meese, E. A. (1986) *Crossing the Double-Cross: The practice of feminist criticism*, Chapel Hill: University of North Carolina Press

Meese, E. A. (1990) *(EX)Tensions: Re-figuring feminist criticism*, Urbana: University of Illinois

Moi, T. (1985) *Sexual/Textual Politics: Feminist literary theory*, London: Methuen

Sellers, S. (1991) *Language and Sexual Difference: Feminist writing in France*, London: Macmillan

Stimpson, C. R. (1988) *Where the Meanings Are: Feminism and cultural spaces*, London: Routledge

Wall, C. A. (ed.) (1989) *Changing Our Own Words: Essays on criticism, theory and writing by black women*, New Brunswick: Rutgers University Press

Warhol, R. R and Herndl, D. P. (1991) *Feminisms: An anthology of literary theory and criticism*, New Brunswick: Rutgers University Press

Further reading

Fuss, D. (ed.) (1991) *Inside/Out: Lesbian theories, gay theories*, London: Routledge

Gornick, V. and Moran, B. K. (eds) (1971) *Woman in Sexist Society: Studies in power and powerlessness*, New York: Basic Books

Humm, M. (1987) *An Annotated Critical Bibliography of Feminist Criticism*, Hemel Hempstead: Harvester Wheatsheaf

Koedt, A., Levine, E. and Rapone, A. (eds) (1973) *Radical Feminism*, New York: Quadrangle

Lakoff, R. (1975) *Language and Woman's Place*, New York: Harper & Row

Miller, N. (1991) *Getting Personal: Feminist occasions and other autobiographical acts*, London: Routledge

Mitchell, J. and Rose, J. (1982) *Feminine Sexuality: Jacques Lacan and the École Freudienne*, London: Macmillan

Modleski, T. (1991) *Feminism Without Women: Culture and criticism in a 'postfeminist' age*, London: Routledge

Offen, K. (1988) 'Defining feminism' *Signs*, 14:1 (Autumn) pp. 119–58

Riley, D. (1988) *Am I That Name? Feminism and the Category of 'Women' in History*, London: Macmillan

Spelman, E. V. (1988) *Inessential Woman: Patterns of exclusion in feminist thought*, Boston, Mass: Beacon Press

Todd, J. (1988) *Feminist Literary History*, London: Routledge

1 Second wave: de Beauvoir, Millett, Friedan, Greer

It is no accident that literary criticism has a central place in post-war feminist writing. Those pioneering texts – Simone de Beauvoir's *The Second Sex* and Kate Millett's *Sexual Politics* – both argue that 'literature' is as important a means of patriarchal power as the family. Betty Friedan's *The Feminine Mystique* and Germaine Greer's *The Female Eunuch* both interweave feminist ideas and cultural criticism. These writers asked major and encompassing questions about literature and culture. De Beauvoir asked why is woman the Other in texts written by men. Millett asked what is sexual politics and how is it represented in literature. Friedan and Greer, although writing in a less thorough-going way, were asking why are cultural stereotypes so potent and why do women accept these stereotypes. In some ways all four writers constructed a new form of criticism as well as asking new questions because they offered new ways of thinking about how these questions could be *approached*. In part, all four writers share one major aim of feminist criticism: how to describe and subvert the cultural repression of women.

All four choose to answer questions about sexual politics by examining representations of sexuality in the contradictory images created by literature and culture. Yet mostly they wrote in isolation from the traditional institution of literary criticism: de Beauvoir's training was in philosophy, Millett's debt was to the sexual historian Steven Marcus, and Friedan was a journalist. Although Millett completed a doctorate and Greer taught at the University of Warwick, their books were unlike traditional academic criticism. They were revolutionary in scope by amalgamating critiques from the social sciences and arts. But what was most revolutionary about all four critiques was the importance each writer attached to the language of sexuality. It is for these reasons that the feminist criticism of de Beauvoir, Millett, Friedan and Greer represents an enormous change in criticism.

Each of the texts is very much part of its own cultural 'moment'. Because issues of women's oppression did not figure in French Left critiques of the 1940s, de Beauvoir focused more on male constraints and is much vaguer about women's alternatives to these. From 1971, when she organised the Right to Abortion Campaign and joined the MLF (*Mouvement de Libération des Femmes*), de Beauvoir has consistently supported radical feminists (Schwarzer, 1984). Millett chose to attack the writers Norman Mailer and Henry Miller because their notions of 'Hipster rape' were popular in the macho libertarian sexual climate of the 1960s. It was the startling conservatism Friedan discovered in women's replies to questionnaires she distributed to Smith College graduates in 1957 which sparked the writing of *The Feminine Mystique*. Greer claimed that *The Female Eunuch* came from the forcing house of the New Left. If the oppressive milieu of post-war culture forced each writer into print, the historical contexts which inspired each writer inevitably shaped their feminism. Yet there is an attractive way in which all four writers refuse the radical chic of their times: for example, Kate Millett bravely attacked the misogyny of Eldridge Cleaver, hero of the American Left.

The distinguishing feature of second-wave feminist criticism is *hybridity* – a multigeneric mixture of cultural and literary criticism. All four critics consistently compare literary images of women with actual social conditions. They create a cultural analysis centring on the female self as a cultural fabrication by male authors. Culture is described as if it is emblematic of social attitudes, and traditional literature is taken to represent masculine emotions and fears. In other words, literature is interrogated in order to confirm each writer's general views about feminine myths.

Literature (or, in the case of Friedan, popular culture) emerges in their work as having an homology or correspondence with the workings of patriarchy. Texts, literary or cultural, are taken to be models of patriarchal power. All four writers engage in a psychosocial critique which is intent on unveiling ideological constructions, 'beliefs' and 'values'.

If their use of a hybrid form links these geographically and demographically distant writers, the titles of all four books are similarly revealing. Each is about sexuality. Indeed, each analysis is pervasively animated by the sense that women's status is sexually determined. For example, de Beauvoir argues that Claudel's character misrepresentations are not the result of poor writing but stem from Claudel's sexual politics. Millett judges texts in relation to the sexual histories of their authors; Swinburne's poetry, for example, is shaped by his impotence. Millett believes that sexual politics even determine a writer's choice of genre. She claims, for instance, that Tennyson wrote fantasy because he was sexually ambivalent. Friedan and Greer assume that popular culture aims, in the main, to restrict women's sexuality to marriage and family life. Yet each text is a *thorough* account of sexual politics.

By taking literature and popular culture to be totally illustrative of social issues – totally incorporative – each critic was able to describe literary or cultural forms as instruments of socialisation. De Beauvoir and Millett focus on male rather than on female authors and argue that women's representations are very similar in otherwise disparate authors. Millett is primarily interested in the 'autobiographical' revelations of male authors represented by their male characters. She therefore examines narrator viewpoint and terminology as if both directly represent an author's ethics. Friedan and Greer take images of women in women's magazines to be documentary evidence of a masculine psychic need for childlike women.

Second-wave criticism has two different approaches. On the one hand, there is the pragmatic experiential writing of Friedan and Greer; on the other, there is the theoretical, politicised criticism of de Beauvoir and Millett. Whilst de Beauvoir and Millett focus on patriarchy itself as the source of sexual repression, Friedan and Greer focus on women's *responses to* patriarchy. The two divergent directions of feminist criticism end in different solutions. Friedan and Greer promote education and consciousness-raising as agencies of change, while de Beauvoir and Millett, although ultimately reformist, speak of radical coalitions between feminism and Négritude, the Black literary movement and lesbianism.

SIMONE DE BEAUVOIR

The architect of second-wave feminist criticism is Simone de Beauvoir. *The Second Sex*, published in 1949, is a now classic study of women's repression and the construction of femininity by men. The title, *The Second Sex*, sums up de Beauvoir's argument that society sets up man as the positive and 'woman' as a negative, second sex or 'Other', an insight in some ways analogous to Virginia Woolf's concept 'Woman as Mirror'. *The Second Sex* works through biological, Marxist and psychoanalytic theories as well as literary criticism to show how all aspects of social life and thinking are dominated by the vision of woman as 'Other'. *The Second Sex* pioneered ideas and techniques acknowledged by feminists from across the range of academic disciplines. Betty Friedan 'Americanised' *The Second Sex*, Shulamith Firestone dedicated *The Dialectic of Sex* to de Beauvoir and Juliet Mitchell called *The Second Sex* the most important of the 'totalising' studies on the oppression of women. Although it is short, 'The Myth of Woman in Five Authors' (that part of *The Second Sex* which is specifically literary criticism), exemplifies de Beauvoir's approach in the rest of the text. De Beauvoir includes literary criticism 'to confirm this analysis of the feminine myth as it appears in a general view' (de Beauvoir, 1972, p. 229). Just as in her fiction and autobiographies de Beauvoir uses long booklists and comparisons with literary heroines like Jo March to establish narrator identity, so in *The Second Sex* she uses literature to illustrate her philosophy.

The theoretical issues raised over forty years ago in *The Second Sex* continue to be central to feminism today. How is woman constructed differently from, and by, men? What explanations from psychoanalysis or Marxism can help women understand this construction? What particular social perspectives does literature offer? And from this can we distinguish between women and femininity in a useful way?

Although *The Second Sex* occupies a crucial place in contemporary feminism, critics have often been less than fair to de Beauvoir's achievement. Early reviewers were hostile. François Mauriac attacked *The Second Sex* in *Le Figaro Littéraire*, and when the heavily edited English translation appeared in America four years later Elizabeth Hardwick said '*The Second Sex* is so briskly Utopian it fills one with a kind of shame and sadness' (Hardwick, 1953, p. 321). Contemporary feminists worry more that de Beauvoir's existentialism and her commitment to notions of transcendence prevent her from understanding the deeper contradictions of desire or eroticism (Walters, 1976; Evans, 1980). But it was precisely de Beauvoir's training in philosophy that enables her to ask the large question 'What is a woman?' and write such a thorough reply.

The Second Sex begins with facts and myths drawn from psychology, history and biology as well as from literature. These include man-made myths from prehistory to the coming of suffrage, in which women are passive objects. Book II describes contemporary Western women, utilising autobiographies as well as psychosocial studies to focus on how women themselves experience social 'reality'. De Beauvoir concludes that woman is constructed 'differently', by men. For de Beauvoir, physical distinctions between women and men have meaning only in social arrangements, so that biological characteristics can explain, but never determine, differences between women and men. It is because women have been denied social liberty that they become narcissists, since the essence of 'femininity' is dependence. What strengthens de Beauvoir's critique is her attention to, and understanding of psychoanalysis and Marxism. The Freudian model de Beauvoir finds too deterministic. Similarly de Beauvoir considers Engel's analysis of capitalism and the oppression of women to be an inadequate explanation for the interaction between the economic and the symbolic oppressions of women by men today. Asked by Alice Schwarzer how she would prefer to be remembered, as a philosopher or a writer, she replied 'I set my store by literature' (Schwarzer, 1984, p. 23). Literature and myth are important because it is there, de Beauvoir argues, that woman as Other is fully elaborated. Describing the work of Claudel, Lawrence and Breton, de Beauvoir shows how each writer describes certain collective myths – of woman as Flesh, as Nature, as Muse. The Other in literature is de Beauvoir's version of Virginia Woolf's 'The Angel in the House'. In literature women act as 'compensation myths' for men: de Beauvoir points out how Henri de Montherlant saw himself as a *deus ex machina*, changing narrative structures in order to create horrifying mother images. Breton, de Beauvoir argues, created women as incarnations of Nature in order to devalue femininity. Even Stendhal, who allows a more humane woman to enter his fiction, still portrays women as dependants.

De Beauvoir gives a more accurate account of Lawrence, for example, than Kate Millett. De Beauvoir claims that Lawrence's representations of sexuality do not simply involve the subjection of women but the transcendence of subjectivity by female *and* male characters. In Lawrence's work men and women use each other instrumentally, with men arousing symmetrical demands in women. For example, de Beauvoir argues that Gudrun's 'masochism' in *Women in Love* is not an expression of innate femininity but is conditioned by her relationship with Gerald. Only the male character who functions as the autobiographical representation of Lawrence himself is permitted subjectivity. Inevitably the 'true woman' which Lawrence offers us, de Beauvoir concludes, is a woman 'who unreservedly accepts being defined as the Other' (1972, p. 254).

Yet, although de Beauvoir's account may be adequate as a feminist phenomenology of literary features, it has some limitations. De Beauvoir describes characters as static entities. Certainly de Beauvoir proves that the male authors she analyses often reveal a belief in a rigid hierarchical society. But the title of de Beauvoir's literary critique 'The Myth of Woman in Five Authors' is very revealing. De Beauvoir paraphrases literature as if it were philosophy. She does not address the issue of why some myths of women are fictionalised at all. By setting out a panoply of male myths and checking them for 'ambivalences' and 'contradictions', like a well-trained philosopher, de Beauvoir is, in effect, checking *internal* consistency in a very atemporal way. In de Beauvoir's analysis the erotic is always mediated by male desire. It is not there as an autonomous state because that would involve de Beauvoir in describing the subjective and the unconscious as a part of literary representations. Yet literature often depends on an imagery drawn from the unconscious as another mechanism for portraying fantasy and desire. It is the parallel which de Beauvoir draws between representation *and* construction – that men need to *represent* (in myth or literature) before they can *construct* women's dependence – which makes her literary criticism so crucial to feminism. What de Beauvoir was able to establish in *The Second Sex* is that male writers share a deep conservatism about women. In other words, de Beauvoir claims, male writers write about women only to learn more fully what they are themselves.

The problem with de Beauvoir's analysis for feminist criticism is not that her interpretations depart from traditional critical vocabulary. It is that, like Millett's, they sometimes depart from the actual world of the novels themselves. She extrapolates women characters too often from the specific contexts of novels, and as feminist critics, we need to look at women existing *within* the worlds of novels as well as outside those worlds. Perhaps de Beauvoir's best legacy to feminist criticism, and what links her with Millett and Friedan, is her contention that women are *never* adequately portrayed by male authors.

BETTY FRIEDAN

Betty Friedan's *The Feminine Mystique* is a pragmatic version of *The Second Sex* and shares the same focus: women's passive acceptance of the cultural stereotypes of femininity constructed by patriarchy. The book is now regarded as a classic of American second-wave feminism which it helped to inaugurate in the late 1960s. As the founder and first president of NOW (National Organisation of Women) Friedan is acknowledged to be one of the pioneers of the American women's movement. *The Feminine Mystique* reveals the private angst which many middle-class white American women were experiencing in the late 1950s as unwaged housewives and consumers. The 'mystique' was Friedan's term for 'the problem that has no name' – the psychic distress experienced by women who had no public careers and were immersed in domestic concerns. Although an overtly populist text, *The Feminine Mystique* is an early version of the kinds of cultural criticism which have been more problematically developed in the writings of Angela McRobbie, Lillian Robinson and Judith Williamson. Friedan focuses on the cultural isolation of American suburban women of the late 1960s. Like Catherine Beecher Stowe before her, who questioned 200 friends in 1846 about the origin of *their* psychosomatic illness, Friedan questioned 200 Smith College graduates about their dissatisfaction with suburban life. *The Feminine Mystique* is a very period text, tied to a moment in Cold War history and the post-war boom, and presents a demographic account of a particular generation. But, although a far less radical writer than de Beauvoir, Friedan was trying to answer a similar question: why did women (albeit affluent college graduates of the late 1950s) narrow the boundaries of their lives to marriage and children?

Friedan, an American journalist whose previous articles had appeared in *Good Housekeeping*, catered to an American fascination with statistics and anecdotes. She writes about the relation between advertising and consumption and women's self and social identities. She analyses popular fiction, 'how to' manuals, and magazines to show how all media collude in stereotyping and conditioning women to accept the restricted roles of homemaker and mother.

Contemporary feminists have attacked Friedan for shrinking de Beauvoir's concepts and endorsing the American dream of individual ambition and competition (Dijkstra, 1980; Eisenstein, 1981). But, although the appeal of *The Feminine Mystique* was to a liberal individualist and affluent America, in observing the process by which Friedan selects and transforms de Beauvoir's more theoretical ideas into a popular language we can witness, problematised, a central dilemma for all feminist criticism: how to be both feminist and yet popular.

The appeal of *The Feminine Mystique* lies most obviously in its easy introduction to snippets of women's history, a simplified Freud, and accounts of familiar aspects of social and educational discriminations. Friedan says that she has no theory, and implicitly suggests that the 'mystique' of suburban American woman stands for women's problems in general. But her basic premise is a belief that individuals can make free choices about lives and careers and that the social history of individuals is evolutionary and progressive. We need to know, not so much why Friedan is addressing such a narrow class group in her obsession with the nuclear family, but how such a cultural analysis clearly satisfied and might still respond to wider feminist concerns.

By comparing the more active personae of women's magazines of the 1930s with those contemporary to her, Friedan argues that the media works to counteract women's social aspirations and achievements. Her explanations are ideological rather than institutional. She describes the way in which women's magazines were serving the political exigencies of post-war America. Magazines, and culture itself, are not a cause of women's oppression but rather the means. They service patriarchal ideology. *The Feminine Mystique* includes well documented interviews and statistics about cultural products, and Friedan starts with these as an anthropologist might start with the observed rituals of a social group, moving from observed point to observed point within a narrow trajectory. Some of her criticisms are based on interesting evidence. Friedan found that American magazines were not creating simple and idealised stereotypes of women but were continually moving between 'genres', creating 'documentary' evidence of feminine stereotypes for their female audiences. For example, the same magazine *Ladies Home Journal* combined picture essays of split-level homes with a social series like 'Political Pilgrim's Progress' about women working to improve playgrounds. Friedan notices the match between form and ideology. Thus, the type size of women's magazines was enlarged and simplified to meet the cruder and simpler image of women being presented in the late 1950s and early 1960s. Since the unconscious is a potent threat to patriarchy (although Friedan would never use these terms), it is not surprising that Friedan found that magazine fictions (which often include dreams) were more stereotyped and less honest than general articles.

If Friedan reads like a product of undergraduate workshops in creative journalism – 'I was on the trail of the problem that has no name' – her understanding of how culture actually functions in American society remains relevant. *The Feminine Mystique* is ideological criticism. A more problematising analysis today would try to analyse women's pervasive psychological need for repeated cultural motifs by deconstructing how such motifs are put together. For example, Friedan quotes the story of 'The Sandwich Maker' – a woman, saved by pregnancy from having to earn money with home cooking – without analysing characterisation or domestic imagery. Friedan ignores the *quality* of images and the fact that these in themselves are unrepresentative of the hard and uncongenial (not only tedious) daily suburban housework, and therefore appealing. A fully feminist reading needs to combine an intrinsic with an ideological reading. Friedan does try to identify the sources of myth creation in her interviews with magazine editors, but she is not able to estimate the impact of institutions or media.

It is when writing about sexuality that Friedan is most revealing. Friedan gives attention to the Kinsey reports about sexual behaviour in the 1950s which shocked many Americans by describing a more diverse range of homosexual, bisexual and heterosexual practices than were believed to be current. Yet like de Beauvoir, Friedan advocates sexual abstinence for career women. Where Kinsey suggested a correlation between sexual pleasure and educational achievement, Friedan's fear of sexuality is evident in her use of extreme vocabulary – love and desire are a 'parasitical softening' (Friedan, 1982, p. 244). Sexuality is always heterosexuality. Friedan's attacks on homosexuals are particularly crude. Homosexuals are 'no less than the female sex-seekers, Peter Pans, forever childlike' (1982, p. 239). Not only does Friedan lack a theory of sexual politics, one of her solutions to the problem that has no name is asexuality, 'to postpone present pleasure for future long-term goals' (1982, p. 214). The vocabulary is telling. Any reshaping of women's culture, Friedan argues, will be by individual not collective effort. Friedan is attracted to strong pioneer women and creates a 'New Life Plan' of hard paid work. 'She must learn to compete, then, not as a woman, but as a human being' (1982, p. 328). After consciousness-raising, Friedan feels, there will be no constraints preventing women from changing their social images. But changing the concept of oneself as a woman is, of course, part of a larger social and class reality. Finally, the ideal woman role model Friedan offers is herself with her 'lifelong commitment to an art' (1982, p. 302).

Because of its popularity *The Feminine Mystique* represents an important 'moment' in feminist criticism. But Friedan's cultural agenda is very limiting. The humanities are crucial to Friedan. Her educational 'shock treatment' comes through 'an intensive concentrated reimmersion *in*, quite simply, the humanities' (Friedan, 1982, p. 324). The organising conference of NOW (the National Organisation of Women set up by Friedan in 1966) chose seven task-forces to investigate discrimination against women. These were in the fields of education, employment, religion, poor women, women's image in the mass media, women's political rights and the family. The list, like Friedan, ignores ethnicity and State power, arguing instead that education is the first vehicle of social change. Friedan's is a superficial solution specifically antagonistic to collective social action. She does not ask women to look at cultural alternatives but remains reformist, accepting intact the academy, its disciplines and canons. Friedan creates an idealised model of women's progress which later feminist critics were to critique.

GERMAINE GREER

The British progeny of *The Feminine Mystique* is Germaine Greer's *The Female Eunuch* published in 1971. The book is arranged in sections which describe historical stereotypes of women all of which, Greer claims, possess characteristics of the 'castrate' – timidity, delicacy and perverted sexuality. Greer describes a range of feminine subjects which she finds in the writing of Blake, Strindberg, Marlowe, Racine, Shakespeare, Sydney, Rabelais and Mailer. She argues that all these writers are aggressively sexual in their work. Greer documents images of women throughout mainstream literature and in popular culture and argues that literature provides clear examples of social roles. For example, she contends that Shakespeare's plays represent in a one-for-one way contemporary views of romance and marriage. *The Female Eunuch* is one of the first British examples of popular culture criticism with Greer's analysis of the stylistic features and themes of popular romance. But, although Greer is making an ideological analysis of aspects of misogyny in culture, her text is very sweeping. Her style – simple paraphrase into a contemporary everyday vocabulary – was dictated by her commissioning editor. Yet it is not the accessibility of *The Female Eunuch* which creates a problem for feminist criticism but rather Greer's deradicalising descriptions.

Why, then, mention *The Female Eunuch* in a chapter on pioneers? Because, like Friedan, Greer was widely read and had a clear impact on feminist thinking.

Greer does not distinguish between different kinds of representations. She gives no materialist or historical analysis. Women are described in terms of contemporary cultural definitions of femininity rather than in relation to race, class or sexual preference. The solution to the issue of women's dependence, for Greer, therefore, is to free women from the destructive *mental* dependence that patriarchal culture induces. Greer's denunciation of cultural manipulation in the name of a more 'authentic' sexuality closely resembles Friedan's agenda even in its choice of chapter titles – 'The Psychological Sell'. But to Greer the possibility of cultural change stems from sexual freedom. Greer even suggests, in the chapter entitled 'Revolution', that women should 'promiscuously' correct false perspectives of femininity through sexual liberation whose first step will be individual revolt. *The Female Eunuch* is very much of its moment; and Greer's subsequent books, particularly *The Obstacle Race*, contain very detailed and sophisticated critiques. Historically, Friedan and Greer played an important role in second-wave consciousness-raising, but feminist criticism needed more complex and comprehensive theories.

KATE MILLETT

The radical subtext of *The Second Sex* becomes the core of Kate Millett's *Sexual Politics*. The book is one of the most influential texts of second-wave feminism. Indeed it was the *cause célebre* following the book's publication – the media-baiting of the Chair of NOW's New York Education Committee, Kate Millett – which forced feminists to add the specific oppression of lesbian women to feminist agendas of the 1970s. The title *Sexual Politics* sums up Millett's theory of patriarchy. She argues that patriarchal power is ubiquitous. There is a deeply entrenched politics of sexuality, beginning with the reproduction of patriarchy through psycho-social conditioning in the family, which operates in all cultural structures. Patriarchy is a fundamental part of all representations because these are permeated by male power. The book made a pioneering synthesis of literary, social and historical images of masculinity. Millett's analysis of the way in which sexist ideologies work in literature paved the way for contemporary feminist literary criticism. Feminist literary criticism has a central role in *Sexual Politics* in which Millett uses critical techniques to analyse gender differences in historical and contemporary discourses. Writing about contemporary literature as if literature is a record of the collective consciousness of patriarchy, Millett revealed the extent of sexism at work in the novels of Lawrence, Mailer and Miller.

She argued that these writers were archetypes of particular social values within capitalism – the values of violence, sexuality and the cash nexus. She challenges the way in which these writers make misogyny attractive (as with Mailer's endorsement of violence against women) and make male values seem the human condition. Millett argues that literature reveals the sexual mastery of men over women in symbols and patterns of dominance and subordination; in other words, that forms of thought and means of expression are made and controlled by men.

There are three kinds of charges in *Sexual Politics*: first, that male writers distort male and female characters; second, that they misrepresent sexuality by associating deviance with 'femininity'; and third, that the narrative structures of fiction represent the structures of masculine culture. The first half of *Sexual Politics* provides the social and political evidence for these critical charges. Here Millett argues that the political power men have over women amounts to a more fundamental political division than class. She provides a range of evidence from biology, sociology, education, anthropology and psychology.

This section is less precise in its use of the language of caste and class than the literary criticism section, and Millett, by playing down feminist alternatives, presents, as a result, a somewhat static picture of patriarchy. As Norman Mailer gleefully pointed out, Kate Millett is an annoying critic. 'A hard-hat has more curves in his head' (Mailer, 1971, p. 119). She paraphrases at length, confuses author with character and generalises to make all-inclusive points. Rereading *Sexual Politics* is a little like watching black and white television after years of colour. But her 'faults' come, I think, from her not knowing her audience. Millett lacked what is now a feminist constituency, and she was trying to create one. Hence, she devotes herself to fiction where sexist themes and techniques are more explicit.

But Millett goes further than simply exposing sexism in one work after another: she provides strategies for interpreting writing form rather than merely denouncing its content. Millett chooses her writers very carefully. Each writes about a particular institution and therefore together they can reveal a range of institutional ideologies, including the American army in Mailer's work and colonialisation in the plays of Genet. Millett's critical technique is one of paraphrase. Millett treats criticism as if criticism is a form of translation designed to change the way in which we apprehend male texts. The key indices to Millett are, then, vocabulary and point of view, and her own vocabulary is full of extremes, words like 'exalts' or 'dazzling', which emphasise the power of language. Millett argues that male characters are authorial surrogates. Mailer's Rojack is 'like one of Faulkner's ancient retainers of a lost cause' (Millett, 1977, p. 16).

Although Millett's methods of literary analysis have limitations (clearest in the way key episodes are not analysed, and often relegated to footnotes), yet by judging everything in terms of identity creation Millett does produce some interesting critical criteria. Particularly intriguing is her notion that genres can be distinguished by the way in which these reveal different aspects of personality. Criticism, she says, is like ego construction: novels represent the id and poetry represents the unconscious (see Millett, 1977, p. 148 for fuller descriptions). *Sexual Politics* makes a psychoanalytic critique of literature as much as a 'deconstructive' one.

The psychoanalytic radicalism of *Sexual Politics* can be highlighted by situating it within mainstream American psychoanalytic criticism of its time and American feminist developments in psychoanalysis (such as they were). It is tempting, when writing about the psychoanalytic milieu of the 1960s, to speak of a split into right and left wing. In Erik Erikson's famous description of women's 'inner spaces', the behaviour therapy of E. G. Skinner and cybernetics of Norbert Weiner, conservative psychiatry was busy translating individual dynamics into those which could function in the practical terms set by American post-war society. A good example here is Erich Fromm's *The Fear of Freedom*. Fromm explains that he analyses the psychological processes operating within individuals only to understand the dynamics of social process. Psychological forces are 'historically conditioned responses to economic change' (Fromm, 1960, p. 252). Fromm and his contemporaries were creating a psychoanalytic ethics for a period of American white male affluence.

The Left counter to this technology of the instincts was to offer the power of the therapeutic. Wilhelm Reich, Norman Brown and Herbert Marcuse emerged as major theorists popular among the disaffected student generation of the 1960s. These writers satisfied a youthful desire for a sexually liberated society. Reich described the extent to which sexual repression is enforced by capitalism; Marcuse proposed the idea of a libidinal morality; there were the hallucinogenic promises of Timothy Leary and Allen Ginsberg. This psychology of alienation has its Baedeker in Theodore Roszak's *The Making of a Counter Culture* (1970). Roszak planned to substitute for Western militarism a 'shamanistic world view', which he drew from a psychotherapy very much concerned with the symbolic vocabulary of dreams. Yet both right- and left-wing solutions ignored the historical *and gendered* dynamics of social psychology.

There was not, as yet, a feminist alternative. Definitions of 'femininity' were set out in Helene Deutsch's definitive two-volume *The Psychology of Women: A Psychoanalytic Interpretation* (1944). Although Deutsch does not claim to trace all women's problems to penis envy, she does claim to have found that successful career women suffer a 'masculinity complex'. Deutsch did not revise Freud's theories of gender identity. Kate Millett, on the other hand, makes a clear distinction between sex and gender. Applying models from psychoanalysis Millett assesses how literature is shaped by sex role ideology. Deconstructing attributes of 'femininity' and 'masculinity' in writing by men, Millett was able to reveal the misogyny of literary constructions.

But Millett does not ignore materialism. She materially situates Henry Miller's descriptions of sexuality by analysing the bourgeois commercialism of his vocabulary. In any case Miller has, Millett argues, a distorted psyche since he is unable to describe sexual behaviour in any realistic way. What Millett particularly resents about Miller's writing is the way in which he objectifies women as prostitutes. Miller's vocabulary, Millett claims, is both bourgeois and sexual (for example 'servicing'). In the 1970s, Millett's argument was a radical attack on Miller's apparent libertarianism. Millett's training in comparative literature enables her to address a wide range of gender constructions as she does in her account of Jean Genet. Genet's aping of 'masculine' and 'feminine' social roles, Millett feels, reveals the essence of what heterosexuals take to be masculinity or femininity. Millett is interested in characters who challenge gender identity like Genet's drag queens, but she also describes the differences between female stereotypes in literature and women in the real world, as in, for example, her account of African women lobbyists at the United Nations.

Millett moves easily between genres comparing 'The Woman Who Rode Away' with *The Story of O* not because Millett herself confuses good and bad writing but in order to clarify the boundaries of literature by contrast with the unfamiliar. Cora Kaplan, among others, has attacked Millett for believing that literature can clearly reveal an author's motivation (Kaplan, 1979). But Millett's critique *is* based on careful reading: she shows, for example, how Hardy chooses different writing modes for different characters on the basis of gender. Millett deplores Hardy's biological essentialism and his belief in hereditary character traits.

There are occasional severe misreadings. Millett argues that Ursula in *The Rainbow* is an example of Lawrence's belief in unfulfilled femininity because he apparently distrusts Ursula's educational values. Since Ursula's educational sympathies, even her teaching techniques, were similar to those of Lawrence himself, as far as we can establish from biographical evidence, then Millett is clearly oversimplifying Lawrence's gender representations. Characters have a more problematic relation to authors than Millett's view that male writers simply inhabit male characters. But the institution of literary criticism is clearly important to Millett. Book II of *Sexual Politics* contains a long account of the history of English criticism in which Millett describes the writings of John Stuart Mill and Ruskin as projections of the unconscious fantasies of Victorian sensibility. The section is a fascinating and unusual ingredient in an American text.

Millett is a very moral critic and a very moral writer. All her writing is part of a quest for an alternative feminist heroic, exemplified in her account of Angela Davis (Millett, 1972, p. 54). *Sita* (Millett's 1977 novel) and *Sexual Politics* balance narrative with interrogative moral debates. Both in her fiction and in her criticism Millett helps us to 'live through' an experience of sexual politics. Life and art in *Sita* are completely interdependent: the narrator's relationship with Sita has to end so that the autobiography can end. The range of literary techniques in *Sita* – its unstable narrator and imagistic repetitive monologues – matches the range of genres in Millett's preference for photographs, scrapbooks and personal notes rather than linear narrative. In *Sita* Millett gives us the all-American feminist, 'all the woman I never was', just as her criticism demolishes the all-American male.

Sita's fluid sexual desire is matched by the juxtaposed columns of Millett's essay 'Prostitution: A Quartet for Female Voices'. Here Millett details the self-perceptions of prostitutes in order to attack the sexual codes of patriarchy, just as in her literary criticism she attacks the sexual codes of patriarchal literature. Millett dislikes the artificiality of both sociological and literary accounts of prostitution. She replaces this artificiality with an innovative choice of form, interweaving the speaking voices of an academic, a teacher, a writer and a prostitute, shifting the speaking voice from column to column on each page to point to the impossibility of fixed social and literary categories (Millett, 1971).

Millett is engagingly open about the purpose of criticism. She tries to bring the private close to the public by calling her readers into her texts. Presumably she herself moved into autobiographical fiction from *Sexual Politics* precisely in order to tie her own private and public worlds more closely together; and in this she anticipates the turn to autobiography by later feminist critics. 'Prostitution' is a deliberate attempt to evade critical categories, the form itself prohibiting the reader from adopting a single response. By directly experiencing the feelings of loss and disfunction recounted by prostitutes we abandon the illusion that writing has discrete genres. Millett's ambivalence and uncertainty about her role as critic are appealing. Millett may deny contradictions as Kaplan claims (Kaplan, 1979, p. 14); and her aim *is* reformist, even evolutionary, since she thinks that feminism can be 'accomplished by human growth and true re-education' (Millett, 1977, p. 363). But Millett could be said to be *the* post-war pioneer of feminist literary criticism. Her expansive understanding of politics – that the personal, sexual life was political – became the fundamental premise of second-wave feminism just as her interdisciplinary, interrogative, autobio-graphical style gave second-wave feminism a new form of criticism.

SUMMARY

What makes these critics pioneers? Primarily it is that they created a new form of feminist criticism. All four made thorough attempts to write a multigeneric feminist criticism by mixing arguments from biology, psychology and historical materialism as well as literary critiques. One of the great strengths of feminist criticism is its challenge to the boundaries of 'literature'. All four texts are pioneering but not without problems for a feminist future. All four critics present a somewhat static notion of patriarchy. For example, although de Beauvoir in particular tried to break the correlation between women and femininity precisely by describing femininity as a construction, there is in her work too absolute a barrier between the sexes. In her autobiography *Memoirs of a Dutiful Daughter* de Beauvoir ignores the value of 'feminine' moments in order to train herself to think like a man, to move into a man's world. In her fiction – for example, *The Woman Destroyed* – she describes a world where women make impossible choices, to be artists or mothers; and where, in any case, they are always vulnerable to the sexual politics of men. Just as women's 'moments' (whether those of childbirth or eroticism) are not central moments in de Beauvoir's autobiographies, so she, together with Millett, Friedan and Greer, gives little space to an alternative world for women. Their criticism is pessimistic not progressive. In these critiques women respond to men rather than act independently of men. In her later interviews with Alice Schwarzer, de Beauvoir regretted not having written more about eroticism: 'I would like to tell women about my life in terms of my own sexuality because it is not just a personal matter but a political one too' (Schwarzer, 1984, p. 84). The fact that eroticism is suppressed in *The Second Sex* is an example of the ideological constraints of post-war French culture as to what can/cannot be written/published. It took later critics like Firestone and Daly to open up these suppressions. The real absence in the work of these critics is a serious attempt to deal with the unconscious. Literature, and hence criticism, is deprived of a whole area of experience. Later critics like Cixous and Spivak redress this imbalance just as the work of Susan Griffin on the juncture of feminism and ecology has enlarged feminist criticism in yet another direction.

All four critics also accept unproblematically a traditional hierarchy of high and low art accepting, for example, a modernist concept, the avant-garde. The institutional nature of literature is not adequately addressed. But many later feminist concerns *are* prefigured. De Beauvoir's account of women's myths foreshadows similar critiques by more contemporary critics such as Ortner and Griffin. Adrienne Rich's theories of lesbian existence and lesbian continuum are in debt both to de Beauvoir and to Kate Millett. The analysis of popular culture by Friedan and Greer prefigures later media studies.

These critics did change literary values and the ways in which we apprehend those values by expanding the content of criticism to include issues that had not previously found their way into criticism. It is this expansion of the field of criticism which is crucial to later feminist criticism. By altering the ways in which we think of culture, the pioneering critiques of de Beauvoir, Millett, Friedan and Greer altered the very experience of reading. Defamiliarising literary experience and incorporating the previously unacknowledged reality of women opened feminist criticism to new horizons.

SELECTED READING

Basic texts

de Beauvoir, S. (1972) *The Second Sex* (1949 1st edition), Harmondsworth: Penguin

Friedan, B. (1982) *The Feminine Mystique* (1966 1st edition), Harmondsworth: Penguin

Greer, G. (1971) *The Female Eunuch*, London: Paladin
Millett, K. (1971) 'Prostitution: a quartet for female voices', in *Woman in Sexist Society* (eds) V. Gornick and B. K. Moran, New York: Basic Books
Millett, K. (1977) *Sexual Politics* (1970 1st edition), London: Virago

Introductions

Donovan, J. (1985) *Feminist Theory: the intellectual traditions of American feminism*, New York: Ungar
Eisenstein, H. (1984) *Contemporary Feminist Thought*, London: Unwin
Evans, M. (1985) *Simone de Beauvoir*, London: Tavistock
Moi, T. (1990) *Feminist Theory and Simone de Beauvoir*, Oxford: Blackwell
Tong, R. (1989) *Feminist Thought*, Sydney: Unwin
Yale French Studies, 72 (1987) *Simone de Beauvoir: Witness to a century*

Further reading

Deutsch, H. (1944) *The Psychology of Women: A psychoanalytic interpretation*, New York: Grune & Stratton
Dijkstra, S. (1980) 'Simone de Beauvoir and Betty Friedan: the politics of omission', *Feminist Studies* 6:2 (Summer) pp. 290–303
Eisenstein, Z. (1981) *The Radical Future of Liberal Feminism*, London: Longmans
Evans, M. (1980) 'Views of women and men in the work of Simone de Beauvoir', *Women's Studies International Quarterly*, 3, pp. 395–404
Fromm, E. (1960) *The Fear of Freedom*, London: Routledge & Kegan Paul
Hardwick, E. (1953) 'The subjection of women', *Partisan Review*, May/June
Kaplan, C. (1979) 'Radical feminism and literature: rethinking Millett's sexual politics', *Red Letters*, 9, pp. 4–16
Mailer, N. (1971) *The Prisoner of Sex*, Boston: Little, Brown
Roszak, T. (1970) *The Making of a Counter Culture*, London: Faber

Schwarzer, A. (1984) *Simone de Beauvoir Today*, London: Chatto & Windus

Stacey, J. (1986) 'Are feminists afraid to leave home? The challenge of conservative pro-family feminism', in J. Mitchell and A. Oakley, *What is Feminism?*, Oxford: Blackwell

Walters, M. (1976) 'The rights and wrongs of women: Mary Wollstonecraft, Harriet Martineau, Simone de Beauvoir', in J. Mitchell and A. Oakley (eds), *The Rights and Wrongs of Women*, Harmondsworth: Penguin

2 Myth criticism

In the 1940s and 1950s many American women writers turned to myths as a means of redefining women's culture and history. Just as in post-war society the definition of what was prototypically feminine became problematic, so in post-war writing women utilised mythic symbols to defy traditional ideas of the feminine. The poet Louise Bogan introduces the wild figures of Medusa and Cassandra into her poems 'Tears in sleep' and 'The Dream'. H. D. (Hilda Doolittle), writing *Trilogy* in 1944, searched through myth and history looking for symbols of archaic rebirth. This enlarged account of femininity appears also in the poems of Muriel Rukeyser who, in *Beast in View* (1944), uses myth to express the ambiguities of woman's condition.

On this territory feminist myth critics have camped, building on and strengthening the work of these poets with histories of myth and fables. Mary Daly, Adrienne Rich, Annis Pratt, Marta Wiegle and critics in the collection *The Lost Tradition* (1980), edited by Cathy Davidson and E. M. Broner, argue that myth is a key critical 'genre'. Yet a precise definition of what constitutes myth and its function in criticism remains problematic. Women *in* mythology are well documented and discussed but generally from male perspectives. Myths represent social issues in imagistic stories drawn from history. Inevitably these stories of the past often present an outmoded set of masculine and feminine characteristics.

Yet ironically one reason why feminist myth criticism might perhaps be more acceptable to the literary establishment than other feminist criticism is because of the 'canonisation' of male myth critics like Empson, Frye and McLuhan. The academic tradition of myth criticism, created by these authors, utilises scientifically organised theories of literature and the symbolic structures of myth.

In *The Anatomy of Criticism*, Northrop Frye amalgamated the empiricist close reading techniques of New Criticism with his sense of 'the archetypal shape of literature as a whole' (Frye, 1957, p. 342). Frye revives archaic doctrines, such as Ptolemaic cosmology, to relate literary criticism to transhistorical forms. Building on Frye, Marshall McLuhan created a mythic structure, which he called the global village, drawn from his own misreading of tribal societies.

The work of these critics was very much in vogue in the academic world of the 1950s and early 1960s. Its success depended on a close analogy between Frye's value-free scientism and the social-scientific ideology of the Cold War period. As a practice it is also racist and patriarchal since it ignores gender and the actual rituals of ethnic groups. In any case, in Western culture 'mythology', as the classicist Sarah B. Pomeroy points out, has tended to mean what was preserved in classical art and literature and perennially reworked. The male modernists – Pound, Eliot and Yeats, for example – escaped from contemporary materialism by a flight into myths of a golden past. There may be traces of Frye's love of classification in Mary Daly's work, yet a greater range of myths needed to be found, scrutinised and reinterpreted from a feminist perspective.

Unfortunately, mythographers simply do not know very much about women's mythology. Very little can be said with certainty about what ritual expressions women themselves performed as opposed to the way women are represented in myths. Just as women poets revised Greek and Egyptian mythology (for example, H. D's *Helen in Egypt*), feminist critics, like Daly, Pratt and Davidson, along with some psychoanalytic critics, have departed radically from traditional criticism by utilising myths not generally derived from the Graeco-Roman tradition. To Northrop Frye, Greek and biblical mythologies represent all the subsequent principles of literature (Frye, 1963, p. 44). Feminist critics aim rather to analyse structures of meaning in myths from many different cultures. A structuralist approach looks for 'codes' in literature and evaluates literary works in terms of the information such codes transmit. The function of critical analysis here is to isolate messages (what Roland Barthes calls a signifying system). The core of feminist myth criticism is a refusal of existing mythical representations of gender and an attempt to find new literary vocabularies often drawn from psychoanalysis. Particularly in books such as Susan Griffin's *Woman and Nature* (1978), feminist myth criticism attempts a more associational, subjective style.

What are the critical concepts and techniques which myth critics use? Mary Daly's challenge is metaphoric. She contests longstanding conceptions of the feminine with progressive ideas of an alternate women's culture. Annis Pratt uses Jungian categories of male and female characteristics and examines women's fiction to 'determine if these works constituted a field that could be investigated as a self-contained entity following its own organic principles' (1982, p. viii). The feminist critics represented by *The Lost Tradition*, as the title implies, are trying to explain how and why the mothers and daughters of literature and myth gradually 'lost' one another.

Black feminist critics make an extensive use of African myths. In Alice Walker's novel *The Color Purple* (1982), Celie's mythical and spiritual quest shows how a woman gains a sense of self-identity from the natural world. Walker subverts Western history by suggesting that the Black mythic is a far truer representation of history than the white accounts. As Henry Gates argues, a Black writer's use of myth often functions as a formula for exploring alternative theories of language (see Gates, Introduction).

What unites all these concerns is the notion that myth can be almost a genre of critical writing in itself. Each of these critics is attempting a more precise way of charting and analysing past, present and future uses of myth and myth's social and literary functions.

Myth critics take a number of different approaches to literature. Although many share a religious background, of Jewish ritual or Roman Catholicism, the stories critics choose to investigate are very different. Marta Wiegle in *Spiders and Spinsters* (1982) concentrates on native American Indian myths using an etymological approach to document crosscultural stories. Annis Pratt remains firmly within traditional academic parameters reading nineteenth- and twentieth-century women's novels in terms of Jungian archetypes and imagery. Adrienne Rich and Mary Daly collect psycholinguistic evidence of women's mythical resources. Critics in *The Lost Tradition* work with the polytheistic myths of the ancient Near East, juxtaposing these with the contemporary culture of native American Indians and white women writing today.

Myth offered post-war writers a comforting structure within which to locate private needs. In the years of the 'feminine mystique' a confusion about sex roles and the status of private life could be addressed by metaphors from myth. In the poetry of Sylvia Plath and Anne Sexton, for example, myths provide a structure of meaning represented by the ambiguous mother images chosen by both writers as poet daughters uncertain about their roles as poet mothers. Mythological figures acted as useful metaphors for each author's maternal focus and sometime private matrophobia. Many women poets explore myths in order to describe supposed aspects of female identity: the Demeter-Kore story is often reworked by women poets exploring the spirituality of mothering.

In the academy feminist myth criticism broke with conventional literary criticism in many ways, while having an ambiguously close relation to the schools of comparative literature in which traditional myth criticism had flourished in the American academic world of the 1960s. The genre offered a radical way of crossing disciplines. Feminist critics utilised myth in both psychoanalysis and literary studies. In *The Reproduction of Mothering* (1978) Nancy Chodorow explores the way in which mother and daughter relations form female personalities. Because male children have to develop their masculinity in a masculine world, that world becomes anything which is not the mother or the feminine. In consequence, the repudiation of the feminine appears, exemplified in traditional mythology in the story of Perseus triumphing over Medusa, who represents the feminine unconscious. A female child, on the other hand, has to be both like, and yet different from, her mother. The mother represents both the childhood the daughter has to reject and, simultaneously, the adult world into which she has to grow. Myths of Medusa or, frequently, Arachne express this ambivalence and differential evaluation. Psychological dilemmas of women can thus be represented in literature through mythical figures, although Annis Pratt argues that 'women find it hard to translate the contents of their unconscious into recognisable symbols and myths' (1982, p. 138). For her, the different psychological experiences of men and women writers create gendered perceptions of mythical archetypes. The radical otherness of women's experience is represented, Pratt claims, in the more arcane symbolism of their fiction. Pratt chooses Virginia Woolf's *To the Lighthouse* as a key example. Mrs Ramsay, Pratt claims, uses myth to call up 'androgynous powers to fertilise her childish husband' (Pratt, 1973, p. 13).

Rather than restricting an area of knowledge to empiricism or positivism, myth consists of images and symbols which are vivid but not always immediately intelligible. Myth narratives aim, not to present coherent explanations of literary and social problems, but to link rituals of daily life with prehistoric symbols in order to explain contemporary events. Feminism has long argued that everyday myths (for example, the myth that all women like strong male protectors) are difficult to refute empirically and that we need to understand the wider symbolic and psychic needs which keep such myths in place.

One of the problems with early feminist myth criticism was its need to rely on traditional theory, particularly on the taxonomy of Erich Neumann. In Neumann's narrative of mythical mothers and daughters, his accounts of power relations between mother and child often simply resemble power relations in his own society. Adrienne Rich attacked Neumann's theories for reinforcing existing stereotypes. She argued that men maintain a culture's rituals to translate their own unconscious fear of women into mythical monsters and – particularly in the Western tradition – into myths of rape and violence to women. Medusa is a traditional symbol of the castrating female, and Rich argues that perhaps part of feminist myth critics' obsession with Medusa can be explained by the internalised gynophobia which women might have as part of our patriarchal inheritance. Dorothy Dinnerstein's *The Mermaid and the Minotaur* (1976) described the way in which women learn and internalise these negative representations.

Feminist critics argue that Graeco-Roman myths are often masculine constructs whose changing narratives reflect changes, both ontogenetic and phylogenetic, only in the male psyche. The main project of feminist myth-critics is to move beyond these constructs, to find perhaps that mythology is originally feminine, or at least to discover the force and outline of early, more specifically female, mythologies. Virginia Woolf's preference for the pre-Greek myths of Egypt and Isis iconography is one good example of a feminist rejecting a contemporary and patriarchal obsession with Greek myths and heroes. This process is also one in which many contemporary women poets engage; for example, the Black lesbian poet Audre Lorde and the Navajo poet Leslie Silko. Audre Lorde points out, however, that Black women poets are not always well served by white feminist myth critics. In 'An Open Letter to Mary Daly' she attacked Daly's description of Black women as victims rather than as sources of wisdom. Mary Daly's *Gyn/Ecology* (1978) is rather a 'vow of derision' against male myths. She argues that the study of myths is important not simply to replace patriarchal myths with feminist versions but to elicit even fresher cultural insights by reversing male myths.

One very strong reason for a feminist focus on myth is the link between myth and orality. Usually myths need to be read aloud slowly since meanings come more from associations than those contained on the page. Oral collective readings bring myths alive, and often restore the immediacy of early myth. It is precisely because myth culture is oral, critics in *The Lost Tradition* claim, that it is likely to respond to women's concerns. In all societies women 'talk-story' (to use Maxine Hong Kingston's phrase) not as mere self-expression but as a way of teaching their children.

Myth can aid minority groups as a vehicle for expressing social reality through analogy or masks. In the literature of Chicana, Black and Jewish women, as Anzaldúa and Wiegle describe, the connections between mothers/daughters, ethnicity and social alienation are often explicitly mythologised. Oppressed groups can seek redress in the reclamation of a mythical identity outside the host culture. Myth provides a psychic escape from the Western tradition while enabling a group to remain physically within. Of course, the reclamation and documentation of feminist myths cannot be seen as an alternative to radical and structural changes in culture. Hence,

Mary Daly is concerned in *Gyn/Ecology* that myth-makers are not associated with anti-intellectualism. She advocates the writing of academic books since, like other critics, she aims to provide women with a historical past which Daly characterises as a 'feminist journeying'. But Daly does propose significant alterations to the categories of traditional criticism. Rather than defining periods or movements in literature (which Daly understands to be specious, intact examples of 'homo-geneous' criticism), she proposes instead that feminist criticism be the 'transmission of our transitions' (1978, p. 23).

Finally, myth can appeal to women because it often portrays the informal and the private experience of women's lives. Traditional critics, like Neumann and Alan Watts, defined myth only as a *public* means of communicating metaphysical or supernatural reality. Currently a revaluation of the mundane is taking place in feminist myth criticism. Wiegle creates an ethnography of native American communication patterns. Daly has made a sociolinguistic study of women's vocabulary. Adrienne Rich has given us almost a macrohistory of legends, autobiography and poetry about mothers. What had previously been dismissed as trivial, ordinary or gossip has been collected by feminist myth-critics and recreated as wives' new tales.

If there are clear and very powerful reasons for Pratt, Daly and Rich to interpret myths, what are the main methods and techniques of feminist myth critics? For most, criticism has a double function. Myth critics argue that literary symbols often make provocative disclosures of writers' psychological conditions. And in turn that these psychological conditions take certain regular and archetypically symbolic forms which may help the reader to understand her own archaic images and pulsations.

MOTHERHOOD

Although, as many anthropologists maintain, there is absolutely no valid reason to proclaim a golden age of matriarchy, feminism has rehabilitated mother/daughter myths. That feminism and motherhood might be incompatible had seemed almost axiomatic to some earlier feminists. For example, Shulamith

Firestone in *The Dialectic of Sex* argued that maternity determined women's social inferiority and lack of economic power.
Later feminists challenged this axiom using myth as a vehicle for
their arguments. Adrienne Rich splits the rhetoric of motherhood into two halves which she named 'experience' and
'institution'. The point of this bifurcation is to enable her to
attack the institutionalisation of motherhood by patriarchy
while celebrating the mythic condition of mothering. Rich writes
about myths since she believes that the realities of motherhood
are obscured by the literary associations brought to it by men.
Traditional cultural icons, she claims, have to be displaced by
the creation of a 'symbolic architecture' of feminism. Rich,
therefore, like Daly, frequently focuses on Demeter and
Persephone, or on other mythical mother/daughter bonds.
While refusing the idea of an historically specific golden age of
matriarchy, Rich argues that a number of fertility and goddess
myths are artifacts of female power.

Annis Pratt, similarly, examines the representation of motherhood in nineteenth-century fiction and argues that this
expresses mothers' 'excessive social power' in Victorian society.
The Lost Tradition examines a whole history of mother/daughter
relationships described in the poems and letters of women
writers. By exploring the personal and mythological aspects
of the intricate and inescapable mother/daughter bond, critics
tried to find more adequate literary representations of female
identity.

Motherhood, then, is the one place from which criticism could
begin to reformulate the representation of women in myth.
Adrienne Rich thinks that one aspect of women's social
construction stems from society's need to romanticise or idealise
'mothers' at the expense of the reality of mothering relationships. Critics in *The Lost Tradition*, by examining difficult mother/
daughter relations in the poetry of Anne Sexton and Sylvia
Plath, seek to find in the double faces of mythical mothers
'the source of our own, specifically female, creative powers'
(Davidson and Broner, 1980, p. 193). In placing the myths of
mothering in the foreground in this way critics were able to start
rethinking representations of sexual difference, since giving
birth is one of the specifically gendered acts.

NATIVE AMERICAN

Myth critics often meditate on psychosexual identity and make social history a mere superfluity. One vivid alternative to this absence is the work of Native American critics and women of colour. *Spiders and Spinsters* is a fascinating synthesis of Native American myths and legends. The editor Marta Wiegle's driving impulse is to give space to the intense, associative, metaphysical ideas of Native American culture. The book is a wonderful, rich collection inviting re-evaluations of Western philosophic and cultural values. Yet the text is imprecise in its generalisations about tribal culture. Aboriginal North American cultures do not offer similar cultural paradigms. As in many cultures throughout the world, men and women in aboriginal North America have separate and complementary cultures. But unlike those in Western religions, myth and ritual in Amerindian religions are often not intimately related. Myths represent the stories of native American religions and are not usually expressed as part of rituals. For native Americans, rituals are the primary mode of religious expression. The institutionalisation of native American religious practices and the cessation of matrilineal culture came not from some simple patriarchal suppression but as a direct result of an economic shift from a mixed to a nomadic economy at the end of the eighteenth century. It is impossible to understand Native American myth without understanding its history of cultural and social discriminations. However, with second-wave feminism, native traditions are being revived which centre on women. For example, women are dancing in the Lakota Sun Dance (Paper, 1983).

BETTINA L. KNAPP

Knapps's *Women in Twentieth-Century Literature* (1989) is a Jungian critique. Jung modified and transformed psychoanalysis by taking it out of the medical realm and into the realm of culture and myth. In addition, Jung's ideas of bisexuality have appealed to many feminists. Yet, broadly speaking, Jung also believed that women's psyches are controlled by Eros, or feeling, and men's psyches by Logos, or the power of judgement. Jung's inability to destabilise traditional gender roles is reflected in Knapp's criticism, particularly in her account of Jean Rhys's rewriting of *Jane Eyre* – her *Wide Sargasso Sea*. Knapp claims that the Black nurse Christophine in the novel is the teacher and protector of Antoinette Cosway (Rhys's 'positive' version of the mad Bertha Rochester) but is entirely a 'Great Mother archetype . . . a timeless and solid and nutritive force unaware' of the powerful role she plays in other characters' lives' (Knapp, 1989, p. 127). Following Jung's defence of stereotypes, Knapp concludes that Christophine 'yields her irrational power to western rationalism' (Knapp, 1989, p. 127). This racist 'myth' clearly should be challenged, and I wish to do so at length to highlight problems of generalism and super-ficiality in Knapp and other myth critics. In *Wide Sargasso Sea* Jean Rhys makes Black Christophine the one character who might free Creole Antoinette from the stereotypes of white settler discourse with songs and patois expressions:

> 'Nor horse piss like the English madams drink', she said, 'I know them. Drink their yellow horse piss, talk, talk their lying talk'. Her dress trailed and rustled as she walked to the door. There she turned. 'I send the girl to clear up the mess you make with the frangipani, it bring cockroach in the house. Take care not to slip on the flowers, young master.' She slid through the door. 'Her coffee is delicious but her language is horrible . . .' (Rhys (1966) p. 85)

This speech constitutes a direct and explicit representation of a Black woman's facility with languages. In defining and con-trasting the cultural signifiers of 'coffee' and 'horse piss' Christophine's speech is governed by the intersection of two languages. Christophine's intercession here has an obvious effect: by switching between the syntactics of dialect, 'talk their lying talk' and the orthography of standard address, 'Take care not to slip . . . young master', she installs difference in the discourse of the text. Christophine constantly interweaves 'standard' and non-standard English, drawing profoundly on a range of styles. The verbal dexterity of this passage does not bespeak Christophine's 'irrational' or 'timeless' authority but suggests that Rhys actively supports Christophine's under-standing that words embody rather than merely represent the

racial characteristics they stand for, by allowing unpara-
phrased 'speechifying'. Rochester's stabilising displacement of
Christophine's dangerous 'code-switching' as 'horrible' reveals
not only that he occupies another language but that he occupies
a different way of understanding the practice and meanings of
languages in the colonial context. Christophine's speeches are
always governed by the doubling of 'vernacular' and 'standard'
English. That she constantly draws attention to the *opposition* of
these codes rather than simply either appropriating received
English or adhering to patois is a clear example of Rhys's faith in
the Black woman/mother as bearer of linguistic variety and as
maker of a more complex dynamic of appropriation. Christophine
is *not* a static, unchanging figure. Christophine's continuous
bifurcation between the rhythms of the vernacular voice and the
limited colonial language is an explicitly thematised example of
Black verbal power. Rhys signals a rupture with conventional
stereotypes because she demonstrates their excess. Christophine
is a visible role model of the Other, self-made into self, in the full
density of otherness with her powerful language and the
medical power of Obeah. Christophine does link Antoinette to a
more complex knowledge made up of magic, earth gods and
Arawak history. There is a strong focus to Christophine
throughout the novel, which begins with the opening description of her specialness and continues in Rhys's sympathetic
portrayal of an alternative and purer Arawak mythology, as
exemplified in Christophine's song 'ma belle ka di maman li'
which deliberately places the maternal in a Black and patois
voice.

Christophine *is* mythical but not in the racist terms which
Knapp supplies. Knapp's inability to deal with textual, historical
and religious representations *in* the text could be said to be a
major weakness of myth criticism, especially Jungian, since
Jung's view was that archetypes appear and reappear without
specificity.

MARY DALY

If motherhood is the main area of knowledge reconstituted by
myth critics, Mary Daly's metaphorical journey into Hagocracy

is another. *Gyn/Ecology* is a territorial examination of the space and architecture of women's prehistory hypothesised as women's future. The issue for Daly is that the language, symbols and concepts of Christian myths and other world religions are masculine. In order to break with this masculine universality women will need to name their own myths. *Gyn/Ecology*, like Virginia Woolf's, *Three Guineas*, is in three parts. The First Passage describes Christian myths and language and their misogyny. The Second Passage describes five international contemporary forms of woman-hating: Chinese footbinding, African female genital mutilation, witch-burning, suttee and gynaecology. In the final Third Passage Daly offers her mythic alternatives to women-hating – 'sparking' – a form of gynetic communication – and 'spinning' – creating a women-identified world.

What, then, are the main elements in Daly's reversal? *Gyn/Ecology* is a major work of myth criticism and a useful key to analysis of the whole genre. The importance of myth criticism, for Daly, lies in its ability to decode literature and culture. She is not intent, in any naive way, on proving that every phallic myth has a precedent in a gynocentric one which antedated it, but she shows that male myths do reverse female tales. Christianity incorporated goddess religions and transformed their symbols into a new mythology stripped of female power. By working through 'A-mazing' tales Daly points to the way in which patriarchy conceals aspects of Greek myth (she cites Apollo's homosexuality) so that it can laud male power. Daly claims that patriarchy also selects particular myths (such as that of Athena) in order to create an emblematic woman more identified with male aims. For Daly a real concern is to expose the ways in which male critics prefer myths which violate gender boundaries, as in the story of Dionysus driving women mad with his femininity. Daly replaces these myths with female images to act as magnets for feminist ideas. Daly prefers metaphor, which she believes is spontaneous, rather than archetype, which is merely reactive – a 'cookie-cutter' of patriarchy.

The problem with Daly's analysis of patriarchal mythology is her often overdetermined idea of gender asymmetry. To make her explanations work, she often reduces women and men to caricatures of themselves and focuses attention away from the social structures of male supremacy onto male behaviour represented in culture. Nowhere is this clearer than in her characterisation of male sexuality as always compulsively violent (a view, of course, shared by other contemporary feminists like Susan Brownmiller).

Daly argues that myths present two features of nature simultaneously: nature regulates women's activities; but nature is also creative. Daly's is a retrospective radicalism. By characterising prehistory as a matriarchy in a total way, Daly makes her retrospective view Utopian, since she gives us no historical evidence of the roles goddesses played in the lives of ancient women. We want to ask what variants of myths were known to women in particular times and distinguish between those that might reflect an historical period and those that might constitute timeless psychological phenomena. *Gyn/Ecology* is an authentic and moving account of myth, yet it is in other ways unreal. Daly's Hagocracy, 'the place we govern' (Daly, 1978, p. 15), remains an idealisation set against contemporary social disorder and hence could be said to evade the actual and bitter contradictions of women's present-day social conditions. However, Daly's ability to attack the sign systems of patriarchy – its language, rituals, myth and symbols – is a powerful and expressive charge.

Daly describes a new women's ecology, a new collective consciousness, both social and literary, which is capable of taking control of an environment in the manner of the myths of prehistory. This is a resonating image of women's power. But it is perhaps not immediately obvious how there could be a radical, socially constituted myth critique when literary myths are often transhistorical, collapsing history into a set of repetitive variations.

But if feminist critics somewhat overemphasise the Utopian aspects of myth, often traditional critics – like Frye and McLuhan, as we have seen – use myth as a displaced version of religion to avoid socially realisable goals. In McLuhan's work myth becomes a fundamental structure of consciousness. He perceives all things in the world, from television to schools, only in their metaphoric dimension. They become significant, therefore, only within McLuhan's schema rather than as a collection of social phenomena in their own right. Similarly Frye turns myths into narrative laws describing comic, romantic, tragic or ironic literature as autonomous verbal structures. In the writings of Claude Lévi-Strauss, there is one key form: the Oedipus myth. In *L'Anthropologie Structurale* Lévi-Strauss describes the Oedipus legend at great length, yet its universal nature goes virtually unquestioned. This obsession with laws is far removed from Daly's or Pratt's interest in myths as dynamic symbols of women's possibilities. Yet, despite Daly's verbal richness, there are problems with myth criticism, both in itself and as a model of literature. As literary criticism it is frequently less than adequate.

ANNIS PRATT

Myth critics believe that criticism should 'overlay' meaning *from* myth onto texts. In this way myth criticism, its practitioners claim, can be both a form of literary appreciation and a form of knowledge. Criticism can translate or reconstitute latent meaning in mythical stories, and can also, and simultaneously, constitute new knowledge about women. This is the aim of Annis Pratt's *Archetypal Patterns in Women's Fiction* (1982). The book examines narrative devices in the work of the Brontës and Edna O'Brien to point to ambivalences in individual authors but also to draw general lessons about the female psyche. Pratt claims that since women writers are often alienated from social time and space, their plots take on a cyclical rather than a linear form. Similarly, Pratt's criticism is itself circular. She starts by describing archetypal images as literary forms that derive from unconscious originals. For example, the representation of passion in the modern novel is still 'dark' as a result of centuries of women's conditioning by men. Pratt argues that literature is both specifically gendered in form and represents, in a one-to-one way, the psyches of female authors.

This 'unconscious' patterning, Pratt claims, shapes fictional structure as well as characters. Plots which use a rise-and-fall wave pattern are 'the raising of erotic expectations followed by an anticlimax of patriarchal misunderstanding' (Pratt, 1982, p. 85). And women's narratives will therefore use recurrent patterns: Pratt cites the rape motif of Daphne and nature myth in *Udolpho*.

Pratt's technique is problematic to begin with, since she refuses to distinguish between narrative ideology (which would relate to specific social institutions) and myth archetype. But she continues to draw universal categories of fiction from the images, symbols and narrative patterns she examines. 'The structure of the new space novel [Pratt is considering lesbian fiction] itself revolves around epiphanic moments, or peak experiences of erotic or metaphysical vision or both of a better world' (Pratt, 1982, p. 109). So that although Pratt describes a very wide range of fiction, her criticism remains narrow. She suggests, not surprisingly, that women writers think differently from male authors because they are socially conditioned to do so. Women writers choose fictional patterns and motifs which enact this difference and persistently use typical and mythical themes. Pratt argues that by understanding these typical literary themes and techniques, we can constitute a body of knowledge about women today. A critique of a whole dimension of literary life is expressed but also reduced.

But there are gains to be had from Pratt and other myth critics. To begin with, her critique is both deconstructive and futuristic. Pratt examines masculine and feminine imagery in *To the Lighthouse*, for example, to clarify the crucial features of power and apotheosis which effect women's social position. She goes on to extend Jung's archetypes, with those more rooted in women's history. It is crucial that feminist critics address myth since, as we have seen, the process of reclaiming and recreating myths is a central activity in the work of many feminist poets. Audre Lorde in particular uses mythological analogies to understand the angry chthonic powers of the goddess figures of prehistory. Critics and poets often describe female mythical divinities in anthropomorphic terms.

But, although a persistent theme in women's fiction is an identification with nature, and vegetation goddesses are among the most prevalent 'culture heroines' of myth, female figures in most of recorded mythology are much more likely to be depicted as destructive monsters. Therefore Annis Pratt admires the writer Fay Weldon precisely because Weldon 'envisions an extrasocietal solution' (Pratt, 1982, p. 70). Yet Weldon's main skill as a novelist (for example, in *The President's Child*) is decoding *existing* social arrangements and the ways in which men often control reality by controlling language and myth.

Understandably, then, institutional forces have less significance to Pratt than personalities. Pratt claims that marriage novels all have the same archetypal images and patterns whether written in the American West or the north of England. Pratt's false universality is evident in her idea, for example, that there is a single marriage debate in fiction covering the entire period of 1870 to 1910. She elides the very dissimilar spinsters of the Brontës and May Sinclair to prove that the spinster archetype is a modern sister of pre-patriarchal virgins. Pratt's flight from real history is clear in the way in which she avoids class or race. Although Pratt does examine some Black novels, she finds merely that 'the limitations of racist stereotypes' 'intensify' gender despair (Pratt, 1982, p. 66). Myth critics often describe race and class oppressions as patriarchal 'motifs' to be swept away by a women's culture.

If implicit racism is one feature of myth criticism, there are other less disturbing features which are equally problematic. Myth critics frequently assume that male myths are inadequate by virtue of their maleness rather than from the power a patriarchal system lends. It seems too sweeping for Pratt to claim, for example, that female authors will always be 'bounded by the all-encompassing, ever-present patriarchal enclosure' (Pratt, 1982, p. 67). She is not able, therefore, to answer the question of whether there is, or can be, a specifically gendered social protest novel. The preoccupation by Daly and Pratt with defining a female sensibility not only leads them to occasional erroneous generalisations about women's writing, but also implies that literary identity reflect only the intractability of maleness and femaleness. In advocating a return to a feminine mythical world these writers sometimes ignore the extent to which femaleness functions as a reflection of any society's given cultural assumptions.

The fact, too, that myth critics offer normative mythical models of women is a little disturbing. Pratt seems always to find that women in fiction are cut off from autonomy, from self-actualisation and ethical capacity. In her view, women are victim figures either succumbing to madness or marriage or frequently to both. Fictional heroines, in other words, are acting out in literature the same characteristics which Phyllis Chesler described of women entering into a 'psychiatric career'. Novels about women's friendships (Pratt examines those of May Sarton) result in excessively punitive denouements. Unlike Nina Auerbach's much more optimistic view of women-bonding, Pratt's case is that a women's space finally has to be beyond the social, not functioning through the social.

SUMMARY

It is obvious from the above accounts that myth criticism has its problems. It undercuts its own positions. It really is not possible to describe patriarchy in any single rhetorical gesture of repressive uniformity. To analyse the cultural embeddedness of gender difference criticism must be able to address at least the following issues: social, historical, religious differences and ethnic identities. No one of these issues is causal, nor is the list complete, but they structure the characters and themes of mythical literature.

In the long run, myth criticism may be more important not to feminist criticism but to creative writing. The creation of new myths in lesbian and science fiction novels, as Joanna Russ says, is an uncharted territory of the psychological and physical potential of women (Russ, 1973). Russ herself, Elana Nachman in *Riverfinger Women* and Bertha Harris in *Lover* create apocalyptic communities of strong, witch women drawing on Amazon myths and prehistorical matriarchies. Similarly Susan Griffin's powerful critique of Western theology, science and anti-environmentalism, *Woman and Nature*, is cast in a lyrical and intuitive form. The book describes the many ways in which patriarchy has used myths drawn from metaphysics and theology and literature (Dante) to formulate the idea of a God who is superior to Nature. Griffin displaces these myths with a growing feminist intensity using traditional myth images – caves, seeds and the elements of water and earth – appropriate to women's vision.

Clearly Daly might argue that in studying a body of myth we are looking less at its narrative contents than at the universal structures. These structures are in a way what myths are about: they are devices for women to think with, ways of organising female reality. But myths must not become focal points for virtually unlimited powers of rationalisation by offering only a static picture of actuality. This undercuts the crucial gain of myth criticism – the way it has informed women poets.

Women's spirituality is today a subject of immense concern to feminists, for we are beginning to recognise the profound and often distressing influence religion has on the role of women in any culture. The more we know about our own culture's dominant myths and the more we know about the myths of cultures other than our own, the more feminism will be able to assess the function of spirituality. In the end, myth criticism can occupy a position in that critical future as long as it is not hermetically sealed from history.

SELECTED READING

Basic texts

Anzaldúa, G. (1987) *Borderlands/La Frontera: The new mestiza*, San Francisco: Spinsters/Aunt Lute Book Company.

Daly, M. (1978) *Gyn/Ecology*, Boston: Beacon Press

Davidson, C. and Broner, E. M. (eds) (1980) *The Lost Tradition: Mothers and daughters in literature*, New York: Ungar

DuPlessis, R. B. (1985) ' "Perceiving the Other-side of Everything": tactics of revisionary mythopoesis', in *Writing Beyond the Ending: Narrative strategies of twentieth-century women writers*, Bloomington: Indiana University Press

Frye, N. (1957) *The Anatomy of Criticism: Four essays*, Princeton: Princeton University Press

Griffin, S. (1978) *Woman and Nature: The roaring inside her*, New York: Harper & Row

Knapp, B. L. (1989) *Women in Twentieth-Century Literature: A Jungian view*, Baltimore, M. D.: Pennsylvania State University Press

Lorde, A. (1984) 'An open letter to Mary Daly', in *Sister Outsider*, New York: Crossing Press

Neumann, E. (1955) *The Great Mother: An analysis of the archetype*, trans. R. Manheim, Princeton: Princeton University Press

Pratt, A. (1973) 'Archetypal approaches to the new feminist criticism', *Bucknell Review*, 21 (Spring) pp. 3–14

Pratt, A. (1976) 'The new feminist criticisms: exploring the history of the new space', in J. Roberts (ed.), *Beyond Intellectual Sexism*, New York: David McKay

Pratt, A. (1982) *Archetypal Patterns in Women's Fiction*, Hemel Hempstead: Harvester Wheatsheaf

Rich, A. (1977) *Of Woman Born*, London: Virago

Wiegle, M. (1982) *Spiders and Spinsters: Women and mythology*, Albuquerque: University of New Mexico Press

Introductions

Allen, P. G. (ed.) (1988) *Spider Woman's Granddaughters: Traditional tales and contemporary writing by native American women*, Boston: Beacon Press

Braxton, B. J. and McLaughlin, A. (eds) (1990) *Wild Women in the Whirlwind: Afra-American culture and the contemporary literary renaissance*, London: Serpents Tail

Christ, C. P. and Plaskow, T. (eds) (1979) *Womanspirit Rising: A feminist reader in religion*, New York: Harper & Row

Hall, N. (1980) *The Moon and the Virgin: Reflections on the archetypal feminine*, London: The Women's Press

Lauter, E. (1984) *Women as Mythmakers*, Bloomington: Indiana University Press

Lauter, E. and Rupprecht, C. S. (1985) *Feminist Archetypal Theory*, Knoxville: University of Tennessee Press

Starhawk (1979) *The Spiral Dance: The re-birth of the ancient religion of the goddess*, New York: Harper & Row

Washbourn, P. (1979) *Seasons of Women: Song, poetry, ritual, prayer, myth, story*, New York: Harper & Row

Further reading

Auerbach, N. (1985) *Romantic Imprisonment: Women and other glorified outcasts*, New York: Columbia University Press

Chesler, P. (1972) *Women and Madness*, New York: Doubleday

Chodorow, N. (1978) *The Reproduction of Mothering*, Berkeley: University of California Press

Dinnerstein, D. (1976) *The Mermaid and the Minotaur*, New York: Harper & Row

Frye, N. (1963) 'The developing imagination', in *Learning in Language and Literature*, Cambridge, Mass.: Harvard University Press

Gates, H. L. (1988) *The Signifying Monkey: A theory of African-American literary criticism*, Oxford: Oxford University Press

Gubar, S. (1979) 'Mother, maiden and the marriage of death: women writers and an ancient myth', *Women's Studies*, 6, pp. 301–15

Lévi-Strauss, C. (1968) *Structural Anthropology*, London: Allen Lane

McLuhan, M. (1964) *Understanding Media*, London: Routledge & Kegan Paul

Ostriker, A. (1985) 'The thieves of language: women poets and revisionary myth making'; in D. W. Middlebrook and M. Yalom (eds), *Coming to Light*, Ann Arbor: University of Michigan

Paper, J. (1983) 'The forgotten grandmothers: Amerindian women and religion in colonized North America', *Canadian Woman Studies*, 5:2 (Winter) pp. 48–51

Pomeroy, S. B. (1975) *Goddesses, Whores, Wives and Slaves: Women in classical antiquity*, New York: Schocken Books

Rhys, J. (1966) *Wide Sargasso Sea*, London: André Deutsch

Russ, J. (1973) 'What can a heroine do? Or why women can't write' in S. K. Cornillon (ed.), *Images of Women*, Bowling Green, Ohio: Bowling Green University Popular Press

3 Marxist/socialist-feminist criticism

To speak of literature and life as two separate phenomena is, for Marxist and socialist feminists, a meaningless distinction. While Marxism embraces a wide range of attitudes and debates – from the 'orthodoxy' of Theodor Adorno and Bertolt Brecht, the dialectical criticism of Lucien Goldmann to the lyricism of Walter Benjamin – in general, Marxism argues that literature is the ideological representation of life experience. 'Marxist and socialist feminism' is not a precise term. While Marxist feminism has traditionally looked to the *material* conditions of literary production, socialist feminists add a focus on the *detail* of women's lives and on women's alternative values. Critics who might be considered as Marxist or socialist include writers like Michèle Barrett who have an explicit interest in the production processes of literature, others who were active in the Communist Party like Tillie Olsen, and many British feminists in cultural studies.

If we look at the development of Marxist and socialist-feminist criticism over the past years in order to assess its contribution, to point to certain weaknesses and to evaluate its future, the problem at issue is the state of Marxist criticism itself as much as uneasy 'marriages' between Marxism or socialism and feminism. Feminists agree, however, that Marxism has something to teach literary criticism about the material conditions of women's cultural products and practices. This enables feminists to interrogate the representation of women's experience in literature in terms of social determinations.

74

Neither Marxism/socialism nor feminism can totally incorpor-ate each other. Among other things, what Marxism argues is that women are defined by the work they do or do not do. Work is the means by which people construct and change their material and imaginative worlds. Feminism argues that women are defined by the sexuality which they express or are repressed by. Sexuality is one means by which social and imaginative experiences are formed.

Yet Marxism and feminism are both theories about the power of the 'real' world and its impact on literary imagination. They both describe how culture relates to class and political change. But a key question for Marxist/socialist-feminist critics is whether Marxism itself can provide intact paradigms for understanding women's literature or whether a new, or modified, mode of analysis is needed. What, if anything, can Marxism teach us about literary form, and what is the utility of Marxist methods of literary criticism?

What Marxism *can* give feminism is a way of analysing literature in terms of the historical contexts which produce literature and which in turn literature helps to produce. Marxist criticism argues that art derives from social-historical processes. Not only this, Marxists understand that, from time to time, literature may be the only available source of historical ideas, feelings and values. The very forms of literature – its imagery, syntax and style – thus have a direct relationship to the ideological world or belief system which it inhabits. In addition, at the centre of the Marxist notion of 'consciousness' is the belief that any group or class becomes 'conscious' of their subordina-tion through critical analysis.

For feminist critics seeking to understand literary representa-tions of women, Marxism offers both a way of linking historical evidence of women's oppression with literary texts and under-standing how writers consciously or unconsciously transpose that evidence into their texts.

Finally, Marxism is so attractive to feminists because it refuses the idea that 'literature' is a distinct bounded form. The repression or misrepresentation of women in writing can be methodically exposed and analysed when you believe, as Marxists do, that writing represents social patterns.

These are very exciting possibilities for feminist criticism. In addition, Marxism draws historical significance from the everyday and hence adds the idea of 'lived experience' to critical thinking. The terrain of literature is massively enlarged. Rather than cultivating sensibility in a tiny minority, therefore, criticism has a much broader project. Indeed the Marxist concept of consciousness depends on a structure of ideology. Marxist and socialist feminists believe that social institutions determine consciousness. By challenging the institution of literature and existing literary relations between writers and audiences, Marxism helps feminism to interrogate and renegotiate the creation of literary value.

But in the writings on aesthetics of Marx and Engels the *significations* of language are not assigned a central or even a distinctive role, and gender itself is never at the centre. Although Marxist literary criticism is not a distinctive approach like structuralism, Left critical theory traditionally favours kinds of writing which plainly express the political aims of the working class, usually characterised as social realism. Marxist literary theorists read literature in relation to social change and the growth of social consciousness. What Lukacs, Gramsci and the cultural theorists of the Frankfurt School (Adorno, Marcuse, Benjamin), Goldmann and Brecht have in common is a concern with the social (not gendered) function of literature in tandem with its 'literary' function.

Echoes of a utilitarian approach to the study of literature can be found in England in the work of the English Marxist, Christopher Cauldwell. The main argument of English literary Marxists in the 1930s was that the function of art had to assist a return to community. Because critics wanted to relate social class and ideology directly to literature, they often avoided detailed textual analysis in favour of finding themes and examples appropriate to the class struggle.

Louis Althusser and Pierre Macherey give a more subtle account of the relationship between ideology and literature in which ideology is not just a theory imposed from the *outside*, but the web of our understanding of the world and of ourselves. The transformation of ideology *within* literature is their focus. According to Althusser, ideology works through systems, representations and the rituals of everyday life. Literature, along with the arts and sport, is a 'cultural state apparatus' and together with ideological state apparatuses (ISAs), which include the Church, Schools and the family, literature colludes in reproducing ideology by 'interpellating' or bringing the subject into being. Althusser defines ideology as our *imaginary* relations to social forces. Macherey adds the suggestive idea that the literary work is continually distancing itself from the ideology contained within it. Gaps or breaks in ideology emerge as 'absences' in literary texts. That is to say, literary texts can be understood by examining their 'absences' as much as their content, since these absences reveal the ideological assumptions which a text finds difficult to voice – for example, the absent centre of whiteness in imperial texts. However, for both critics the subject is unified, conscious and ungendered.

One example of how feminism has extended Marxist theory is the work of Julia Kristeva. While Althusser 'translated' Lacan into a Marxist account of the ideological construction of the subject, Kristeva initially develops a materialist analysis into a psychoanalytically based theory able to deal with *gendered* subjectivity. Kristeva attempts to show, by linking Freud and Lacan with Marxism, that literature cannot simply be understood in material terms but that criticism must take account of how woman as subject is constituted in language. Since Kristeva is considered in detail in chapter 4, suffice it to say here that she emphasises the gendered and potentially revolutionary nature of literary language. She argues that all social activity should be treated as signifying systems; as a series of texts that reveal a 'dialectical' relationship, as Marxists argue, between female experience and literary sign systems.

In Marxism and socialist feminism the Marxist indictment of capitalist repression is changed into a revolutionary account of women's existence. For example, the Marxist-feminist critic Christine Delphy suggests that each woman has within her a dialectic between feelings and existence which she can manifest as social language or as literary imagination (see Delphy, 1984).

Marxism itself, as Kristeva and Delphy argue, cannot be incorporated directly into feminism. There are problems with its categories and with the way in which it constitutes subjects. To take the question of language first: if Macherey's work is useful to feminists, since he argues that texts are never complete but are written around silences, there is a way in which women themselves are silent in Macherey's books. The problem with Macherey is that, although for him literary texts constantly undercut their own values, he does not address *gender* values. Marxists tend to theorise the roles of subjects descriptively in relation to class rather than moving from ideology to question the whole foundation of symbolic language itself. Hence Marxist critics' continual preference for the realist text in their obsession with nineteenth-century novels.

Marxist theory and criticism have a more developed history than have Marxist or socialist feminism: this brief background is intended simply as a grid of points within which to locate feminist constructions of Marxist criticism. The feminist critics I shall now describe may not necessarily themselves outline all these priorities but they are attempting to formulate a Marxist/socialist-feminist critical method when analysing literature and culture.

TILLIE OLSEN

Tillie Olsen is generally acknowledged to be the major contemporary Marxist-feminist critic. Deborah Rosenfelt argues that Olsen's work is part of a socialist literary tradition extending from Charlotte Perkins Gilman to Alice Walker (see Rosenfelt, 1985). In *Silences* (1978) Olsen describes the relation between class and creativity in the work of Rebecca Harding Davis and many other writers who 'are women in our Century'. Olsen wrote *Silences* not as a form of close textual analysis or as some dense theoretical account but as a mixed generic form juxtaposing multiple quotations from writers worldwide with her own autobiographical musings in the manner of Virginia Woolf's *A Room of One's Own*.

Key themes dominate all of Olsen's writing: the power of language and the importance of difference (in gender, race and class). The management of these themes demands a narrative strategy characterised by mixtures and interfusions. For example, in *Tell Me A Riddle* Olsen subverts the distinction between 'high' and 'low' art by implying affinities and similarities between Russian literature, folk art and revolutionary songs, all of which vivify the Russian Jewish immigrant, Eva.

Throughout her work Olsen constantly interweaves the voices of workers, Black and white, mothers and those published writers Olsen admires, juxtaposing these voices to show the impress of history.

JULIET MITCHELL

In Britain the opening argument came more directly from feminist politics with Juliet Mitchell's article 'Women: The Longest Revolution' published in *New Left Review* in 1966. Mitchell's crucial contribution was to recognise the ultimate centrality of economic forces yet describe as equally significant other aspects of women's experience. Mitchell's work at this stage is theoretical rather than literary critical, but in the literary essays collected in *Women: The Longest Revolution* (1984) she draws on Althusser to describe how literature and culture are a material force in patriarchy and how the ending of *patriarchal* ideology therefore needs a cultural, as well as a social, revolution (see chapter 5, 'Psychoanalytic criticism').

LILLIAN ROBINSON

To describe the relations between culture and the social world is the objective of Lillian Robinson. In *Sex, Class and Culture* (1978), her collected essays, Robinson believes that it is futile to develop a feminist critical theory unless this proves adequate to women's history. She enlarges the boundaries of criticism to examine 'low' and 'high' art by mixing pieces about the television show 'What's My Line?' with those about Virginia Woolf. Her essays continually move back and forth between literary and social events by describing autobiographically how that relation operates in her own political and literary activity. Robinson argues that literature describes women's social roles and focuses on the question: what are the social effects of literary conventions?

'Criticism: Who needs It?' is a good example of Robinson's approach. The essay is about her home town Buffalo, and she describes its ethnic and class groups before describing cultural features. Robinson places her own autobiography ethnographically to expose the gap that she feels exists between contemporary critical concerns and the everyday life of women in a typical American town. It is clear that Robinson expects feminist critics to respond to social as well as to literary forces. Her technique is basically one of juxtaposition and she provides very 'readable' accounts of historical romance and soap operas. Although Robinson starts with a specific use of Marxist theory – for example, applying Marx's analysis of commodity fetishism to works of art – her criticism sometimes suffers from the reflectionist fallacy of traditional Marxism. Phrases like 'social experience is not only different from private experience but, that, acknowledged or not, it is the dominant force in the making of art or criticism' seem to accept a sharp division between the public and the private, a division which feminist criticism works to reject (Robinson, 1978, p. 60).

This early version of Marxist-feminist criticism is to some extent cultural criticism in the sense that Robinson describes literature as a social agency not as a symbolic representation of psychic needs. As a Marxist feminist Robinson takes care to avoid prioritising avant-garde writing in any hierarchy of literary value. She argues that literature should reflect a total culture not just the culture of a restricted literary elite. However, if Robinson disparages formalist aesthetics, she does make unconscious value judgements. While arguing that literature as an institution should widen its brief to include media studies, Robinson herself accepts the literary canon when she says that her essays on 'low' culture stem from her more private interests. If Marxist-feminist literary criticism does not deal with the relation between psyche, gender and aesthetic form, then it remains just an epistemology.

MICHÈLE BARRETT

What methodology could feminist critics use that would link literature's institutional practice with literary artifacts? Michèle

Barrett finds one answer in literary contexts. In *Women's Oppression Today* (1979) Barrett sets out the theories which underpin her cultural criticism in 'Feminism and the Definition of Cultural Politics' and other writings. Barrett argues for a historical approach over what she calls the biologistic arguments of writers like Shulamith Firestone. In challenging the apparently universal and transhistorical categories of Firestone, Barrett is calling for a more complex construction of subjectivity. Literature cannot provide a single site for that construction since, although we may learn a great deal while reading about the ways in which meaning is constructed in a particular historical period, 'our knowledge will not add up to a general knowledge of that social formation' (Barrett, 1979a, p. 98). For Barrett, it is the context, as much as the genres of literature which forms a basis for analysis.

There are obvious problems for literary criticism in Barrett's construction of Marxist building-bricks. If literature can provide only one (of many) 'sites for the construction of ideological processes' we could ask: why bother with literature at all? (Barrett, 1979, p. 97). Barrett might answer that, although cultural practice is not a privileged site, it is an essential site and helps us to understand the bounds within which particular symbolic means are constructed.

Women's Oppression Today is firmly based in Marxist feminism. Barrett's argument is that literature grows if it engages in a living dialogue with many different cultural products. We have solved one problem – the isolation of literature from determinations surrounding literary practice – but are immediately into another. We are no nearer the material reality of literature itself. How do we set about reading fantasy symbols and metaphors – the textual surface of literature – within a Marxist framework?

The source of that more difficult critique, Barrett claims in 'Feminism and the Definition of Cultural Politics', can be found in a concept of skill. Barrett travels from the England of Charlotte Brontë's *Shirley* to the America of Judy Chicago's *The Dinner Party* deconstructing distinctions between art and other cultural products like soap operas in a feminist critique. Her premise is that the sex of an author is not a reliable guide either to the meaning of a text or to its feminist potential. Judy Chicago fails Barrett's test because Chicago worked in an apparently hierarchical, dictatorial manner. As in traditional Marxism, mode of production is all. But Barrett does acknowledge that art is ambivalent and contradictory and is not simply a result of production processes (Barrett, 1982, p. 41). Barrett is justifiably antagonistic to feminist critics (her example is Elaine Showalter) who separate the activity of reading (consumption) from that of writing (production), but her own alternative is perhaps problematic. Feminist literary criticism should identify 'levels of aesthetic skill in the construction of works of art' (Barrett, 1982, p. 52). While Barrett's argument is an attractive alternative to the elitism of traditional criticism, she leaves open very large questions. What about reader reception? How do we judge skill?

The notion of skill is an idealist suggestion which does not come to grips with aesthetics directly. Michèle Barrett seems to describe a reading experience not in the formulation of literary experience but in deciding what can be saved from the terrain of 'literature' for feminist politics. Barrett has worked hard to link theories of historical materialism with literary representations of women. She provides crucial insights in particular into the relation between the class position of Virginia Woolf and Woolf's system of literary values in her pioneering edition of Woolf's writings (Barrett, 1979b). It is Barrett's insight into Woolf which is my reason for comparing Barrett with another feminist Marxist and deconstructionist, Gayatri Spivak, who has also written extensively about Woolf. The comparison will highlight the different cultural concerns of Marxist feminism. Barrett and Spivak's accounts of Woolf are not only by two very different critics but read as if they were about two very different authors. Barrett starts from the question 'What are the consequences for the woman author of historical changes in the position of women in society?', and her aim is to analyse the historical determinants of Woolf's literary/critical productions. Barrett's is a fascinating and complex analysis of the relation between Virginia Woolf's lack of formal education, her critical reception (or lack of it) by male critics, her domestic isolation and the inevitable effect of these forces on Woolf's work. Barrett links Woolf's writings on sexuality to Woolf's ideas about male belligerence and fascism and to Victorian bourgeois sexual morality. Although Barrett fully fleshes out a psychoanalytic critique in her later criticism, here she prefers to interpret Woolf's commitment to female difference in social rather than psychoanalytical terms.

Sexuality and its multiple forms are Spivak's very 'different' point of departure (as I discuss in detail in chapter 6, below). Her critique is, like much of American criticism, heavily in debt to Lacan and Derrida (whom Spivak translated and introduced to American audiences). But in her early essays Spivak focuses more explicitly on the relation between Marxism and deconstruction. Spivak's essay also illustrates the debt many feminists owe to their undergraduate training in rhetoric and linguistics. Spivak focuses on Woolf's allegory and verbal dexterity. Spivak argues that *To the Lighthouse* deliberately superimposes two allegories, the grammatical and the sexual. These are present, Spivak claims, in Woolf's two languages: the language of art and the language of marriage. By an extended pun on the word 'copula' – a pivot of grammar and a sexual activity – Spivak makes a Derrida-like business of the different uses and meanings of single words. Spivak does not offer Barrett's thorough cultural history but rather a use of what Raymond Williams called Keywords, words which can represent key cultural moments. The differences within Marxist feminism could not be clearer. Barrett's criticism appears to be illustrative in its welding of social and literary concerns. Spivak's criticism appears to be formalist and assumes an agreed notion of the avant-garde. Both critics offer helpful ways of reading Woolf.

By taking a text more overtly focused on sexuality like *Orlando* we could (following Barrett) describe Orlando's development and gender changes in relation to the literary and historical moments she/he encounters. The critical focus here would be Orlando's attack on Victorian culture and masculinity. Conversely (following Spivak) we could describe *Orlando* as a deliberately uncommitted narrative, whose biographer 'slips away' textually revealing the impossibility of fixed gender identities. Since Woolf describes gender difference primarily physiologically, this reading would focus on the subtext of physical violence and on Orlando's response to this in his/her mixture of interrogative and interior analysis.

Both approaches are forms of Marxist-feminist criticism and are good examples of how two models can complement rather than cancel each other out. Where critics like Spivak, informed by psychoanalysis, understand that meaning always lies in the *process* of the text, to British Marxists the text often seems to be a 'souvenir' of social experience. However, presumably all texts historicise a writer's fantasies rather than simply 'remember' these. If we ignore contradictions in the surface of discourse, we preclude discussion of the dialectical interplay of conscious creation and subconscious intent. If we read literature as a representation of ideology, we blot out what is literary about literature. The process of negotiation of meanings, of identification and reassurance is both an internal process in a text and has to do with our own subjectivity.

A way around the problem for British Marxists and socialists is to treat the socially situated reader as discursively constructed *by* the text. This has been one of the great strengths of British feminist work on soap operas and the media. The objective of much of this criticism has been to address the paradox that popular culture enjoyed by women speaks to women's pleasure at the same time that it seems to put pleasure at the service of the patriarchal family. *Feminism for Girls* provides a good example of this approach (McRobbie, 1981). Angela McRobbie and other critics in the collection detail the kinds of discrimination experienced by adolescent girls as represented in and constructed by the literary and visual styles of teen magazines and other forms of popular culture. The focus here is on the reception and subversion of imagery. The approach can be characterised as semiotic and analyses depictions of reality or unreality as modes of signification. Much of this criticism is ethnographic, asking questions about mainstream culture and the creation of alternative 'female' cultures. Although British Marxist and socialist feminists have enlarged the boundaries of what we can call 'literature', there are weaknesses in the approach as an explanation of literary patterning. By describing ethnographically forms of popular culture, critics are tempted to refuse an aesthetic hierarchy of 'good' or 'bad' representations. Meaning, then, can only be the result of a changing interaction between particular verbal forms and socially constructed readers. While the notion of meaning, as an ideological force is often very well demonstrated, the focus on ideology often ignores the issue of literary value.

BIRMINGHAM CENTRE

Feminists at the Birmingham Centre for Cultural Studies were some of the first critics to question the relation between cultural and social practices in terms of the lived experience of readers (see Hall *et al.*, 1980). The group focused on 'the popular' in a radically new way, producing concrete research about ideas of the popular and the interaction between literary texts and women from different classes. Methodologically this led Marxist-feminist literary criticism to its more ethnographic approach, moving from close formal readings of texts to the lived reception of texts. 'Women, Feminism and Literature in the 1930s' and the study of Barbara Cartland and Winifred Holtby in *Culture, Media, Language* (Hall *et al.*,1980) do not analyse texts in depth but, following Althusser, look at the process of literary production and the interpellation of (or hailing of) readers by texts. This is accomplished by a mechanism of identification. That is to say, characters in a text call upon the reader to identify her or himself as an ideological subject. The Birmingham Centre approach, as I shall have to call much of British Marxism, searches popular narratives, like Barbara Cartland's *Blue Heather*, for motifs (of home and marriage) which relate to social concerns. The Birmingham Centre pioneered a collective approach both to feminist criticism and to research methods in general. It mapped different cultural practices and aimed to mobilise these. In Britain Marxist feminism has worked to reconstitute 'community' in an active involvement in women's writing groups outside the academy – for example, the women's groups 'Human Voices' and 'Commonplace Workshop' (see Worpole, 1982). Although this represents a radical departure for feminist literary criticism, another way of reading romance would be to use deconstruction to read a romance text as a set of relations with other texts. This is an equally helpful critical approach because romance vocabulary is as much to do with readers' expectations of form (four-letter words are added to

Women's Weekly romances when published as books to attract a wider readership) as with the Birmingham linkage of reader expectation with lived experience.

MARXIST-FEMINIST LITERATURE COLLECTIVE (MFLC)

While the 'culturalist' approach of the Birmingham Centre focuses on a woman reader's relation to literary form, the Marxist-Feminist Literature Collective (MFLC), although no longer writing as a group, did interrogate aesthetic form in terms of constructions of women. While the overriding concern of the Birmingham Centre was with material production, adapting Althusser and Macherey, the MFLC focuses on the material results of that production.

In 'Women's Writing: Jane Eyre, Shirley, Villette and Aurora Leigh' the MFLC propose to transform traditional Marxist criticism. They do this by describing the marginality of women's literary practice, and find representations of that marginality in the situations of female characters. The group looks at two key points of articulation in the nineteenth-century novel: marriage and paterfamilias. The Brontës and Barrett-Browning, the essay claims, by excluding their heroines from conventional family structures, create plots which deliberately interrogate the patriarchal ideology of Victorian life. Rather than simply equating character representation with authorial point of view, the location of feminism, the collective claims, is to be found not in what characters *say* but in what they cannot say – in the awkward moments when speech is denied or repressed.

Yet it is sometimes difficult to imagine each text in the terms which the group provide, particularly since they ignore features crucial to feminist criticism like female friendship in *Shirley*. They describe women's consciousness as passive with an apparent foregrounding of the 'real'. A more adequate analysis of textual moments would be to look at texts as bundles of discourses, not silences, bound in different ways. Some discourses would relate to other texts gone before, some would anticipate responses to come. Literary ideology would be located less in a specific *form* and more as a series of effects.

The problem stems ironically from the very success of British Marxist/socialist-feminist history. Contemporary British feminism was generated by the work of feminist historians, like Sheila Rowbotham, which predates feminist literary criticism. Feminist historians introduced new historical techniques; Rowbotham, for example, uses autobiography. In 'The Public Face of Feminism' other feminist historians examine suffragette autobiographies as important historical documents because it is autobiographical modes of writing, they argue, that pose the question central to feminism: the relation between the 'public' and the 'private' (Davis *et al.*, 1982).

By acknowledging the role of 'unwitting testimony' in the writing of women and men, feminist historians often resemble literary critics. For example, Davis *et al.* take the gaps, absences and tensions of historical discourse to be evidence of repressed feminism. However, there is one major absence in feminist history – the *literary* text itself. Imaginative literature is still not being widely used by feminist historians as source material. Feminist literary criticism argues that autobiography, popular text and literature are all vehicles for the production and reproduction of forms of consciousness.

MARY POOVEY

The attempt to treat a text as a more densely orchestrated unity of writing practices comes in Mary Poovey's *The Proper Lady and the Woman Writer* (1984). Poovey takes up where Lillian Robinson left off, by examining each writer's career and ideology as part of her literary practice. Poovey's focus could be characterised as Marxist feminist. She states that the terms in which femininity is publicly formulated by Mary Wollstonecraft, Mary Shelley and Jane Austen are determined by familial and economic relationships and dictate the way in which femaleness is experienced in their work. Where Robinson finds ideology to lie in the social *context* of the text, Barrett in the *production* of the text, the Birmingham centre in the implied *reader* of the text and the MFLC in *absences* in the text, we now have the *woman author herself* as a textual construct.

Poovey chose to write about Mary Wollstonecraft, Mary Shelley and Jane Austen, she says, because these writers represent in literary form a 'critical phase in the history of bourgeois ideology' (1984, p. xv). The French Revolution, she points out, explicitly challenged English patriarchy. To Poovey, it is women above all who naturalise discrepancies in lived experiences – the differences between promises made and the material world.

However, Poovey prefers Jane Austen to Mary Shelley because Austen could 'resolve' the ideological contradictions left unresolved in *Frankenstein*. Yet often a narrative closure might be compensatory for a woman writer rather than aesthetically valuable. Perhaps more significantly, Poovey makes a rather overgeneral use of the term 'ideology'. Since her usage includes politics, economics, literary practices and institutions, we could ask 'Is there anything non-ideological now?' While Poovey's interpretation of ideology is an attempt to escape the social reductionism of some traditional kinds of Marxism, it creates terminological difficulties when we want to distinguish literary practice from literary institutions. This is a common weakness in much of Marxist/socialist-feminist criticism. By proposing, as Poovey does, a vague extra discursive reality in some social totality, 'ideology' becomes an imprecise concept, an imprecision corrected in her later text, *Uneven Development*.

SUMMARY

The methods of Marxist/socialist-feminist literary critics often resemble a tricky balancing act. Marxist criticism focuses on social and cultural production, often without analysing differences between women and inherent contradictions in the subject 'woman'. Of course there is a material world out there, but literature inevitably involves, to some extent, a subjective perception of the world. Marxist and socialist feminists often ignore the fact that textual material is a form of materialism. Feminist criticism stresses the positionality of the subject and her history as part of literature, not external to literature. Representations have their own specificity. To take an obvious example of the difficulty in practice, how do we analyse representation of the family in novels by writers like Buchi Emecheta? The Birmingham Centre argues that the family is not 'natural' but a socially constructed institution. But for the Black woman writer in patriarchy, the family is a site of a more vibrant politics and culture (see chapter 7 'Black feminisms').

Other oppositions to Marxist and socialist feminism appear in the work of radical feminists like Adrienne Rich. Lesbian criticism seems to require a different set of priorities from those in Marxist and socialist feminism. Rich and others describe psychic domains ignored or trivialised in traditional criticism. Radical feminism poses the question (where this chapter began) of whether feminist criticism can be simply and easily assimilated into a Marxist agenda, or whether it requires a new critical method. Much of what has been said about Marxist and socialist feminism indicates the absolute priority of analysing social production along with literary productions. Yet only a feminist criticism that addresses the psychic as well as material representations of class and gender can begin to account for textual representations in their complexity.

The attempts to bring together Marxism and feminism perhaps raise more questions than they answer, but they do represent a sustained and often very polemical enterprise. In Marxist and socialist feminism, certain major themes and leading ideas stand out. Marxist and socialist feminists continually focus on the ways in which representations of gender and representations of institutions such as class and the family interconnect. For example, the British socialist feminist writer, Zoe Fairbairns, describes the relations between women's oppression, the State and reproduction in her widely read novel, *Benefits* (1979). Fairbairns paints a horrific picture of a future State where women are paid (benefits) to stay at home, limiting their horizons to the family and to reproductive roles.

Taken together, these themes and ideas indicate the important contributions made by Marxist feminists to literary criticism. The practice of group writing in itself represents a quite significant break with traditional critical practice. In addition the Marxist feminist linkage of literature and history breaks with traditional literary history and its lists of transhistoric great books. Marxist feminism attends to popular romance and the media. Added to this, Marxist feminism rejects the distinction between a knowing woman subject and the known woman object – the division between subjective and objective discursive postures. In other words, Marxist feminism offers us the possibility of a more open dialectic between our reading pleasures and the historically precise conditions in which we read.

SELECTED READING

Basic texts

Barrett, M. (ed.) (1979a) *Virginia Woolf: Women and writing*, London: The Women's Press
Barrett, M. (1979b) *Women's Oppression Today*, London: Croom Helm
Barrett, M. (1982) 'Feminism and the definition of cultural politics', in R. Brunt and C. Rowan (eds), *Feminism, Culture and Politics*, London: Lawrence and Wishart
Davis, T., Durham. M., Hall, C., Langan, M. and Sutton, D. (1982) ' "The Public Face of Feminism": early twentieth-century writings on women's suffrage', in R. Johnson *et al.* (ed.), *Making Histories: Studies in history, writing and politics*, London: Hutchinson
Delphy, C. (1984) *Close to Home: A materialist analysis of women's oppression*, London: Hutchinson
Hall, S., Hobson, D., Lowe, A. and Willis, P. (eds) (1980) *Culture, Media, Language*, London: Hutchinson
Kristeva, J. (1980) 'From one identity to an other', in *Desire in Language: A semiotic approach to literature and art*, Oxford: Blackwell
Marxist-Feminist Literature Collective (1978) 'Women's writing: Jane Eyre, Shirley, Villette, Aurora Leigh', *Ideology and Consciousness*, 3 (Spring) pp. 27–49
McRobbie, A. (ed.) (1981) *Feminism for Girls*, London: Routledge and Kegan Paul
Mitchell, J. (1984) *Women: The Longest Revolution: Essays in feminism, literature and psychoanalysis*, London: Virago
Olsen, T. (1978) *Silences*, New York: Delacorte Press

Poovey, M. (1984) *The Proper Lady and the Woman Writer*, Chicago: University of Chicago Press

Poovey, M. (1988) *Uneven Development: The ideological work of gender in mid-Victorian England*, Chicago: University of Chicago Press

Robinson, L. (1978) *Sex, Class and Culture*, Bloomington: Indiana University Press

Robinson, L. (1983) 'Treason our text: feminist challenges to the literary canon', *Tulsa Studies in Women's Literature*, 2 (2:1) pp. 88–98

Spivak, G. (1987) *In Other Worlds: Essays in cultural politics*, London: Methuen

Introductions

Campion, M. and Gross [Grosz], E. (1991) 'Love's labours lost: Marxism and feminism', in S. Gunew (ed.), *A Reader in Feminist Knowledge*, London: Routledge

Donovan, J. (1985) 'Feminism and Marxism', in *Feminist Theory: The intellectual traditions of American feminism*, New York: Ungar

Kaplan, C. (1986) *Sea Changes: Essays on culture and feminism*, London: Verso

Rosenfelt, D. (1985) 'From the thirties: Tillie Olsen and the radical tradition' in J. Newton and D. Rosenfelt (eds), *Feminist Criticism and Social Change: Sex, class and race in literature and culture*, London: Methuen

Tong, R. (1989) 'Marxist feminism' in *Feminist Thought*, Sydney: Unwin

Further reading

Althusser, L. (1975) *Lenin and Philosophy and Other Essays*, London: New Left Books

Eagleton, T. (1976) *Marxism and Literary Criticism*, London: Methuen

Eagleton, T. (1978) *Criticism and Ideology: A study on Marxist literary theory*, London: Verso

Fairbairns, Z. (1979) *Benefits*, London: Virago

Macherey, P. (1978) *A Theory of Literary Production*, London: Routledge and Kegan Paul

Mulford, W. (1983) 'Notes on writing: a marxist/feminist viewpoint', in M. Wandor (ed.), *On Gender and Writing*, London: Pandora

Rowbotham, S. (1983) *Dreams and Dilemmas: Collected writings*, London: Virago

Worpole, K. (1982) *The Republic of Letters: Working class writing and local publishing*, London: Comedia

4 French feminist criticism

Where second-wave critics Kate Millett and Mary Ellmann focused on sexist stereotyping in literature, later feminists questioned the construction and underlying assumptions of language as well as literature. In the 1970s a number of feminist writers, mainly in France, began to describe not simply the sexism of literary constructions but the sexism of systems of thought underpinning the construction of 'literature'.

The term 'French feminism' applies to a number of writers and critical approaches to literature ranging from the psychoanalytic to the utopian. Many Anglo-American critics are disappointed that French feminist thought in translation is dominated by the writings of Julia Kristeva, Luce Irigaray and Hélène Cixous. Toril Moi claims that there are many other French writers engaged in important feminist critiques; for example, Antoinette Fouque (Moi, 1987, p. 107). Yet few would deny that the idea of a 'woman's language' has been aired in literary studies because of the work of Kristeva, Irigaray and Cixous on language and subjectivity over the last twenty years. The reception of French feminism by Anglo-Americans in the late 1970s was greatly helped by the publication of *New French Feminisms*, an anthology of important extracts from a range of French feminist critics.

What links these three writers is a shared belief that our structures of understanding are coded in and by our language. All three critics are deconstructionists in the sense that they believe that systems of language are systems of power built on internal contradictions which can be sought out and deconstructed or taken apart. By focusing on the *processes* of language, particularly on the acquisition of language by the infant, French feminists aim to deconstruct patriarchal discourses. At the heart of all French feminism is de Beauvoir's concept of the 'Woman as Other'. Like de Beauvoir, contemporary French feminists believe that feminine language is repressed – is itself the 'Other' of social and cultural speech. So that in spite of their differing views of femininity and masculinity, and of feminism itself, Kristeva, Irigaray and Cixous share a number of ideas and techniques which are distinct from those adopted by many Anglo-American critics and others.

LANGUAGE

The problem is that traditional criticism has made literature into an institution ruled by the regulations of genres and histories. Yet writing (*écriture*) is defined as much by its practice as its past. How then can questioning the relationship between feminine language and literature enable women to deconstruct the historical values of that institution? Hélène Cixous would argue that language is a dynamic system, not a stable body whose elements need to be classified and organised. She studies the interaction of signifiers (words) and signified (concepts), of texts and readers in order to break their traditional connections. For example, Cixous suggests that all forceful women writers give birth to words flowing in accord with the contractual rhythms of labour (Andermatt, 1977). The tempo of women's writing, in other words, will be in cadence with *lacunary* moments and 'jets of letters'. There are many other possibilities. Carrying memories of our bodies women will, in any case, read texts in a different way from men. Cixous asks questions which implicitly carry with them gendered values. What sexual politics are represented in the relations between an authorial voice and a heroine? Is a woman writer creating stylistically the questions she poses theoretically? The markers are a writer's intimacy with her heroine or her doubts about the ability of language to represent gender adequately.

It is not surprising that a search for a feminine language should begin in France. In French philosophy (for example, existentialism) language is always more than a cultural concern.

Simone de Beauvoir, in *The Second Sex*, describes the importance of philosophical assumptions about language to writers choosing representations. The newer trends in feminist criticism are much indebted to her ideas, whether or not they diverge from them. The creation of a feminine language by French feminists must be seen in this intellectual context where the transformative powers of language are always part of the intellectual agenda. The French language itself could not better represent an example of the suppression of the feminine with its 'mute e'. Kristeva, Cixous and Irigaray all oppose phallocentric language – what Kristeva calls the domain of reason and judgement – but they envisage different forms of resistance and different ways of moving ahead. What they agree, however, is that language has been the central mechanism by which men have appropriated the world. The linguistic means by which men colonise women, they argue, is that men devalue sensuality in favour of symbolism.

SUBJECTIVITY

How then are the symbolic discourse of men and its signifying practices to be resisted? Julia Kristeva uses psychoanalysis to help her clarify her concept of the semiotic discourse, or instinctual drives, a phase of sensual language occurring between mothers and children before children enter into the symbolic, or formal, language of society. Irigaray and Cixous, more radically, use psychoanalysis to formulate a discourse which, by expressing women's sexuality, can deny male egress. If female physiology is, for Irigaray or Cixous, a source of critical metaphors, they do not describe this language in any idealist sense. Rather they reflect on women's discourse in order to change the phallocentric order of culture.

The key questions concern: the role of language in literary forms; the specific linguistic representations of masculinity and femininity; and what alternative representations can be constructed. Literature is central to these concerns because literature often represents dreams and the unconscious; literature *is* the accumulation of subjectivity; and literature's discursive formations provide spaces/absences – or moments – when other kinds of subjectivity might be represented. It is French feminist critics, more than other critics, who tackle the question: how do we express female subjectivity when, as yet, there is no literary language which is unmarked by tradition and by patriarchy? In her work on the Brazilian writer Clarice Lispector, for example, Hélène Cixous displaces and expands critical languages by inventing a new critical vocabulary, making puns of Lispector's name – for example, 'claricing'.

WRITING THE BODY

One other, and major, distinction between French and Anglo-American feminist critics is a French immersion in texts by men, particularly those of European philosophy and psychoanalysis. Luce Irigaray in particular focuses on male not on female theorists as she deconstructs the work of Plato, Hegel and Freud among others. Drawing on biological theories of knowledge, Irigaray opposes the humanistic idea of a universal ungendered subject with a mythical female subjectivity. Where many Anglo-American feminist critics prefer to describe the *social* construction of femininity, French feminists search out feminine styles of writing derived from their readings of literary and philosophical texts. To efface a masculine, linear style Irigaray claims that critics will need to utilise female imagery because only a symbolism created by women (for example, the female auto-eroticism of lips) can *speak* to other women. It is this countering of traditional critical vocabulary by metaphors of the female body which distinguishes French feminism from other critical approaches. Responses to French feminism inevitably revolve around issues of essentialism and questions of metaphor. Are French critics like Cixous and Irigaray trying to create a *literal* female erotics or is this a metaphorical vocabulary for the inexpressible – a women's language? Cixous argues that a successful feminist criticism must write woman's body, must adopt sex-specific rhythms and desires. Julia Kristeva similarly sketches the links between the *materiality* of language – its general formations – and its meaning.

ÉCRITURE FÉMININE

These arguments and techniques have come to be known as *écriture féminine*. The term has a number of different definitions of which I will highlight those by Kristeva, Irigaray and Cixous. In *écriture féminine*, critics focus on the specificity of female sexuality and on a relationship between sexuality and writing style and forms. The publishing firm of *des femmes* in Paris gave institutional support to these ideas throughout the 1970s and 1980s by publishing a number of key texts of *écriture féminine*. The starting point of this criticism is that women's actual physical desires, if represented in writing, might constitute a counter language. These desires are for the most part unconscious. Building on Freud's notion that the unconscious is represented in disruptions of syntax (or slips of the tongue) critics argue that similarly women's 'unconscious' might disturb the ordered syntactics of traditional literary criticism. Each French critic draws out of *ecriture féminine* a different literary possibility. While focusing on texts by men, Kristeva argues, in *The Revolution in Poetic Language* (1984), that a kind of language exists in the pre-linguistic experience of early infancy. Irigaray prefers the term *parler femme* (rather than *écriture féminine*) because *parler femme* is defined by its *mode* of address (speaking *to* women) rather than its *form* of address (*what* or *how* one speaks). In 'La Mystérique' Irigaray suggests that the writings of mystics are an alternative language, while Cixous, in *The Newly Born Woman* (1987), listens to the voice of the hysteric. Julia Kristeva's aim is to intersect the psychosexual with the linguistic, and she integrates Marxist, Lacanian, and structuralist and poststructuralist approaches. The main focus of Kristeva's literary analysis is on avant-garde writing, in particular on the work of Joyce, Artaud, Mallarmé, Proust and Lautremont. In their writing Kristeva finds representations of what she calls the semiotic or the early sign system of child and mother. This is one of the sources of *jouissance*, or a totality of enjoyment – sexual, spiritual, physical and conceptual. Feminine sexual pleasure (*jouissance*) cannot be expressed in the symbolic or linguistic rules.

Sometimes Kristeva appears anti-feminist, particularly in her attention to the work of Georges Bataille. Similarly Hélène

Cixous draws on Derrida in her key essay 'The Laugh of the Medusa', using deconstruction to avoid describing women as the negative of men. She mixes autobiography with sentence fragments and portmanteau words and in her fiction speaks freely in a 'feminine' voice of female body rhythms, as she does in her novel *Angst*.

Luce Irigaray's attempt to write a language of the body is methodologically similar to those of Kristeva and Cixous, but she adds other elements to their approaches. In her early work on senile dementia, Irigaray observed key gender differences between male and female patients in the relation between their language and their unconscious. As Margaret Whitford points out, if the unconscious can be heard in slips of the tongue then it is not surprising that gender can speak (see Whitford, 1991). In *This Sex Which Is Not One* (1985) Irigaray models Alice's adventures through the looking glass. 'Le miroir, de l'autre côté' is not in one style but in a mixture of discourses, body descriptions and occasional silences.

Perhaps only in France would writers reply so fully to the questionnaire 'Does writing have a sex?', sent out as early as 1974 by *La Quinzaine Littéraire*. The answers reveal explicitly the issues involved in *écriture féminine*. The periodical asked whether writers when writing are conscious of gender and whether that influences the text. Some writers, like Marguerite Yourcenar, largely evade the issue by suggesting that the content of a piece would determine the role gender might play. For example, if a writer was describing her experiences as a mother autobiographically, then clearly gender would be a factor, but not necessarily otherwise. Nathalie Sarraute thinks that writers would choose to emphasise masculine or feminine qualities if they wanted to possess these. However, the notion that writing *has* gendered qualities stays intact in the replies (*La Quinzaine Littéraire*, 192, August 1974).

MONIQUE WITTIG

The most exciting example of *écriture féminine* is the work of the writer Monique Wittig. Wittig is a French writer, now living in America, who is attempting to construct a new language.

Wittig's writing career spans thirty years, from her first novel *L'Opoponax*, published in 1964. She is probably best known for her novel *Les Guérillères*, written during the political turmoil of May 1968, which describes the possibility of a new language for women, based on fragments of writing. But it is in *Lesbian Peoples' Materials for a Dictionary* (1979) that Wittig names a new feminist lexicon. To create a new erotic discourse Wittig takes language away from patriarchy; for example, she does not use conventional linear arguments. Wittig does not document in an unpoliticised way the details of women's bodies but encourages her readers to rethink the relation between language and identity. One of her devices is to experiment with pronouns and nouns. In this way, Wittig splits a text's subject. In the *Dictionary* she goes so far as to reject the name 'woman' altogether since it means 'one who belongs to another'.

In this brief introduction I cannot hope to assess the full significance of *écriture féminine* which would require describing its extensive use by writers such as Antoinette Fouque, Annie Leclerc and others, as well as analysing *écriture féminine*'s mixture of Lacanian and deconstructive techniques. One major problem implicit in *écriture féminine* is the danger of universalism. Not only does *écriture féminine* somewhat efface history and praise women's libidinal experience at the expense of woman's social experience but to date it is resolutely Eurocentric. Its descriptions of libidinal power do not include Black representations, feminist or otherwise. As Gayatri Spivak points out, 'the limits of their theories are disclosed by an encounter with the materiality of that other of the West' (Spivak, 1990, p. 11).

Yet these critics have made a major contribution to feminist criticism by focusing on fundamental issues in psychoanalysis and language. They take language seriously. They describe the ways in which patriarchy uses verbal minutiae to create and maintain cultural values. Above all, they address questions of difference by insisting on a fundamental difference for women's language – a language which is no longer constructed as the negative, with women the complement of men, but one which is radically non-unitary, grounded in female anatomy. As Cixous maintains, 'It is impossible to *define* a feminine practice of writing . . . It will be conceived of only by subjects who are breakers of automatisms' (Cixous, 1976a, p. 883).

JULIA KRISTEVA

Julia Kristeva is a practising psychoanalyst and linguistic critic who came to Paris from Bulgaria in 1968. Kristeva's work is shaped by her studies with Barthes and his creation of a theory of semiotics in the late 1960s and early 1970s. Semiotics is the study of how linguistic structures and imagery create meaning in many diverse forms including advertising, media, and everyday speech as well as in the arts. From her doctoral thesis, *La révolution du langage poétique*, Kristeva graduated to a chair in linguistics at the University of Paris VII. The thesis was an ambitious mixture of Marxism and psychoanalysis together with semiotics and linguistics which Kristeva utilised to create a thoroughgoing account of poetic language. She describes how her theory of language derives from the distinction made by psychoanalysis between the imaginary and the symbolic orders.

In psychoanalysis, Kristeva states, what constitutes the role of the subject in language is his penis or her lack of one. Kristeva opposes this trajectory with her subject who is constituted before 'the castration phase', in the semiotic – a space of privileged contact with the mother. In French 'la sémiotique' is 'semiotics', the science of signs, and Kristeva starts by using 'le sémiotique' to refer to the organisation of instinctual drives as they affect language. Kristeva devotes a major part of *La révolution* to describing differences between the semiotic and the symbolic and I will merely summarise the main arguments. The semiotic and the symbolic are the two forms of language which a subject 'speaks' or signifies, with the semiotic being a pre-symbolic language. Kristeva argues that the semiotic is a time when children have an all-encompassing relationship to the mother achieved through gestures, aural and vocal rhythms and repetitive patterns. The significance of these ideas for feminist criticism lies in Kristeva's argument (following Freud and Lacan) that because individual subjectivity is constructed in a mothering relationship, women's close identification with mothers and mothering creates in us a more ambivalent relation to the symbolic or metalanguage.

If castration marks out the symbolic contract, Kristeva asks, what can woman's place be in such a sacrificial order of language? The answer for women is to subvert the symbolic and its social codes and paternal function. We must, she claims, find a discourse closer to the body and emotions, to the unnameable which is repressed by the social contract. Kristeva is interested in exploring the ways in which language, and particularly language in literary texts, can call up this early subjectivity. Kristeva argues that, far from being marginal, the semiotic is 'revolutionary', because it acts *on* the symbolic and allows a new vision of subjectivity, one which is rhythmical rather than linear in development.

But if the semiotic is basically a pre-symbolic oral life we could, in turn, ask Kristeva: what connection can there be between a semiotic process and literary form? Kristeva's answer is that if the semiotic occurs in a previous time chronologically to the symbolic, it is also simultaneously present as the subtext of symbolic discourse. Obviously I cannot assess in detail the whole of Kristeva's extensive account of subjectivity and signification and her critique of avant-garde literature and Western art. However, Kristeva's argument that the subject's development as a speaking subject is present as a rupture of the symbolic (for example, a deviation in grammar) is intensely relevant to feminist criticism. The semiotic occurs in literature as a pressure on symbolic language: as absences, contradictions and moments in a literary text. Kristeva found in analysing the modernist techniques of Joyce, Céline and Mallarmé, how the social and the symbolic are structured and in particular the way in which subjectivity is determined.

In 'Psychoanalysis and the Polis' Kristeva analyses the novels of Louis Ferdinand Céline. She focuses on two main features: the segmentation of sentences and syntactical ellipses. This is the locus of emotion, or where the semiotic will appear. Not only does Kristeva provide us with specific critical techniques, she is also concerned to provide specific aesthetic criteria. Great writers, she says, are those who can immerse their readers in the semiotic. The task of critics is to help writers and readers find this crisis in the symbolic function of literature itself. For example, in her analysis of Mallarmé, Kristeva traces the semiotic in Mallarmé's use of ellipses (. . .) and in his use of sounds which resemble children's murmurs. Modernist poetry in particular, Kristeva discovered, depends on the semiotic in its irregular rhythms, its attention to dreams and in the way in which it ruminates on its own processes and incorporates other forms of writing.

Kristeva calls this process of incorporation *'intertextualité'*. Kristeva defines intertextuality as the adoption of sign systems from the media, art and so forth, by literature (or by any other cultural system). She believes that all texts are mosaics of references to other texts, images and conventions. Her argument, in *Desire in Language* (1980), is that intertextuality is the place of plurality and subversion. Kristeva developed this argument from her interest in the work of Bakhtin, the Russian formalist. Kristeva was one of the first critics in France to write about Bakhtin. In his work Bakhtin claims that language is not made up of abstract words but is structured by 'dialogic' intercourse, or characters entering into dialogue with an author. This is Bakhtin's central metaphor. Bakhtin categorises the various forms of 'dialogism' in Dostoevsky's work and suggests that 'dialogism' marks the moment when a plurality of voices exists in any literary place. In *Problems of Dostoevsky's Poetics* (1984) Bakhtin describes literature as representing a struggle between languages which subverts a social (or patriarchal) belief in universal truth. Characters in novels embody the social differences of languages (which are inevitably shaped by the sexual differences which shape society). Bakhtin's relevance lies in his recognition of the unequal distribution of power in language and the need for oppositional tactics. So that although Kristeva, like Bakhtin, rarely mentions women writers, Bakhtin's ideas helped Kristeva to understand how literature reveals a complex subjectivity.

In 'Women's Time' Kristeva went on to examine the historical development of concepts of gender difference and their impact on linguistic structures in general. Kristeva describes several historical representations of sexual difference. The symbolic becomes 'masculine' history which is linear time and Kristeva equates the 'feminine' with cyclical or monumental time. All language, according to Kristeva, is sexually differentiated. 'Masculinity' retains, and indeed celebrates, logical connections and linearity (the symbolic). This singularity is challenged by the semiotic which contains the 'feminine' drives or voice tones. Changes to dominant histories will therefore depend not only on new political practices (in 'Women's Time' Kristeva discusses feminism, modernism and terrorism) but on new forms of language which will value the feminine. With the publication of *Pouvoirs de l'horreur* (1980) Kristeva made a psychoanalytic examination of literature in terms of three emotional states: literature, melancholy and love in relation to mothering. What Kristeva proclaims is the indelible association of women's bodies with language, whether in texts written by women *or* by men. The concept of 'woman' or 'the feminine' is both a metaphor of reading and part of the topography of writing and Kristeva poses this as a deliberate alternative to paternal metaphors or symbols. The most fruitful example of 'the feminine' to Kristeva is the representation of motherhood in Western culture (Kristeva, 1980a). The subject's special relationship to the mother manifests itself in art or literature through a heightened tension between the semiotic and the symbolic. Like other feminists writing about motherhood, Kristeva is very aware of difficulties inherent in any definition of the feminine which depends on motherhood. Kristeva suggests however that the man-subject is as much a product of the interrelation of motherhood, the semiotic and discourse as the woman-subject is. The problem is not Kristeva's 'essentialism' but rather her displacement of social and political concerns. She seems, at points, to be arguing that a linguistic disruption by the semiotic is as great a revolutionary gesture as radical political practice. In addition, it would be misleading to assume that Kristeva's writing is free from sexual hierarchies. As Diana Fuss, Elizabeth Grosz and Teresa de Lauretis among others point out, Kristeva has characterised the lesbian as a 'bad object' (see Fuss, 1991, p. 183). At the same time, however, Kristeva has forcefully drawn attention to those moments in literature where women can deny patriarchy even if this occurs primarily in 'the eruption of the semiotic', or across the border into 'Freudian' hysteria (Kristeva, 1980b, p.125).

LUCE IRIGARAY

Like Kristeva, Irigaray is an émigré who also trained as an analyst. She taught in the department of Psychology at Vincennes and studied with Lacan at the *Ecole Normale Supérieure* until the publication of *Speculum of the Other Woman* (*Speculum. De l'autre femme*, 1974) ensured her expulsion both from Vincennes and from Lacan's seminars. Irigaray's main project is to investigate the relation between writing and subjectivity, specifically feminine sexuality. Irigaray argues that the language we use routinely is shaped by masculinity; for example, the way we concentrate on finding the 'right' word or precise meaning. To Irigaray, women's sexuality is a form of language and a feminist criticism which ignores women's sexuality ignores the multiple possibilities a new language of the body makes available.

Irigaray's work revolves around a key question: how can women speak, or even think, in a language which is inherently anti-woman? Irigaray's main aim, therefore, is to change our language structure, vocabulary and forms of representation. What is at stake for Irigaray, unlike Kristeva, is not only the *place* of feminine subjectivity/sexuality but the *ways* in which female sexuality might create new forms of knowledge. For example, since writing acts as a privileged entry into the unconscious it can reveal aspects of femininity. Like Cixous, Irigaray adopts an ambitious experimental vocabulary and syntax. While for Kristeva intertextuality is a characteristic of all texts, Irigaray makes a determined use of intertextuality, ranging across the disciplines of psychoanalysis, philosophy and literature. Carolyn Burke describes Irigaray's writing career as falling into roughly three phases. First is the stage of *Speculum* and *This Sex Which Is Not One* (1977) in which Irigaray brilliantly explored the misogyny of male philosophers from Plato to today. The second stage starts with the last part of *This Sex*: 'When Our Lips Speak Together' and moves into the more poetic essays *Le Corps – à corps avec la mère* (1981). Irigaray wrote her influential essay *Amante marine* (1980), moving into her third phase with *Sexes et parentes* (1987) among many others, all of which 'rewrite' language by such strategies as including sentences without subjects and conditional verbs.

Speculum argues that all the main systems of Western knowledge are shaped by masculinity. The title 'Speculum' is a metonymy for language. Where Lacan describes the acquisition of language as a recognition in a mirror, Irigaray describes language as a speculum – a *sexual* reflector.

It is tempting not to ask the obvious questions. If 'woman' is absent in male discourse, how can she speak in books? This problematic – the enunciation of 'the feminine' in discourse – is Irigaray's main concern. In *Speculum of the Other Woman* she examines polarities of masculine/feminine as represented in analogies, repetitions and oppositions in discourse. Through endless word-play Irigaray aims to create a place in writing where opposites might creatively fuse. 'Don't worry about the "right" word. There isn't any. No truth between our lips' (Irigaray, 1985, p. 213). Sentences often include blanks and ellipses. Irigaray counters a masculine language of 'rights' with the female metaphor of 'lips', creating feminine openness and auto-eroticism. Irigaray offers women a syntactically startling language as an alternative to what she regards as Lacan's exclusion of female expression.

This Sex Which Is Not One is a collection of essays which reject patriarchal language. This is clear in the way in which Irigaray organises the book. Passages are not linked by a single linear argument but woven by metaphorical ideas repeated through-out the book.

> If we don't invent a language, if we don't find our body's language it will have too few gestures to accompany our story . . . Be what you are becoming, without clinging to what you might have been, what you might yet be. Never settle. Let's leave definitiveness to the undecided; we don't need it. Our body, right here, right now, gives us a very different certainty. (Irigaray (1985) p. 214)

Irigaray's style is both oral and written at the same moment, moving from consecutive sentences to the direct command, 'Never settle'. The plural pronoun 'we' brings in the reader. The most crucial aspect of the book is Irigaray's repeated use of references to the female body which here is represented as a singular *shared* experience between author and reader, 'our body'. Even in this short extract, we can see how Irigaray addresses many of the theoretical ideas of French feminism – refusing structures and rejecting the negative role given to femininity by our culture. Western discourse, Irigaray claims, has for too long used its solidity to beat out feminine fluidity.

This is the central and knotty problem which Irigaray has been addressing since *Speculum*: how to create a language in which women can speak. In what is regarded as the finest piece of *This Sex Which Is Not One* – 'When Our Lips Speak Together' – Irigaray argues that women's language will reject binary hierarchies such as subject/object. Irigaray's ideas have been strongly criticised. Monique Plaza has accused Irigaray of endorsing the eternal feminine. Other feminists attacked Irigaray's 'essentialism'. One issue is the extent to which Irigaray falls into the trap of idealism, the stick with which she herself beats male philosophers. Jane Gallop defends Irigaray by arguing that Irigaray *uses* metaphor rather than simply *reflects* biological givens. Other critics (for example, Christine Holmlund) have found Irigaray's lesbian erotics to be richly evocative. In general, feminist literary critics appreciate Irigaray's use of double syntax – the idea that under the masculine logic of a sentence there might be a feminine 'unsaid' perhaps hidden in elemental metaphors of earth, fire and sea, the subject matter of *Amante marine*.

Yet Irigaray does not ignore the relationship between criticism and forms of political practice. Although concerning herself with subjectivity and sexuality, Irigaray thinks through feminist questions to some logical end; that is, she perceives that women's oppression exists both materially and in the very foundation of the language through which material meaning is acknowledged. Irigaray's specific contribution to literary criticism is that she forces us to see 'femininity' as much more of a rhetorical category than a 'natural' one. Irigaray fundamentally deconstructs realism. The critic can no longer be simple-minded about literary names or identities when identity is fluid. Like other feminist work on mother/daughter relationships (for example, that of Kristeva and Adrienne Rich) Irigaray's opposes the 'hopelessness' of realism with the hope of defining a self in relation to m(other).

To Irigaray the relationship between infant and mother is an issue of fantasy. Fantasy does not mean 'illusion' but part of an individual psychic reality. Irigaray's concept has advantages for feminist literary criticism. For example, once aspects of the early relation of mother and infant are read as fantasy then questions of the imaginary, of desires can be added to psychosocial accounts such as Nancy Chodorow's *The Reproduction of Mothering* (1978; see chapter 2). As a result, the female identities we look for in literature can be multiple.

Irigaray asks a double question: what is sexual difference and (simultaneously) <u>how is sexual difference intervening in the act of reading?</u> Literary criticism has to ask both questions, and it has to define difference while trying to discover the answers. One way is to threaten the authority of the patriarchal code, to find signifiers of 'masculine' or of 'feminine' in texts which no longer fit into the social or institutional codes of their period. For example, following Irigaray, Shoshana Felman describes how, in Balzac's *Adieu*, the text itself questions a masculine need for the authority of proper names (see Felman, 1975). Balzac, Felman argues, is staging theatrically Stephanie's 'recognition' of her lover Philippe in order to tell us, unconsciously, that patriarchal naming is illusory. By showing how the cultural process of name-giving is no longer working in an individual text, feminists can disrupt the authority of naming.

Irigaray's *Amante marine* equally disrupts the symbolic by finding a language in elemental metaphors of earth, fire, air and water which provide a truer materiality for women's language. As she said as early as 1977, 'there should no longer be separation: Sex/language on the one hand, body/matter on the other, then perhaps another history would be possible' (Irigaray, 1977, p. 76).

HÉLÈNE CIXOUS

Cixous was born in Oran, Algeria in 1937 and Cixous's punning reference to the town figures as a metaphor of exile in *Vivre L'orange*. Her immediate family represent that more significant exile to Cixous, an exile from language with her German/Jewish mother and a Mediterranean, French-speaking father.

Cixous is a critic, novelist, playwright and director of the Centre d'Etudes Féminines which she founded in 1974 at Paris VIII, Vincennes. Cixous's main project, both in her writing and in her teaching, is to explore the relation between women's bodies and writing; but her influences have been hugely diverse. Her readings range from Shakespeare, German Romanticism

(Kleist) through to the contemporary Brazilian writer, Clarice Lispector.

The manifesto of *écriture féminine* is generally regarded to be 'The Laugh of the Medusa', written by Cixous in 1975 and published in *L'Arc* in an issue dedicated to Simone de Beauvoir. Cixous's first task is to deconstruct masculine structures of knowledge. Like Wittig, Cixous attacks patriarchy by attacking patriarchal language. The only alternative to male domination, Cixous says, is to construct a women's language which can exemplify sexual difference. If the overall aim of *écriture féminine* is for women to write with their bodies, Cixous manages to make this aim more precise by attention to myths. In 'Castration or Decapitation' she begins by telling stories – the stories of Hera, of Chinese Wives and of Sleeping Beauty. These are stories, Cixous claims, about the relation between women's names and their sexuality. Little Red Riding Hood is the little clitoris – the female sex with her little jar of honey caught in a forest of male metaphors. Cixous calls the classic dualist oppositions of activity/passivity superior/inferior in symbolic systems a kind of male war. She finds a critical focus here of the relation between knowledge and power.

What women have to do, Cixous says, is to bring about a shift in the metalanguage, or the idea that meaning is universal and homogenous. First, they should attack the institutionalisation of language in universities and disciplines where 'doing classes' is like military service – a way to keep women in the service of men. Next, women should learn how to read for themselves women-centred texts. How can we do this? By creating, Cixous claims, a new site of language, a feminine Imaginary shaped by the libido and spoken about in 'savage' tongues. Hence Cixous is continuously interrogative. The main feature of this feminine textuality will be its endlessness. There is no beginning and no conclusion to a female text. Cixous believes that there is a link between feminine language and the language of the marginalised – children/hysterics. One way in which the two come together is when language reveals the unconscious in slips of the tongue and wordplay. Cixous's writing is therefore often associational with multiple pronouns. Clearly Cixous is interested as much in the *féminine* as in *écriture*, as she demonstrates by publishing with feminist presses.

In 'The Character of "Character" ' (1974) Hélène Cixous claims that it is only with the removal of 'character' altogether that the question of the nature of fiction can come to the fore. Characterisation, Cixous suggests, is the mechanism by which literary criticism 'markets' literature to a reader. Characterisation is, by necessity, a kind of social coding and connotes conformity, even censorship. Feminist psychoanalytic critics refuse the idea of a whole knowable subject. It is, in any case, an impossible notion to use in analysis. To support her argument Cixous cites the example of Virginia Woolf creating multiple subjects in a single passage in *The Waves*. Cixous's own fiction transforms literary genres and avoids set characterisation in favour of images of characters and sketches of ideas. Feminists have to destroy logocentrism and choose to read the subject as 'an effort of the unconscious . . . which is unanalysable, uncharacterisable' (Cixous, 1974, p. 387).

Cixous's critique of Joyce is a good example of this new kind of reading. In 'The Exile of James Joyce' Cixous argues that Joyce's main innovation lies in his representation of subjectivity in a non-linear narrative. Similarly Cixous praises Edgar Allen Poe's 'The Imp of the Perverse' because Poe disrupts conventional subjectivity by attention to the unconscious. In Cixous's own work, she mixes styles to compound the subjectivity of the autobiographical with the theoretical. In *Souffles*, for example, Cixous makes many allusions to Jean Genet, creating him as a character and combining this with ironic accounts of major Western texts interspersed with fantasies and autobiography further fragmented by the inclusion of blanks and disordered type. The title, of course, suggests the power of her body represented by breathing and continuous movement.

Cixous's attention to the reader and her eagerness to dialogue with authors rather than appropriating them, is one of the main techniques of *écriture féminine*. Cixous, like Kristeva, takes her notion of 'dialogue' from Bakhtin. It is in *Vivre L'orange* that Cixous's experimentation with a range of genres and critical forms bears fruit. If Cixous's aim is to represent the grammar of female sexuality so that each text might correspond to a woman's psychic needs, her work on the Brazilian writer, Clarice Lispector, offers an imaginative example. *Vivre L'orange* is the culmination of Cixous's many years of work on Lispector.

The orange – a pun on Oran (her birthplace) and je – is also a symbol of the elements – of blood, moisture and light. Morag Shiach has drawn attention to similarities between the styles of Cixous and Lispector in the way in which both writers use visual images to powerful effect 'and particularly the emotional weight of colour, texture and light' (Shiach, 1991, p. 67). *Vivre L'orange* exemplifies Cixous's aim to write a criticism in which readers can let themselves be 'read' by the text. In a discussion with Catherine Clément published at the end of *The Newly Born Woman* which they co-authored, Cixous describes how this might function. She suggests that critics focus on those elements of the text in which authors themselves confirm the presence of a reader.

The Newly Born Woman explores the revolutionary possibilities implied by these new critical ideas. Following Cixous, feminist criticism could move from linear narrative into fairy story or myth. Feminist criticism could avoid the practice of 'ownership' and endless detail of the lives of characters by writing in a language closer to the body which can set in motion different styles and different representations.

SUMMARY

French feminist criticism is engaged in a major critical project of deconstruction and revision and it is also a creative material project – a place of attack and also of reconstitution. The history of language, the established disciplines of literature and philosophy, and the frameworks which support all of these, are major sites of power in patriarchy. In Western culture language has a particular and historically determined power. Language determines the ways in which we perceive gender and come to know ourselves as gendered beings and the ways in which society perceives gender and creates gendered subjects. *Ecriture féminine*, whether it takes the form of Kristeva's semiotic or a new syntax like Irigaray's ellipses, offers an alternative to that existing order.

It is not surprising that most of the early texts of second-wave feminism focus on language, or the lack of language (for example, *The Dream of a Common Language*, and *Silences*), nor that many of the major feminist critics have been poet/creators (for example, Hélène Cixous, Adrienne Rich and Luce Irigaray). It is likely that any attack on Western philosophy, linguistic and literary theory will encourage the development of a women's culture as well as encouraging a new feminist criticism. Italian feminist criticism, for example, with its dramatic anti-institutional politics has been most responsive to the ideas of French feminism. Critics such as Carla Lonzi and her associates in the Milan Women's Bookshop Collective attempt the kind of symbolic revolution which *écriture féminine* encourages. Italian critics have seized on French feminism's egalitarian concept of 'entrustment' – of exchanges between women of different generations. For example, the Milan Bookstore Collective developed an experimental method of literary critical 'entrustment'. Here working groups treat texts as 'puzzles' to be deconstructed and rearranged according to extratextual personal associations and interpretations, a form of psychotherapy akin to Cixous's textual 'therapies'. Italian feminist critics are also in debt to the central theme of French feminism: that women can obtain symbolic authorisation only from a female source.

SELECTED READING

Basic texts

Cixous, H. (1974) 'The character of "Character" ', *New Literary History*, 5:2, pp. 383–402
Cixous, H. (1975) *Souffles*, Paris: des femmes
Cixous, H. (1976a) 'The laugh of the Medusa', *Signs*, 1:4 (Summer), pp. 875–93
Cixous, H. (1976b) *The Exile of James Joyce*, London: John Calder
Cixous, H. (1979) *L'Heure de Clarice Lispector précéde de Vivre L'orange*, Paris: des femmes
Cixous, H. (1981) 'Castration or decapitation', *Signs*, 7:1 (Autumn) pp. 36–55
Cixous, H. and Clément, C. (1987) *The Newly Born Woman*, Manchester: Manchester University Press
Irigaray, L. (1977) 'Women's exile', *Ideology and Consciousness*, 1 (May), pp. 62–77

Irigaray, L. (1980) *Amante marine. De Friedrich Nietzsche*, Paris: Minuit. A section of this is translated as 'Veiled Lips', *Mississippi Review* 11:3 (1983) pp. 98–119

Irigaray, L. (1985a) *This Sex Which Is Not One*, Ithaca: Cornell University Press

Irigaray, L. (1985b) *Speculum of the Other Woman*, Ithaca: Cornell University Press

Kristeva, J. (1980a) *Desire in Language: A semiotic approach to literature and art*, Oxford: Blackwell

Kristeva, J. (1980b) *Pouvoirs de l'horreur*, Paris: Seuil

Kristeva, J. (1981) 'Women's Time', *Signs* 7:1 (Autumn), pp. 77–92

Kristeva, J. (1982) 'Psychoanalysis and the polis', *Critical Inquiry*, 9:2 (September) pp. 77–92

Kristeva, J. (1984) *The Revolution in Poetic Language*, New York: Columbia University Press

Marks, E. and Courtivron, I. (eds) (1981) *New French Feminisms*, Hemel Hempstead: Harvester Wheatsheaf

Wittig, M. (1992) *The Straight Mind and Other Essays*, Hemel Hempstead: Harvester Wheatsheaf

Wittig, M. and Zeig, S. (1979) *Lesbian Peoples' Materials for a Dictionary*, New York: Avon

Introductions

Andermatt, V. (1977) 'Hélène Cixous and the uncovery of feminine language', *Women and Literature*, 7:1

Andermatt Conley, V. (1992) *Hélène Cixous*, Hemel Hempstead: Harvester Wheatsheaf

Duchen, C. (ed.) (1987) *French Connections: Voices from the women's movement in France*, London: Hutchinson

Fletcher, J. and Benjamin, A. (eds) (1990) *Abjection, Melancholia and Love: The work of Julia Kristeva*, London: Routledge

Grosz, E. (1989) *Sexual Subversions: Three French feminists*, Sydney: Allen & Unwin

Jouve, N. W. (1991) 'French feminisms', in *White Woman Speaks With Forked Tongue*, London: Routledge

Lechte, J. (1990) *Julia Kristeva*, London: Routledge

Moi, T. (1985) *Sexual/Textual Politics*, London: Methuen

Moi, T. (ed.) (1987) *French Feminist Thought*, Oxford: Blackwell
Sellers, S. (ed.) (1988) *Writing Differences: Readings from the seminar of Hélène Cixous*, Milton Keynes: Open University
Sellers, S. (1991) *Language and Sexual Difference: Feminist writing in France*, London: MacMillan
Shiach, M. (1991) *Hélène Cixous: A politics of writing*, London: Routledge
Whitford, M. (1991) *Luce Irigaray: Philosophy in the feminine*, London: Routledge
Wilcox, H., McWatters, K., Thompson, A. and Williams, L. R. (eds) (1990) *The Body and the Text: Hélène Cixous, reading and teaching*, Hemel Hempstead: Harvester Wheatsheaf

Further reading

Bakhtin, M. M. (1984) *Problems of Dostoevsky's Poetics*, Manchester: Manchester University Press
Burke, C. (1987) 'Romancing the philosophers: Luce Irigaray', *The Minnesota Review*, 29 (Fall) pp. 103–14
de Lauretis, T. (1989) 'The essence of the triangle or, taking the risk of essentialism seriously: feminist theory in Italy, the U.S. and Britain', *Differences*, 1:2, pp. 3–38
Felman, S. (1975) 'Women and madness', *Diacrits*, (Winter) pp. 2–10
Fuss, D. (ed.) (1991) *Inside/Out*, London: Routledge
Lonzi, C. (1974) *Sputiamo su Hegel*, Milan: Scritti di Rivolta Femminile
Plaza, M. (1978) ' "Phallomorphic Power" and the psychology of "woman" ', *Ideology and Consciousness*, 4 (Autumn) pp. 4–36
Spivak, G. (1990) *The Post-Colonial Critic*, London: Routledge

5 Psychoanalytic criticism

Since May 1968 the barriers between the disciplines psycho-analysis, philosophy, literature and linguistics have come down in the academy. The most dramatic reworking of the academic map comes in the texts of Julia Kristeva, Monique Wittig, Hélène Cixous, Luce Irigaray and (in America) Mary Daly. All these writers share a desire to destroy not only a tradition of humanistic criticism but also the very language in which this is transmitted. In *Les Guérillères* Monique Wittig claims to 'screen every word'.

The dialogue between feminist criticism and psychoanalysis is invaluable for several reasons. While not all feminist criticism shares similar concerns with psychoanalysis, both address common themes: the psychic relation of mothers, fathers and children; the relation between sexuality and its expression; the instability of identity shared by authors and readers. Second, both share similar methods: they treat their texts, whether the unconscious or novels, as kinds of codes and as representing the 'unsaid' in everyday life. Both expect dreams, displacement and transference to explain individual feelings. Psychoanalytic literary critics focus on authors' and characters' motivations and on the hidden areas of texts as well as on readers' responses to these.

It is psychoanalysis which puts the 'feminine' into *'écriture féminine'*. Critics describe the relation between the female libido, woman's unconscious, and their representation in female discourse. Psychoanalysis has shaped the more exciting and energetic feminist criticism of the 1970s and 1980s. The texts of Kristeva, Cixous, Wittig or Daly could not have been written thirty years ago. It is only very recently that psychoanalysis has shown criticism how 'the feminine' is consciously produced and organised in language. When the question 'What does feminist criticism learn from psychoanalysis?' is put, Kristeva, Cixous and Irigaray might answer that we learn to oppose the phallic symbols that have structured Western thought and writing with women's body experiences as decoded by psychoanalysis.

Juliet Mitchell's *Psychoanalysis and Feminism* (1974) is the first feminist text to explore fully the theories of Freud, Lacan, Laing and feminism for explanations of women's experience. Mitchell argues that although Freud might be misogynist (as Millett and other critics claimed) he was shaped as we still are shaped today by a patriarchal culture. Freud's understanding of the feminine *in* patriarchy, Mitchell argued, is therefore still a relevant and important theory. The problem with a Freudian psychoanalytic construction of femininity *per se* is that it overlooks important contemporary changes in women's sexuality and culture.

The concept of *écriture féminine* derives from psychoanalysis and addresses this issue. Since so many feminist critics accept the possibility of an analogy – and a very attractive one at that – between the female psyche and women's writing (*écriture féminine*), it is important to examine this analogy in detail to see how well it can answer the question: is there a woman's language which speaks of psychic experiences ignored or devalued by the dominant discourse? The discipline of psychoanalysis offers useful starting points. Psychoanalytic criticism articulates a problem that is inherent in all feminist criticism: that of linking the place of the social with what are private, perhaps even totally individual, feelings.

Psychoanalytic criticism is one of the most valuable and fruitful additions to feminist literary theory. If we make a list of the major feminist critics, we find that Kristeva, Cixous and Irigaray from France, Heilbrun, Mary Jacobus, Gilbert and Gubar, Spivak, Hirsch and Felman from America, and Coward and Mitchell from England are all indebted to psychoanalysis, albeit in very different ways. While psychoanalysis is not *just* about the construction of femininity through language, what psychoanalysis *does* is to offer a reading of the feminine rooted not entirely in the social construction of femininity (which nevertheless organises the feminine), nor entirely in biology, but through language and subjectivity. Indeed, even in 'purely' medical psychoanalysis, case studies of the private lives of women, their fantasies and early experience are initially read *as* language before being read as medical symptoms. Even those preverbal experiences of the unconscious or the semiotic are constituted linguistically, as it were, by psychoanalysis.

Psychoanalytic cases as well as literary criticism have a tendency to be written as texts. Both openly reveal their status as fiction without, of course, abandoning their search for a 'true' meaning in the discourse each examines. Psychoanalysis tries to read the 'text' of each subject in terms of her dreams and style of speech among other things. To do this, it focuses in particular on 'literary' forms – on absences, distortions and slippages – which may provide access to hidden parts of a subject's personality. Literary criticism does something very similar. By examining metaphors, similes and absences in the literary text it tries to reveal the hidden subtext of an author.

There are challenges which psychoanalysis and feminism together offer to traditional literary criticism. The greatest challenge both make is to the unity of the subject. Psycho-analytic critiques, like feminist criticism, involve the writing of many rich and random multiple realities. Another, and crucial, challenge is to the traditional relations of art, politics and society. There need no longer be a hierarchy of value in which one or other area has a more privileged status in explaining an individual psyche or text. The popular text (for example, women's magazines) may be as useful as a modernist novel in offering explanations of women's desire. Feminism itself, both as a political movement and as a literary practice, is analogous to psychoanalysis. Both use a model of repression. Feminists think that aspects of women's sexual experience are often repressed or 'unconscious'. Consciousness-raising in feminist groups is like the bringing 'up' of the repressed into consciousness in therapy or the raising of the subtext in literature – all ways of learning about the previously unexpressed effects of patriarchy.

What are the main modes of feminist psychoanalytic criti-cism? There are several different forms which include Freudian theory, Lacan and object/relations analysis among others. The

French feminist Julia Kristeva focuses attention on the semiotic/ preverbal time of mothers and infants and defines patriarchy as the symbolic. The semiotic involves the organisation of instincts by rhythm and intonation and precedes the imposition of the symbolic, a system of meaning created in language. The American feminist Ellen Moers uses the term 'symbolic' in a more conventionally Freudian sense to mean the textual representations of women's unconscious desires. Juliet Mitchell, influenced in addition by R. D. Laing and by Winnicott, describes a phenomenology of childhood and its relation to female identity.

Feminist psychoanalytic criticism is thus very rich and multiple. It includes study of the psychodynamics of women characters and women authors (Moers, Gilbert and Gubar), a psychoanalysis of textual metaphor (Spivak, Mitchell, Jacobus) and study of the psychodynamics of readers reading. Yet writing about gender difference is central in *all* psychoanalytic theory, not just in feminist criticism. It would be wrong to treat feminist criticism in isolation from this general background. Norman Holland, Herbert Marcuse and Harold Bloom also address cultural assumptions and political power as ideologies within discourses to be decoded with the aid of psychoanalytic models. But there are differences in focus and method which mark out the feminist critique.

The literary criticism of orthodox Freudians has tended to focus on the notion of an individual author's, or individual reader's, single experience. In his *Holland's Guide to Psycho analytic Psychology and Literature-and-Psychology* (1990), t American critic Norman N. Holland argues that literature alert the reader to his (sic) unconscious fantasies. But, of co Holland does not offer the equality of response between and critic which is often stimulated by shared feminist re Indeed, Holland claims that his criticism is a scientific d single and distinctive literary identities in texts. Simi psychoanalytic critic Simon Lesser in *Fiction and the L* (1957), argues that literature serves mainly to re hence stabilise a unitary reader. The multiplicity experience has no space here. In contrast, the syn and Freud created by Marcuse and the Frankf examine individual consciousness as part of shared, capitalist, relations but tends to leave little space for the unique case histories of particular subjects as women do in their autobiographies. Harold Bloom has greatly influenced American feminist criticism with his interpretations of Freud's Oedipus complex in *The Anxiety of Influence* (1973). If other male identity theorists assume that constancy is a desirable goal for writing development, Bloom, in effect, rewrites literary history in terms of the Oedipus complex by arguing that all poems represent a poet's deliberate misinterpretations of a precursor poem or poet. Yet Bloom's theory, too, is an inadequate basis for feminist criticism. Not only does Bloom focus only on male poets, he seizes on a quantitative notion of sublimation, or feelings of ecstacy. That is to say, Bloom assumes that the value of a poem stems from the amount of sublimation a poet exposes in his (sic) poem.

Feminist criticism, on the other hand, prefers models which are not locked either into an opposition between the individual and the collective nor into a quantitative piling up of literary experience, but rather are able to think about discontinuities in a ¬ically different way. In 'Women's Time' Julia Kristeva ¬sts that feminism represents the arrangement of new ¬n a new time. Kristeva's is an arresting and useful Like Kristeva we can ask feminist psychoanalytic ¬hat place do you speak psychoanalytically about

¬ Sandra Gilbert and Susan Gubar would ¬ak from the place of female friendship ¬es and symbols of nineteenth- and ¬ Kristeva would answer that she ¬mother and the semiotic. While ¬ther is a central focus in much ¬ll aims to speak from the ¬n finds a very 'different' ¬us heroine. Cixous and ¬ent a whole morphology ¬popular culture enlarge ¬hodynamics of women

FREUD AND LACAN

Yet the influence of Freud is enormous if only because his concepts and vocabulary have transformed everyday thinking and writing. Freud himself was a literary critic and took certain themes and topics from literature to use as psychoanalytic models. The Oedipus complex from Greek tragedy is one obvious example. There are crucial connections between feminism and Freud and Lacan which must be spelt out. Rather than briefly recapitulating the theories of Freud and Lacan and hence oversimplifying their ideas, I will simply consider their import to feminism. Freud, for the first time, made the very status of femininity the centre of Western theoretical discourse. Psychoanalysis began by trying to understand how femininity (and masculinity) came about through analysing the individual histories of female patients. Freud, in systematising manifestations in these case studies, offers objective knowledge about how femininity is experienced in each woman's mind. It was Freud who changed the interpretive strategies of medical psychology from a use of sight (the main technique of Charcot in the 1880s) to a use of the ear and hence to language. By separating psychoanalysis from biology, Freud shifted attention from physiology to the spoken and subsequently the written word.

Freud's terms and concepts are crucial to literary criticism for several reasons. First, Freudian concepts describe patterns and give explanations for the way in which characters behave. Second, Freud articulated the significance of pleasure and desire in the formation of the individual psyche and he marked out ways in which these instincts could be understood through an analysis of dream symbolism, metaphors and condensation. For example, in Zora Neale Hurston's novel *Their Eyes Were Watching God* Hurston argues that, for women, 'the dream is the truth. Then they act and do things accordingly' (Hurston, 1986, p. 9). Like psychoanalysts, Hurston's women characters know that dream metaphors and images represent the inexpressible or repressed elements of their lives in a displaced form.

Similarly, for Lacan, the unconscious is structured like a language. Lacan, like Freud, reads subjects as texts. We grow as children, Lacan says, by making imaginary identifications, but such identifications are always difficult and will often be fictive. The first stage of our ego identity comes from the sight of ourselves in a mirror – an image which in itself blurs subjectivity and objectivity. The second stage is when we enter into the 'symbolic' order; that is, we begin to use language to create our identity as 'myself' and 'I'. The unconscious also, Lacan claims, is 'a sliding' of what he calls signifieds and signifiers; that is, a mixture of fixed meanings and metaphors. 'Masculinity' and 'femininity' are constructs, metaphors, in some senses a language.

It is clear that feminism's deconstruction of language is in debt to the analysis of psychic imagery begun by Freud and continued by Lacan and others. To Lacan the unconscious reveals the fictional nature of sexual categories. Lacan develops his account of subjectivity in reference to the idea of a fiction. It is this relation between language and fantasy that attracts feminist critics to Lacanian analysis. Language, Lacan argues, is what identifies us as gendered subjects. The acquisition of identity and hence subjectivity occurs only as we enter into speech. Lacan gives feminist literary criticism a useful concept of subjectivity. Not only is a girl identified through her language, rather than by innate biology, but Lacan suggests that the idea of a coherent subject is itself a fiction. Sexual identity is always unstable; it is susceptible to disruption by the unconscious and disruption manifests itself in the discontinuities and contradictions of everyday language. Additionally, the idea of femininity will always be open to redefinition.

The ways in which Freud and Lacan link psychoanalysis and language are useful for feminist psychoanalytic criticism. Freud's model of interpretation has another immense advantage for feminists. It is halfway between a purely interpretive method – providing a single meaning through the connection of stable terms – and a method which questions the interpreter herself. In other words, both the author and the critic in the act of literary interpretation are, like the analysand and the analyst, interpretable objects.

Yet Freudian and Lacanian psychoanalytic critiques clearly pose problems for feminism. It is the Oedipus complex in Freudian and Lacanian theory which forces us into a symbolic order. Language (and hence literary criticism), in simple terms, is controlled by the law of the Father, or masculine syntactical order. Female metaphors are in a realm outside the symbolic – in romance, fantasy or transcendental imagery. For example, Irigaray's descriptions of women's semi-confidences, exclamations and 'babble' would be outside the symbolic. Feminist literary critics cannot, therefore, simply celebrate female metaphors because this implies accepting patriarchy as a superior symbolic. As we shall see, Julia Kristeva to some extent evades the issue by placing an imaginary, feminine 'literary' world in pre-symbolic, pre-Oedipal patterns which she calls the 'semiotic'. Although this does establish a source of 'difference' in something other than a castration complex, a further problem remains. For Lacan there is no prediscursive reality, and therefore for feminists to privilege that world is to assign femininity to an archaic form of expressivity.

In its current attempts to question radically and 'deconstruct' a range of psychoanalytic practices, feminism encounters the major challenge of contemporary thought. The challenge is common both to psychoanalysis and to feminism: how can one speak from the place of the Other? How can women in literature, or for that matter men, be thought about outside an existing masculine/feminine framework? According to Derrida, Western metaphysics depends on a system of opposites (presence/absence, identity/difference) with the 'positive', usually masculine, term being of greater value. In other words, how can women break away from the logic of oppositions?

ELLEN MOERS AND SANDRA GILBERT AND SUSAN GUBAR

Ellen Moers in *Literary Women* and Sandra Gilbert and Susan Gubar in *The Madwoman in the Attic* argue that novels are primarily narratives about the location of gender identity. These critics suggest that women's writing carries a certain knowledge about the repressed and unconscious features of women's identity. All three critics trace the psychodynamics of character representation in fiction. They build on the earlier writings of the American psychoanalyst Karen Horney among others. In 'The Dread of Women' Horney described anxiety images in the poetry of Heine and Schiller which, she claims, reveal men's secret fear of women and caused men to write about 'a feminine type which is infantile, non-maternal and hysterical' (1932, p. 360). Contemporary critics, using similar techniques, opposed these alienating models of women, with literary examples of mothering and female bonding as a potentially positive source of female identity. Redefining Sartre's dialectics of Otherness and Lacan's concept of the mirror stage, feminist critics were able to show how mothers and daughters and friends mirror each other in literary imagery. In their textual analysis of these psychoanalytic images, feminists showed how 'the reproduction of mothering', in Nancy Chodorow's terms, is also mirrored in the production of the daughter's text.

Ellen Moers's *Literary Women* (1977) is a classic example of the psychodynamic approach. *Literary Women* links each author's biography with particular images or themes in her work. For example, Moers links Christina Rossetti's creation of vivid and brutal masculine goblins in 'Goblin Market' to her supposed incestual or sororial abuse by her brothers as a child. Moers translates aspects of female culture into a problematic relation between female consciousness and forms in female writing. She claims that there are specific female modes (for example, the Gothic), specific female myths (such as birthing in *Frankenstein*) and specific female symbols (like Anne Frank's bird).

Literary Women does open up a new way of thinking about the literary conflicts of women writers, and how these were resolved. Ellen Moers describes the warmth and regard which women writers had for each other; for example, George Eliot and Harriet Beecher Stowe, and Emily Dickinson's debt to Elizabeth Barrett Browning. But Moers describes literary forms in very functional ways and mainly for their function in the characterisation of white heterosexual heroines. The drawback to Moers's project is her very uncritical assumption of a writer's intention. Critics like Elly Bulkin also attack Moers as racist and homophobic since she centralises Western, white heterosexual writing (see chapter 8, Lesbian feminist criticism).

Sandra M. Gilbert's and Susan Gubar's *The Madwoman in the Attic* (1979) develops Moers's model. They describe the works of Jane Austen, Mary Shelley, the Brontës, George Eliot, among others, and claim that it is in images (of enclosures, of doubles, of disease and madness) that women writers strategically reveal their cultural and social anxieties. *The Madwoman in the Attic* is one of the most cited texts in contemporary feminist criticism. This is because not only does it firmly 'save' writers like Emily Dickinson from patriarchal critics but it attempts to create a feminist poetic. The book throws out a number of interesting ideas: that women writers are closest to characters they detest, that their images represent anxieties about their own creativity. But the form of *The Madwoman in the Attic* is revealing. Its 718 pages show how much Gilbert and Gubar depend on paraphrase rather than on precise analysis. They go from writer to writer with no concluding chapter. It is a curiously static text which gives little sense of why we should read one writer more than another.

Gilbert and Gubar's choice of a narrative rather than analytic form is partly due, as the authors themselves admit, to its derivation from a course they taught at Indiana University. Similarly, Patricia Meyer Spacks's *The Female Imagination* (1977), which also adopts psychoanalytic themes, is organised around teachable titles which can encompass a variety of otherwise disparate works. For example, her titles of 'power' and 'passivity' resemble Gilbert and Gubar's 'angel'.

These American feminist critics utilised psychoanalysis in the main to interrogate images of femininity. Certainly female stereotypes are obvious features of Western literature. But not only do these provide vague handles for literary criticism, they also lock in the disparate qualities of any text to crude polarities. Charting the psychodynamics of characterisation uncontextualised does not explain why one stereotype is more significant than any other. More important are the metaphysical implications of the 'female heroine' approach of these American critics. By conceptualising the female heroine as an integral subject coincident with her own consciousness, such critics suggest a unitary subject.

In a more general way, the dilemma shows that feminists needed more sophisticated conceptual instruments to define subjectivity than simply to use symbols of character identity. Important theoretical questions about women's representation have been addressed in a different psychoanalytic direction by Hélène Cixous, Mary Jacobus and other feminist critics. For example, Mary Jacobus has utilised a wide range of concepts drawn from Freud, Lacan and Melanie Klein to analyse literary texts. *Reading Woman: Essays in Feminist Criticism* (1986) addresses representations of sexual difference in Western art, in Freud and Lacan as well as in women's writing. Similarly, Elizabeth Abel in *Virginia Woolf and the Fictions of Psychoanalysis* (1989), as the title might suggest, looks at the connections between Woolf, Freud and Melanie Klein in psychoanalytic debates (of the 1920s and 1930s) about matriarchy and patriarchy. Current feminist psychoanalytic criticism focuses on maternal relations in literature supported by ideas and theories drawn from object relations psychotherapy. This is the approach best known perhaps in the work of the American critic, Nancy Chodorow, which argues that the infant's relation to the mother shapes gender identity causing boys to become men by being 'not-the-mother' and girls to become women by 'reproducing mothering'. As a result men often separate from others while women remain connected to others in the world.

By offering clear explanations for the ways in which masculinity and femininity are constructed in the West, object relations theory could account for different literary representations of masculinity and femininity. If women writers have intense and ambivalent relations with their mothers or mother figures this would be represented in their work. Object relations theory has been utilised by Elaine Showalter, Ellen Moers and Marianne Hirsch among others to describe the influences women writers have on each other's work. Feminist psychoanalytic literary criticism was matched by feminist historians intent on examining women's friendships in earlier centuries. For example, Carroll Smith-Rosenberg's early and very influential essay 'The Female World of Love and Ritual' (1975) traced the interdependence of American women diarists.

Marianne Hirsch's book *The Mother-Daughter Plot: Narrative, Psychoanalysis, Feminism* (1989) builds on this historical work, utilising object relations theory in order to analyse contradictions and articulations in texts about mothers and daughters. She assesses three periods/styles: realism (the nineteenth century), modernism, and matrifocal relations in the work of American Black writers such as Alice Walker and Toni Morrison.

Hirsch argues that the maternal is continually being repressed in women's writing but that in Black women's writing the mother begins to represent 'herself'.

JULIET MITCHELL

Juliet Mitchell on the other hand believes that the literary power of the novel lies in its portraits of hysteria. In contrast to *The Madwoman in the Attic*, Mitchell does not seek to endow madness with romantic glamour. Hysteria cannot provide a social reality for women; it is simply that the place of hysteria in literary texts is another 'place' to which the psychoanalytic critic must attend.

In her literary essays Juliet Mitchell builds on the work of Phyllis Chesler in *Women and Madness* and other psychoanalysts. Chesler mixes statistical data about mental health with subjective accounts by individual women and sets these in the context of literary excerpts from the novels and autobiographies of women writers. Chesler aims to let women speak for themselves rather than be spoken for. Mitchell argues that the problem with Kristeva's concept of the semiotic is that it has its own space set up by patriarchy because the semiotic occurs *before* a child's entry into the symbolic. In order to be published, Mitchell claims, women writers use a masculine language to talk about female experience. Inevitably their symbolic 'order' will always be 'hysterical'.

Mitchell offers two kinds of psychoanalytic insights in her criticism. The more important because more theoretically thought out is her idea that woman's style is 'imprisoned' in traditional discourse. The focus here is on syntactics. But right from the beginning of her work Mitchell uses another psychoanalytic technique which is the more conventional, but no less useful, translation of narrative plot into psychoanalytic life history. She describes *Wuthering Heights*, for example, as a series of stages, of composite crises, represented metaphorically in Catherine's adult life. Again, when reading George Meredith, Mitchell constructs an existential phenomenology of Meredith's treatment of childhood (Mitchell, 1984). The focus here is on structure. Mitchell's argument is that narrative form as well as character representations will simultaneously define femininity. Mitchell attempts both a psychodynamic analysis of character and a psychoanalytic critique of textual structures. Mitchell's psychoanalytic critique focuses on relationships, on metaphors of Lacanian games and Winnicott's mirror imagery, and Mitchell turns to psychoanalysis to pose a question central to feminism: where is 'difference' constructed in a literary text? Mitchell's answer is in the place of hysteria because hysterics articulate both the acceptance of and a refusal of sexuality in contemporary culture.

CAROLYN HEILBRUN

While Mitchell's approach has the advantage of making it impossible to read literature outside of a consideration of gender construction, earlier critics had tried to free sexuality from gender restrictions and step outside gender divisions into androgyny. For example, in *The Second Sex* Simone de Beauvoir described the sexually androgynous figure. But to de Beauvoir, androgyny implies masculinity (her word is 'brotherhood'). Carolyn Heilbrun in *Toward a Recognition of Androgyny* (1973) was the first feminist critic after Woolf to examine concepts of androgyny to subvert existing representations of masculine and feminine traditional literary criticism. In a line from Virginia Woolf's *A Room of One's Own* Heilbrun claims that 'androgyny' is useful to feminism because it moves away from Freud's notion of bisexuality, which reinforces gender difference as binomial. Heilbrun claims that androgyny circumvents literary patterns of dominance and submission associated with rigid gender paradigms.

Heilbrun examines the psychology of sex differences as these are represented in literary descriptions of transsexualism and cross-dressing. Androgynous representations, Heilbrun says, do not reflect authorial confusion about gender. The problems of female identity in women's poetry and prose are rarely difficulties in knowing one's gender; more frequently they are difficulties in learning what being a female means culturally. While more contemporary feminist writing sees androgyny as problematic, androgyny theory offers the view that sex roles are societal constructs which can be abandoned. There is, of course, a significant nineteenth-century tradition of writing about androgyny and transvestism; what was new in Heilbrun's work was her argument that androgyny could name not what is sadly fixed but what could be fluid. Many female modernists, including Woolf, Stein, Barnes and McCullers, create fictional universes that question traditional assumptions about gender ascription and identity. In that work, and in the more contemporary writing of Ursula LeGuin, the androgynous future to Heilbrun represents the hope of Utopia.

GAYATRI SPIVAK

Another concept which feminist criticism could utilise is the concept of absence. The best example of a psychoanalytic criticism which attends to absence is the writing of Gayatri Spivak. In 'The Letter as Cutting Edge' Spivak suggests that any critic who has read the main texts of psychoanalysis has learned that language is made up as much by its absences as by the substance by which the absences are framed. The critic's task, Spivak claims, is to discover the rhetorical slips and dodges in texts. The follower of Lacan would interpret these textual gestures as the eruption of the Other into the text of the subject. Spivak argues that the job of a feminist psychoanalytic critic is to look at imagery and signifiers of desire in a topological cross-hatching of the text. Sometimes Spivak is very diagrammatic about these symbological lexicons, but she does allow psycho-analysis to help her question 'overt' meaning in a text. In her earlier work, Spivak argues that psychoanalytic criticism is caught in a double bind. Psychoanalysis frequently has to break with apparent sense to dig deeper into the psyche, yet literary criticism must operate as if the critic is making a sensible interpretation. What can criticism do? Spivak's solution is to name frontiers, borders and boundaries where the text becomes a subtext. In addition, she suggests feminist criticism should use psychoanalytic vocabulary to try for a frontier style, breaking the boundaries of formal criticism.

SUMMARY

Psychoanalytic criticism changes our perception of popular culture. A key focus of psychoanalytic criticism is on romance fiction. Popular literature has great appeal to readers and part of that appeal derives from a use of repetition. In psychoanalysis pleasure and desire are discussed in terms of compulsions and repetitions. Psychoanalytic criticism is therefore of particular value in analysing textual repetitions and in decoding 'compulsive' literary strategies such as avoidance and subversion.

Romance is founded on absence – on frustration about what will happen next. Tania Modleski in *Loving with a Vengeance* (1982) utilises psychoanalysis to show how films and mass-produced narratives contain elements of resistance. A psychoanalytic framework has proved very useful to feminist critics of the romance; for example, in Kristeva's account of desire in *Histoires d'amour* or in Beauman's more anecdotal account of popular fiction. In *Female Desire* (1984) Ros Coward investigates the imaginative dimensions of romance and female complicity in the creation of a culture of romance. Romance fiction can be read as a fantasy of women's repressed narcissism. Romance is a major category of the feminine imaginary. By centring on the question of pleasure, psychoanalytic criticism helps us to understand why the vicarious satisfaction of psychic needs (created in women by a patriarchal culture unable to fulfil these) are often satisfied by romance fiction.

Debates about romance fiction polarise between Marxist critics like Ann Snitow (1984), who feel (however sympathetically) that romance keeps women in their socially and sexually subordinate place, and critics like Janice Radway (1983) who refuse this restricted notion of female false consciousness. I instance this final example of feminist debate not so much to investigate its topography but because it summarises many of the main issues of a psychoanalytic critique. Snitow argues that romance fiction is a mirror image of pornography since women's price for emotional intimacy is passivity. Women enjoy romances, Snitow argues, by accepting a delimited invitation to artificial warmth. Radway, on the other hand, thinks women when reading resist any 'regulation' of female sexuality in the

Harlequin texts she considers, because they read ironically, and 'enjoy' the inherent instability of gender.

The scene of this critical debate is itself a repetition of psychoanalytic motifs. For example, Snitow focuses on what in the text invites in a reader and Radway on what in the text resists sexual identity. Romance offers a sense of self-identity only through a precise sequence of cliff-hanging moments. Similarly psychoanalysis narrates the topography of the unconscious in a set chain of signifiers. Both centre on the ownership of interpretation. Romance critics ask: is the reader 'owned' by romance or does she own her own reading? In psychoanalysis the subject is both invited to interpret herself and be interpreted. In some ways this describes the role of the mother in Audre Lorde's *Zami*.

Feminist psychoanalytic criticism continues to focus on motifs of mothers and daughters in women's writing: Elaine Showalter's recent interest in the psychoanalyst Melanie Klein (see Showalter, 1990) focuses on the restorative, therapeutic aspects of 'maternal' writing paralleled in the work of other critics such as Nancy Miller, and Rachel Blau DuPlessis. Throughout the 1930s, 1940s and 1950s Melanie Klein analysed the primitive mental stress created by early mother/infant relationships. Klein describes imagery from the pre-Oedipal world of instinctual experience which shows again how our unconscious symbols and representations are gendered. One good example of a literary representation of the pre-Oedipal occurs in Jean Rhys's *Wide Sargasso Sea*. Rhys makes a stark contrast between the dreams of Antoinette Cosway (Rhys's version of Charlotte Brontë's mad Bertha) and those of Rochester. Whereas Antoinette's dreams reach back into her earliest memories of primal energy symbolised as a forest, Rochester's dreams are nightmares where he experiences a loss of ego.

Psychoanalytic criticism gives feminism elbow room. Using psychoanalysis to investigate desire, gender identity and linguistic constructions feminists can deconstruct the gender hierarchies of literature and the gender hierarchies of society. Juliet Mitchell even claims that psychoanalysis is an exemplary instance of Gramsci's 'optimism of the will' since its aim is to change will. At a simple level psychoanalysis describes a multiplicity of female expressions and interpretations. The challenge facing feminist criticism today is nothing less than to 'reinvent' critical language. What psychoanalysis offers feminism are ways of rethinking phallocentric structures.

SELECTED READING

Basic texts

Abel, E. (1989) *Virginia Woolf and the Fictions of Psychoanalysis*, Chicago: University of Chicago Press

Coward, R. (1982) 'Sexual politics and psychoanalysis' in R. Blunt and C. Rowan (eds), *Feminism, Culture and Politics*, London: Lawrence & Wishart

Freud, S. (1983) *The Standard Edition of the Complete Psychological Works of Sigmund Freud*, trans. J. Strachey, London: Hogarth Press

Gilbert, S. and Gubar, S (1979) *The Madwoman in the Attic: The woman writer and the nineteenth-century literary imagination*, New Haven: Yale University Press

Hardwick, E. (1953) 'The subjection of women', *Partisan Review*, May/June

Heilbrun, C. (1973) *Toward a Recognition of Androgyny*, New York: Harper Colophon

Hirsch, M. (1989) *The Mother-Daughter Plot: Narrative, psychoanalysis, feminism*, Bloomington: Indiana University Press

Horney, K. (1932) 'The dread of women', *International Journal of Psychoanalysis*, XIII, pp. 348–60.

Jacobus, M. (1986) *Reading Woman: Essays in feminist criticism*, London: Methuen

Lacan, J. (1977) *Ecrits: A selection*, London: Tavistock

Mitchell, J. (1974) *Psychoanalysis and Feminism*, Harmondsworth: Penguin

Mitchell, J. (1984) *Women: The longest revolution*, London: Virago

Modleski, T. (1982) *Loving With A Vengeance*, Hamden, Conn.: Anchor Books

Moers, E. (1977) *Literary Women*, Garden City, NY: Anchor Books

Radway, J. (1983) 'Women read the romance', *Feminist Studies*, 9:1 (Spring) pp. 53–78

Showalter, E. (1990) '*Mrs Klein*: The mother, the daughter, the thief and their critics', *Women: A Cultural Review: Special Issue Positioning Klein*, 1:2 (November) pp. 144–9
Snitow, A., Stansell, C. and Thompson, S. (eds) (1984) *Desire: The politics of sexuality*, London: Virago
Spivak, G. (1987) 'The letter as cutting edge', in G. C. Spivak, *In Other Worlds*, London: Methuen
For Cixous, Irigaray, Kristeva references, see previous chapter on 'French feminism criticism'.

Introductions

Gunew, S. (ed) (1991) *Feminist Knowledge: Critique and construct*, Parts IV and VI, London: Routledge
Keitel, E. (1989) *Reading Psychosis: Readers, texts and psycho-analysis*, Oxford: Blackwell
Rigny, B. (1978) *Madness and Sexual Politics: Studies in Brontë, Woolf, Lessing and Atwood*, Madison, Wis.: University of Wisconsin Press
Rowly, H. and Grosz, E. (1990) 'Psychoanalysis and feminism', in S. Gunew (ed.), *A Reader in Feminist Knowledge*, London: Routledge
Wright, E. (1984) *Psychoanalytic Criticism: Theory in practice*, London: Methuen

Further reading

Bloom, H. (1973) *The Anxiety of Influence*, New York: Oxford University Press
Brennan, T. (1989) *Between Feminism and Psychoanalysis*, New York: Routledge
Chesler, P. (1972) *Women and Madness*, New York: Doubleday
Coward, R. (1984) *Female Desire*, London: Paladin
Felman, S. (ed.) (1977) *Literature and Psychoanalysis*, special issue of *Yale French Studies*, 55/56
Felman, S. and Lamb, D. (1992) *Testimony: Crises of witnessing in literature, psychoanalysis and history*, London: Routledge
Gallop, J. (1982) *The Daughter's Seduction: Feminism and psycho-analysis*, Ithaca: Cornell University Press

Garner, S. N. *et al.* (1985) *The (M)Other Tongue: Essays in feminist psychoanalytic interpretation*, Ithaca: Cornell University Press

Holland, N. (1990) *Holland's Guide to Psychoanalytic Psychology and Literature-and-Psychology*, Oxford: Oxford University Press

Lesser, S. O. (1957) *Fiction and the Unconscious*, Boston: Beacon Press

6 Poststructuralism/ deconstruction/postmodernism

INTRODUCTION

By the late 1960s, many literary critics had moved away from the view that the history of literature had a progressive evolutionary shape, continually and smoothly moving from movement to movement, period to period, and they were beginning to identify the discursively specific ways in which literary language figured men and women in very *systematic* patterns.

Structuralism is the science, or critique, most concerned to describe these systematic patterns and identify the structure (*langue*) of meaning in texts and how it operates through organised rules and conventions. Ferdinand de Saussure's *Course in General Linguistics* (1915) showed that language, and hence literature, obeyed certain rules and that these rules could be systematised. Saussure called these rules a generative grammar. Following the work of Saussure, structuralists transformed many disciplines. For example, the feminist anthropologist Mary Douglas, examined structures of differences, taboos and rituals in societies throughout the world and argued that these structures construct culture and language.

With the publication of Kate Millett's *Sexual Politics* (1970), the founding of the National Organisation of Women in America and the British Women's Liberation Movement, and the student revolts of 1968 in Paris, a profound shift occurred in conceptions of women, culture and subjectivity, and therefore a profound shift in assumptions about the power and forms of language. Beginning to identify the powerful ideologies shaping language, the *his* of history, as a crucial form of women's oppression, feminists refused to *isolate* language systems, or indeed literature itself, from the political conditions of their production. So, as Katie King points out, it is no accident that academic theorists discovered the destabilising tools of poststructuralism at the same time that in the United States feminists were elaborating issues of difference (King, 1990). Critics turned to poststructuralism because it offered a grand critique of contemporary culture.

POSTSTRUCTURALISM

Poststructuralism focuses on how literature and its languages work within particular cultural and educational frameworks. Poststructuralism 'deconstructs' or debunks structuralism's faith in measuring systems in isolation from the authority and power structures that control those systems. In other words, poststructuralism has made us aware of the ways in which men and women are absent from or included in representations, depending on who owns or speaks the language of representation.

No language or literature can ever be 'free' from the conditions which produce it. For example Négritude, which was a form of independent black culture and writing developed by the Martiniquan poet Aimé Césaire, was also part of the colonial world in which it first evolved. As Wole Soyinka argues in *Myth, Literature and the African World*:

> Négritude, having laid its cornerstone on a tradition, however bravely it tried to reverse its concepts (leaving its tenets untouched), was a foundling deserving to be drawn into, nay, even considered a case for benign adoption by European ideological interests. (Soyinka (1976) p. 134)

It was Michel Foucault, the French poststructuralist critic, who comprehensively analysed the way the languages (discourses) of medicine, criminology and sexuality control and define women and men through the power of 'experts' who articulate such discourses. Foucault's histories of madness, medicine, prisons and sexuality have been influential in literary criticism, history, philosophy and the social sciences. The concept of language, or discourse, which he developed in *The Archaeology of Knowledge* (1974) focuses on the rules which allow certain languages to form. Discourses are statements collected in 'discursive formations' of knowledge called 'fields'. Statements can include maps, descriptions, calculations and experiments. 'Real' language is what is permitted to be true by the people and institutions who control the formation and development of language. An extreme example here is Foucault's argument that hysterics are *given* the language of hysteria by changes in the power and institutional structures of medicine. Changes in forms of language are therefore not necessarily progressive.

Foucault's poststructuralist formulations are very appealing to feminist literary critics because Foucault locates the rules which control patriarchal/sexist linguistic definitions and terminology. Poststructuralism's theorising of subjectivity is particularly attractive to feminist criticism. Poststructuralism offers a way of understanding literary processes and the construction of gender as simply that – constructions. If gender constructions can be 'deconstructed' by literary critics then gender identities in writing, as in any other form of social expression, might at some time be 'free' of misogynist constructions.

Feminism shares with poststructuralism its attack on universal values and its desire to explore multiple kinds of discourse. Both examine literary and social texts, not only in terms of what these texts *describe*, but in terms of what they do to *hide* their own ideologies. To feminist poststructuralists the question of literary value, of choosing great books by great writers (a choice given the title 'the canon') is not a self-evident question, and the answers which traditional literary criticism provides are, to poststructuralists, a matter of class and gender-based forms of control and power.

Literary texts are placed in grids or hierarchies of value in examination and educational curricula. Because these powerful hierarchies cannot be undone by simply replacing texts by men with texts by women or by creating an alternative canon (useful though this activity can be in raising the status of women writers), feminist poststructuralists point to wide-ranging practices of challenging the canon. For example, the writer Jean Rhys transformed Charlotte Brontë's *Jane Eyre* into *Wide Sargasso Sea* to challenge the racist image of a mad Creole woman.

Challenges to notions of a unitary cultural or literary identity come from several directions. They can be found in French feminism's focus on gender difference; for example, Luce Irigaray and Julia Kristeva describes a maternal language, called the semiotic, which is 'outlawed' by the symbolic or written language. (This idea is examined in chapter 4, above: French feminist criticism.)

Since the 1970s, poststructuralism and feminism have made the most radical breaks with humanism and structuralism. What emerges from that decade is a shared set of concerns. Both critiques examine, in an interdisciplinary way, how key texts, from Freud's essays through to media advertising, might direct everyday thinking. Both respond to canonical texts such as nineteenth-century realist novels with challenging and interrogative accounts. Both work to dethrone the authority of the author and the narrow range of 'great' writers studied in the academy. As a result, both critiques highlight the *processes* of literary production. While Marxist criticism, most of all, could be said to focus on production processes – whether those processes are making TV sets as capitalist objects or TV shows as capitalist fodder – feminism includes what society denies and Marxist critics frequently neglect: the gendered subjectivity of production. Feminism asks who is speaking, and who is reading. In feminist poststructuralism these questions often involve fictions of the narrating 'I' and the supposed reader. Take this passage from the first chapter of Maxine Hong Kingston's novel *The Woman Warrior*:

> The emigrants confused the gods by diverting their curses, misreading them with crooked streets and false names. They must try to confuse their offspring as well, who, I suppose, threaten them in similar ways – always trying to get things straight, always trying to name the unspeakable. The Chinese I know hide their names; sojourners take new names when their lives change and guard their real names with silence. (Kingston (1976) p. 5)

Kingston clearly shows that, in addition to immigration controls, *language* displaces people. Names have meaning only from their political contexts and uses: what words need to be said to those in power. The narrator's speech is characteristically poststructuralist because it tells us about the history of Chinese immigration and then immediately contests the limits of that history by drawing attention to language as an act of construction which never names the 'unspeakable'.

Poststructuralists (for example, Roland Barthes and Hortense Spillers (see the section on Spillers below)) would argue that a character like Kingston's narrator intimates her own production or characterisation as 'knowledge-for another' (see Spillers, 1991).

Despite Kingston's emphasis in this novel on confusions of naming and speaking, she also paradoxically claims that the speaking act *is* important, *has* meaning. Kingston's summoning or 'interpellation' of subjectivity in the confused worlds of Los Angeles, China and Stockton (for example, by enabling the English-speaking reader to enter the mind of a non-English-speaking Chinese woman) is the work of the novel and it is also the work of feminist poststructuralism.

There are obvious convergences between poststructuralism and second-wave feminism, both in terms of their starting dates and in terms of shared techniques. Both date from approximately 1966–1970. Following Pierre Macherey's *A Theory of Literary Production* (1966), Jacques Derrida published *Of Grammatology* in 1967; Roland Barthes converted his semiotic theories to the poststructuralism of *S/Z*, and Michel Foucault's *The Order of Things* and Jacques Lacan's *Ecrits* were published in 1966. These critics inaugurated a radical rethinking about the basic assumptions of literature such as the idea that literature actually says what it means. The deferral of meaning by texts and the absences or *marginalities* in texts are, for Derrida, the inescapable features of all language. Feminists attack women's situation of marginality – the absence of women in social institutions, or in texts. Society's choice of certain social groups as marginal or 'Other' is a choice that feminists and poststructuralists condemn.

The 1970s, then, represent a widespread feeling in Western critical thinking, concerning the ineffectiveness and inappropriateness of single literary theories and a growing sense that multiple and different voices needed to be heard. The feminist recovery of hitherto underrepresented forms of the feminine occurred in psychoanalytic theory (Kristeva, Irigaray, Cixous) as well as in literary criticism. These critics' fundamental goal was to show how gender relations are created and expressed. The single most important contribution of feminist poststructuralists to literary criticism is to make us think deeply about the existence or absence of race and gender relations in literature. Feminist critics warmed to poststructuralism because only poststructuralism seemed to recognise the processes controlling the ways in which women are represented misogynistically in literature – for example, the convention in nineteenth-century novels of ending women's independence by marriage or death – and because poststructuralism attacks these conventions.

In contrast to modernism and humanism, poststructuralism favours open, decentred texts where theory can mix with fiction and high culture can mix with low. In traditional literary criticism authors are thought to 'own' the books they write. Poststructuralism, on the other hand, ridicules the idea that texts simply carry the messages of authors. It would be absurd to say that Milton's *Paradise Lost* has the same meaning today as it had when Milton wrote it or that we should, or even *can*, read it in the way in which Milton wished. Authors are there in texts as 'functions', as effects. Texts cannot be understood in terms of the author's supposed biography or intention alone. Poststructuralism prefers writing which is ironic and full of multiple signifiers; writing like that of Virginia Woolf and Laurence Sterne. But although all poststructuralists claim that literary language is bound up with other cultural languages, only feminist poststructuralists specifically centralise issues of gender and subjectivity. This is because feminism is committed to meaning-making, to representation, to creating a social space for women. So that although feminism and poststructuralism share many concerns – a questioning of elitist aesthetics and an urge to confuse traditional disciplinary boundaries – feminist poststructuralism diverges from mainstream poststructuralism in several crucial ways. Feminist critics often utilise autobiography, either their own or that of the author they are describing, in their attempts to contextualise the enunciative or spoken situation of the text. Feminist criticism in the 1970s was often defined as the search for the 'authority' of experience (see chapter 1). Many feminist critics then asserted that the personal and historical experiences of a writer would explain the 'truth' of her writing. Feminist poststructuralism moved away from this faith in realism; away from, for example, the notion that a character gains a self-identity simply from a quest for social place or status. But feminist poststructuralism often attends to the trappings of realism – interior monologues, coherent characterisation, heuristic plots – to point to the importance of a woman's point of view even while agreeing that point of view is always constructed. Literary texts often provide good examples of these concerns. For example, Toni Morrison's *Beloved* is often described as a poststructuralist novel but Morrison defines her narrative strategy in this and in her other novels as a kind of 'literary archaeology' which relies on individual memory and autobiography (see Morrison, 1987, p. 109). In addition to a more complex response to realism, feminist poststructuralism mixes different languages: Margaret Atwood, for example, brilliantly ironises terms from women's magazines and TV commercials, and poststructuralism reconstitutes notions of high/low art. An obsession with allegory, with the aesthetic, lies deep in the heart of feminist poststructuralist criticism, evident for example in the punning title of Julia Kristeva's *Histoires d'amour*. Another and key feature of feminist poststructuralism is the interdependence of Black and white critiques.

White feminist poststructuralists (for example, Elizabeth Meese) often cite a debt to Afro-American literary criticism, while the major feminist poststructuralists are Black (for example, Hortense Spillers and Valerie Smith). In addition, both white and Black feminist critics betray an interest in feminist anthropology and feminist Utopias; for example, Rachel Blau DuPlessis has introduced anthropological ideas into her criticism. Thus, the contradictions of feminist poststructuralism (individual identities versus open endings) are not necessarily resolved, but rather are held in ironic tension. They are represented by what DuPlessis calls 'the form of the desk, the tote' in opposition to Ezra Pound's 'codes, a great man's laws' (DuPlessis, 1990, p. 9).

Feminist poststructuralism belongs neither to feminist theory nor to literary criticism but mingles both in a deliberately self-reflexive, often autobiographical manner. There are similarities here between poststructuralist criticism and feminist fiction by Jean Rhys, Margaret Atwood and Angela Carter. Angela Carter's *Nights at the Circus* (1984), for example, in its eye-witness account of a nineteenth-century bird woman, teaches us that the evidence of history and literature is social texts,

constructions. British poststructuralism, like other British feminisms, is more socially focused than its American or French
counterparts. Ros Coward, for example, deconstructs mecha-
nisms in popular culture such as magazines and television
programmes as well as analysing psychoanalytic theory. In
Female Desire (1984), she looks at implied patterns of desire in a
whole range of cultural artifacts including health and fitness
guides. Coward attempts a psychosocial critique of textuality,
acknowledging that culture is a complex discursive network of
popular, elite and medical languages. Coward lays a greater
emphasis on popular culture's dominating ideologies than do
American critics with their greater attention to mainstream
literature. But it is with Afro-American criticism that feminist
poststructuralism develops a fully politicised practice of open
reading. Here feminist poststructuralists turn from a focus on
multiple signifiers to a focus on key words in texts, because, as
Hortense Spillers claims, it is in locating the power of what
Spillers calls the 'terministic cruxes' that Black feminism can
transform poststructuralism. For example, the British Black critic
Hazel Carby, now resident in America, analyses the term, the
'Black Other', as a writing *subject*, rather than as the victim figure
described by white critics. In *Reconstructing Womanhood* (1987),
Carby describes the careers of nineteenth-century Black women
writers such as Ida B. Wells and Anna Julia Cooper. Carby
shares several concerns with poststructuralism: she attacks the
essentialism of traditional criticism – for example, the notion of a
universal Black 'woman' – by describing the different verbal
powers and perceptions of these Black women writers. In a
poststructuralist use of mixed genres Carby places Black
women's writing against the dominant political and religious
languages of the nineteenth century which these writers both
reflect and interrogate. Similarly the Black American feminist
poststructuralist Valerie Smith, in her reading of Harriet Jacobs'
Incidents in the Life of a Slave Girl, shares Carby's interest in the
complicated relations between acceptable and unacceptable
representations of sexual and racial otherness (Smith, 1987). For
example, when describing the colonisation of the Black female
body by white slavers both critics brilliantly juxtapose
nineteenth-century fiction with contemporary racist theories
and feminist theory to reflect on strategies of difference.

HORTENSE SPILLERS

Hortense Spillers is an Afro-American author of several very influential essays. Spillers's work crucially links a Black feminist poststructuralist account of Black history, (for example, she exposes the way in which slavery deconstructed, degendered and destroyed black women) together with poststructuralist theories of language and signification. Indeed, one of the most important contributions of Black feminists to poststructuralism is this rigorous recasting of poststructuralist theory in terms of race. The carefully chosen title of Spillers's early essay 'Interstices: A Small Drama of Words' (1984) hints at the need for a new criticism – one which reads between the lines. In this impressive example of feminist poststructuralism, Spillers describes representations of Black female sexuality and argues that these representations seem to be forms of theatre performing dominating (white) mythologies. Spillers tackles the rhetorical features of contemporary feminist non-fiction writing about sexuality, and the relative absence of Afra-American women in such texts. She gives a radically different account of sexuality from the one provided by contemporary white feminists, attacking specifically Shulamith Firestone's *The Dialectic of Sex*. Spillers's main theme is the rift between 'the body' and 'the flesh' in cultural productions. In other words, the rift between the ungendered Black female (in culture) and Black flesh as a primary focus of white domination. The Black body functions as an absence in white feminism. For example, it is a sign of unrepresentability in the white feminist iconography of Judy Chicago's huge art work *The Dinner Party*. Chicago's collection of dinner plates representing great women of the past has only one Black woman – Sojourner Truth. The plate has been attacked by other Black feminists (for example, Alice Walker) as being irredeemably Eurocentric in both its assumptions and iconography. This is because Chicago chose to portray Sojourner Truth's tears rather than to represent her sexuality – her vagina – as Chicago represented all the other feminist thinkers in her exhibition. Spillers believes that only an adequate representation of both the Black body *and* Black voice, or language, can be the 'chief teaching model for Black women of what their femaleness is' (Spillers, 1984, p. 80).

Spillers's allegiance to poststructuralism in this essay is clear in her belief that Blues music crosses the binary of subject/object. She describes the female Blues voice as a series of gestures (or signifiers) which articulate 'kinship to other women' (Spillers, 1984). What attracts her to the Blues is its obvious connection to Black history on the one hand, and its less obvious but equally significant tie to 'double consciousness' on the other. The Blues stand as a trope, as a metonymy, of difference. The two tropes in Spillers's essay which come to stand most centrally for difference, then, are 'body' and 'dancing voice'. One thinks here of Foucault's notion of the body as an object of knowledge and hence power. Foucault would argue that representations, or descriptions, of bodies change from era to era, not because bodies themselves change shape dramatically but because authorities change the conventions of body representations for political reasons. Yet Foucault is prone to describing history as a disconnected collection of discourses. Spillers's feminist poststructuralism, on the other hand, is firmly materialist. She concerns herself with 'living bodies in material scenes'; with Black history; and with the careers of specific Blues singers such as Bessie Smith and specific women slaves. Spillers deliberately revises poststructuralism to allow the *experience* of Black women singers and their autobiographies to have a space. If anything marks Spillers's approach it is her belief that isolated lexical features (here 'stone' and 'solid') can carry a 'community of notions' (Spillers, 1990).

Her essay 'Notes on an Alternative Model: Neither/Nor' (1987) is also an impressive poststructuralist performance. Spillers begins by looking at configurations of the mulatto/a, and its contradictory paternity embedded in public consciousness. The mulatta is a metonymy for Afra-American issues in the United States today. The mulatta figure exists first for the male Other, the Black man; next, her history and body exist for, indeed are created by, white patriarchy. The gender of the mulatta is, in any case, a cultural *construct* historically because the reproduction of mothering was denied to Black women slaves who were often forbidden to rear, or 'gender' their offspring. Spillers brilliantly highlights how the politics of racism depends on a complex interaction with 'multiple signifiers' of Black women and men. In poststructuralist fashion she deftly weaves theory and fiction, using, for example, the concept of the three dimensions of alterity from T. Todorov's *The Conquest of America* to deconstruct Francis Harper's 1893 novel *Iola Leroy*, and the writing careers of Frederick Douglass and William Faulkner. Alterity, according to Todorov, has three dimensions: the axiological level where an I and the Other are distinguished, the praxeological level or distancing of the Other by the 'superior' I, and the epistemic level – admitting ignorance of Others. Todorov's theory, which Spillers interweaves with Black fiction and autobiography, pinpoints for her the ways in which African men and women are misrepresented historically.

The success of Spillers's use of 'terministic cruxes' in explaining the violent dispossessions of racism can be gauged in her punning essay 'Who Cuts the Border?' (1991). The slippery title refers to a private, autobiographical moment of indecision about cutting the border of grass between her house and the next door church, but quickly Spillers metamorphoses the incident into an allegory of the borders of American capitalism. Here Spillers's texts are again Faulkner's *The Sound and the Fury* and *Absalom, Absalom!* together with the work of Hegel and 'Our America' by José Martí, the nineteenth-century leader of the Cuban Revolutionary Party.

Spillers's essay is stunning in its reach, in its poststructuralist welding of theory and fiction, but also for its teasing apart of key signifiers in dominant discourses. Spillers looks at the term 'Caliban', its associations with cannibal, its sign as a geographical contact between Africa and America as well as its representation in seventeenth-century and contemporary writing. From *The Tempest* through to today the character Caliban always represents difference, animality and separation or absence from the civilised, the white norm.

Spillers pays a constant poststructuralist attention to the surface of her essay, to make clear her own textuality. Phrases such as 'from what angle does one insert . . . the "I's"/"eyes" of this collection of writings' recur, showing Spiller's debt to Lacan and to his idea that gazing establishes for us who/where we think we are. The mirror phase is Lacan's significant contribution to contemporary psychoanalysis. At about six months of age an infant is absorbed by its own image and that of others. The mirror phase provides a child with a potential individual identity – an external, spatial image. Following Lacan, Spillers deconstructs the overdetermined representability of 'Caliban'. She also reads politically by focusing on the key features or ways in which bodies, race and gender intersect. For example, like Paulo Freire, Spillers makes ideological interpretations of key words, laying bare their political meaning. Freire's teaching programme (developed in adult literacy schemes in Latin America) involves a concept of 'dialogic education' in which students, by deconstructing key words in their everyday lives, are able to define political features and then learn language. Freire believed that if a student chooses such words, these could expose for him or her the complex political world in which s/he lives and which barred her/his access to language (Freire, 1972).

Freire did not address questions of gender explicitly but he believed that the essence of liberation lies in the acquisition of words. By focusing on names and meanings which control their social realities the illiterate are liberated. Spillers adopts a similar process of political alphabetisation. Throughout all her essays she examines how racism draws fundamentally on key terms – 'mulatto', 'border', 'Caliban'. In poststructuralist manner, yet much like Freire, Spillers invites her reader to share in her punning and wordplay. For example, she often points to verbal associations in texts and to the root or derivation of a term. And, like other feminist poststructuralists (and Freire), Spillers wants her search for alternative signifiers of women's knowledge to be the basis of utopia. But if Spillers reads the history of the degendering of captive Black men and women through the lens of poststructuralism, she also politicises poststructuralism by focusing on the key terms (mulatta/Caliban) by which gender, race and sexuality are controlled by white power.

SUMMARY: POSTSTRUCTURALISM

The way in which poststructuralists deconstruct fixed representations of women has been criticised. Christine Di Stefano and Seyla Benhabib, among others, fear that poststructuralism 'leads to a theory without addressees, to a self without center . . . Is not a feminist theory that allies itself with poststructuralism in danger of losing its very reason for being?' (Di Stefano and Benhabib, 1989, p. 369). Their argument is that feminist politics depend on a notion of specific constituencies of women with whom feminists identify.

Poststructuralism, on the other hand, argues that terms such as 'author', 'self' and 'experience' are not stable. In addition, the association between poststructuralism and other European theories often seems imperialistic. The poststructuralist love of decentring, deconstructing and open endings, seems to many feminists to threaten the legitimacy of a worldwide movement dedicated to creating a social space for constituencies of women. But feminist literary critics do use poststructuralism positively to disrupt the literary canon. They have uncovered new writing by women and reconstructed cultural and literary categories and denaturalised sexist images.

Poststructuralist theory, though not the theory of its feminist followers, is criticised most vehemently by Barbara Christian (1989) as a 'race' which ignores material culture. Christian's argument is that the literary world, by which she means the American academy, has been taken over by professional theory-creating critics, and that this white academic hegemony has silenced women of colour, symbolised for Christian by the term 'minority discourse'. As she points out, Black women have central roles in much writing in the world, if not in the American academy. Black women have continually speculated theoretically about the world, although for the most part in stories, proverbs or what Christian calls 'hieroglyphs' – forms different from Western logic. Hence, Black theory has not been recognised by the academy just as Black people have been refused entry to academic institutions (see chapter 7, Black feminisms). Christian specifically attacks the status of the canon which Spillers also refuses in her accounts of slave documents and other extra-literary texts. In Spillers's amazingly complex bridging of race/gender/psychoanalysis/history, material life and culture are not in opposition. The choice of Spillers's essay subtitle 'Neither/Nor' does not signal indecision. Rather, Spillers's Black poststructuralism, informed by Lacan, permits her the possibility of affirming race as a representational category. 'Neither/Nor' addresses the material contents of racist names and labels together with the way in which these names can never fully represent the precise historical or literary realities of Black women.

DECONSTRUCTION

Deconstruction is the belief that universal concepts and the conventional boundaries between opposed concepts or binary opposites such as Black/white, man/woman, culture/nature must be taken apart, or deconstructed, in order for us to understand the (political) processes such terms represent. The basis of all literary criticism is that texts never actually mean what they say or say what they mean. More specifically, deconstructionists argue that literary meaning is 'constructed' through contrasts between binary opposites such as Black/white and that the choice of one of these terms as positive (usually white) depends on the negation or oppression of the opposite term (usually Black). The object of deconstruction is to pull apart the processes of production which create and naturalise these oppositions; to deconstruct, for example, the ways in which we have come to think that culture follows and is superior to nature. Patriarchal society, feminist deconstructionists go on to argue, sets up oppositions between men and women linked to other oppositions such as nature/culture in order to create specific meanings of gender; for example, that it is not natural for women not to want children. These naturalised character-istics are quite unrelated to actual biological or psychological features of women. Inevitably cultural representations in literature and the media encode, or are built on, these oppositions and in turn cultural representations affect the way we feel about our sexual identities and those of others. The focus of deconstructive literary criticism, then, is on those moments in books when such oppositions are seen to be in contradiction. This is the point at which, deconstruction argues, meaning seems to go beyond its binary limits. By demonstrating that these binary oppositions, of Black/white, inside/outside, are constructions – are not natural or innate to language and meaning – deconstruction shows how such representations appear true or natural only because their *process* of representa-tion, their coming into language, is effaced and made invisible by culture.

Deconstruction was initiated by Jacques Derrida, the French philosopher whose ideas influenced American as well as French feminists – for example, Barbara Johnson, Julia Kristeva, Luce

Irigaray as well as Gayatri Spivak, Derrida's translator, in whose writings deconstruction is a major critical strategy. In *Of Grammatology* (1976), his most significant work, Derrida focuses on Rousseau and examines the violent hierarchies of 'nature/ culture' and 'speech/writing' in Rousseau's work. Derrida gives the term 'logocentrism' to Western philosophy's elision of meaning with words (or logos). Along with its logocentrism, Derrida attacks two other features of Western philosophy: its phallocentrism, or belief in unitary male values, and its dualism, or belief in binary oppositions. Derrida developed a practice of close reading looking at key metaphors and words, often called copulae, such as 'difference' and 'woman' which enable texts to operate meaning. At the École des Hautes Études en Science Sociales Derrida teaches a form of interdisciplinary research which explicitly addresses the politics of texts. In his recent work (for example, in 'Racism's Last Word', 1986) Derrida lays increasing stress on challenging the 'last word' of racism – apartheid – and shows how a system of political apartheid obviously depends on a language of deep-rooted binary opposites.

This brief summary cannot do justice to Derrida's complex and sophisticated arguments but aims to make clear what is involved in a deconstructive reading and why deconstruction might attract feminist critics. What relevance does deconstruction have to feminism? First, Derrida makes clear that metaphors of 'woman' and 'difference' are 'used' in texts phallocentrically; that is, to reinforce a masculine perspective. Deconstruction argues that metaphors are hierarchically ordered but in addition it promises that these hierarchical oppositions (such as man/ woman) are unstable and could be contested. One obvious similarity, then, between feminism and deconstruction is that, like feminism, deconstruction is attracted to those areas of meaning which traditional literary criticism has regarded as less important, such as metaphors of gender; and like feminism, deconstructive critics work together with the reader in a shared uncovering of the ideological patterns which shape aesthetic forms. Deconstruction, and Derrida in particular, have been attacked for ignoring the idea of human agency. Yet French feminism (discussed more fully in chapter 4, above), informed by deconstruction, focuses on language precisely because language is the mechanism by which women have been 'deauthorised'. In turn, French feminists aim to create a woman's language (*écriture féminine*). Their task is to question how male/ female oppositions are produced by language and how 'woman' is always the negative or supplementary term. Julia Kristeva and Luce Irigaray, in particular, have utilised deconstruction to describe the gendering of language and subjects. In brief, they argue that the feminine is represented in language by process, by heterogeneity and fluidity, whereas the masculine is repres- ented by fixed terms such as binary oppositions. So that the deconstruction of fixed terms encourages the development of more fluid or feminine processes. French feminism, following Lacan, has created a theory of the entry of the subject, or individual, into language (logocentrism). Here the imaginary is a time when the subject has no sense of him or herself separate from the world, and in particular from the mother. Kristeva calls this moment the semiotic or a rhythmic association between mother and child which is replicated in literature but hidden under oppositions. Gradually the child learns to differentiate itself from others and enters into the patriarchal, or symbolic, world of differences (nature/culture, woman/man).

Because logocentrism opposes reality to the imaginary, and objective to subjective, Luce Irigaray, in particular, works to deconstruct logocentrism with her free play of meanings and associations. Her style is deconstructive because her arguments depend on parodying and pulling apart coded opposites in the writings of Freud, Hegel and Plato:

> We have to reject all the great systems of opposition on which our culture is constructed. Reject, for instance, the opposition: fiction/truth, sensible/intelligible, empirical/transcendental, materialist/ idealist. All these opposing pairs function as an exploitation. (Irigaray (1983) p. 9)

Irigaray analyses the inequality of these opposing pairs showing how 'woman' is always the inferior term. American feminist deconstructionists, influenced by French feminism, also often focus on male writers. For example, Shoshana Felman argues that Balzac was attracted to realism because realism relies on gender oppositions and yet critics writing about Balzac fre- quently avoid discussing these gender oppositions (Felman, 1977). Consider the example of Sula in Toni Morrison's novel *Sula* (1973). She may be said to highlight the difference between symbolic and presymbolic ways of signifying. Morrison describes Sula as having 'no center' or ego. Morrison disrupts the symbolic, or social meaning of language by representing Sula's body with silences and 'howls'.

For Black feminism the implications of deconstruction are profound. Because deconstruction argues that the literary text is not a 'pure' realm uncontaminated by social pressures but instead suggests that Black/white binaries are socially constructed, then clearly Black is not naturally derived from, or supplementary to, white except in the fantasies of white racists. Again, consider the example of *Mules and Men* by Zora Neale Hurston: the book is a fascinating account of Black lives, stories and culture in Eatonville, Hurston's home town. It is also a complex account of the problems and possibilities involved in representing Black townspeople to a presumed white reader. In other words, Hurston deconstructively attempts to *represent* 'difference' but wants to *refuse* oppositions such as insider/outsider, nature/culture or rural Blacks/urban whites. Hurston achieves this brilliantly by creating herself as a fictional figure – Hurston the narrator, a continually self-reflexive character. This allows *Mules and Men* to be taken over by the multiple voices of the townspeople and Hurston refuses authorial distance. Hurston undercuts the fixed terms of Black/white by invalidating the certainty of distancing and the conventional gender and racial metaphors, references and terms likely to be used by her white readers.

GAYATRI SPIVAK

One of the most important contemporary feminist deconstructionists is Gayatri Spivak, whose careful attention to issues of race and gender is uncompromising. Spivak focuses on displacements of meanings in texts in order to prove how figures of speech in Western writing often obliterate the viewpoints of 'Others'. In her essays Spivak is not specifically concerned with deconstructing the work of male philosophers nor with attending only to women's writing. Instead she concentrates on the practices of 'comprador', or imperialist, languages. Spivak shows how patriarchal language is organised around particular racist and sexist oppositions, and how these oppositions occur also in Third World economics, but are subverted in texts by Third World women (Devi) as well as in texts by white Western women (Woolf). Spivak's work marks a significant new direction for deconstruction. Her most important collection, *In Other Worlds* (1987) contains her writings about Woolf, Wordsworth, feminism, Subaltern Studies and the writer Devi, among other topics. Before turning to that collection it will be helpful to start with Spivak's own assessment of her deconstructionism in 'Feminism and Deconstruction, Again' (1989). In this essay Spivak claims to be motivated by a desire to assert the fluidity of the term 'woman'. Feminism, she argues, should use the critical techniques of deconstruction but give up its attachment to the specific name 'feminism' for the problem/solution of founded programs (psfp), also named 'writing' (Spivak, 1989, p. 206). As Spivak argues in this essay, deconstruction is useful to feminism, first *technically* and more specifically for its suggestion that 'the subject is always centred' (Spivak, 1989, p. 214). Spivak claims that this centring is always an *effect*, and therefore that *particular* names for women, or historical determinism, will fail feminism, unless we use deconstruction to help us to stage the scene, or moment, of that centring. Spivak's attachment to deconstruction is clear in her continual references to the term in interviews (see Spivak, 1990).

As we have seen, poststructuralism and deconstruction share similar characteristics: an interest in irony, multiple signifiers, open discontinuous structures and a mixture of genres; for example theory/fiction, popular culture/high art. Feminist deconstructionists, in addition, forcefully centre on women's subjectivity by focusing on autobiography, diaries, and the ethnography of women's daily lives. Spivak's essays fully articulate these concerns. *In Other Worlds* examines relationships between theories of literature, women and political disenfranchisement. In 'Unmaking and Making in *To the Lighthouse*' she is responding, as she says, to 'the reactionary sexual ideology of high art' not simplistically by substituting low for high, or rejecting or excusing the canon but by borrowing from Foucault in order to examine *To the Lighthouse* in relation to the perspectives of 'agents of knowledge'. So, for example, Spivak argues that *To the Lighthouse* is structured around the rivalry and partnership of Lily and Mr Ramsay who have different systems of knowledge and therefore power (picture/ womb versus lighthouse/phallus). Spivak's debt to Foucault is clear in her continuous use of terms such as 'fields'. For example, she defines feminism as 'situational, anti-sexism . . . a heterogenous field' (Spivak, 1990, p. 58). Like Derrida, Spivak examines how modernist writing objectifies women. For example, Yeats uses Latin, Spivak claims, to keep women out, to neutralise their importance. Spivak interweaves deconstruction and feminism in other ways: for example, in her use of irony. As she puts it 'into the élite theoretical *ateliers* in France, I bring news of power-lines within the palace. Nothing can function without us' (Spivak, 1987, p. 221).

The use of irony is Spivak's key deconstructive device. She puns on terms such as copula/copulation and associates this with hinge/unhinged (Woolf's 'madness') in order to interweave critically the Ramsay's marriage with Woolf's marriage of art and literature. In 'Unmaking and Making in *To the Lighthouse*' Spivak is faced with the problem of dealing with Woolf's politics of representation (outside of psychoanalysis). The solution she adopts is to explore the book as a huge allegory of grammar, sexuality and autobiography. As Spivak herself explains, she is frequently exercised in 'allegorizing such a situation' in her critical essays (Spivak, 1990, p. 15).

So far from vaulting *above* the ordinary linguistic features of a text, Spivak goes out of her way to call these decisively into play. She focuses on allegory in order to set up a tension between allegorical features and other characteristics of the text. Her major allegory, throughout all her writing, is from Subaltern Studies. Subaltern Studies involves the analysis of South Asian history and culture by a group under the editorship of Ranajit Guha. 'Subalternity' Spivak takes to be a 'dangerous signifier' of the repressive dominance of white Western thinking. It is a major allegory of the displacement of the gendered and colonised, or subaltern, subject, by the imposition of 'narratives of internationalism and nationalism' (Spivak, 1990, p. 142). Spivak refuses to answer the question 'whether the subaltern can speak?', silenced as s/he is by the epistemic violence of the West, because she claims the question cannot ever be answered. Instead Spivak prefers to describe the *place* of a speaking moment combined with an account of the speaking *person*. As a good deconstructionist, Spivak attacks the notion that knowing more about an author will explain a text. Rather she sets up 'allegories' of reading, looking, for example, through the lenses of Marxism and liberal feminism to ask what their theories can reveal about colonialism.

What Spivak's essays offer is the *problem*, not the solution, of representation: 'The radical intellectual in the West is either caught in a deliberate choice of subalternity, granting to the oppressed either that very expressive subjectivity which s/he criticizes, or, instead, a total unrepresentability' (Spivak, 1987, p. 209).

One of Spivak's solutions to this impasse is to adopt some of the techniques of postmodern anthropology, searching, for example, for communal modes of representation or revolt (Spivak, 1987, p. 219). Yet there are problems for deconstruction in using allegories. This can catch deconstructionists in the very structures which their critical efforts are designed to subvert. Allegories, however well intentioned, cannot avoid representing structures. The key point of an allegory is its ability to frame meaning. Allegories are not open-ended and fluid in a deconstructive sense but usually very organised literary patterns which have precise meanings. Yet if Spivak's interest in allegories is not without its problems, allegories are also sometimes useful. Allegories do not need to be tied to an author's intention – they can take on a life of their own, revealing a text's blindness or hostility to issues of gender and race. For example, in post-colonial writing the construction and demolition of houses can be an evocative allegory of the political problems of post-colonialism itself (as in Janet Frame's *The Edge of the Alphabet* (1962)). As Rosemary Jackson argues in *Fantasy* (1981), allegories highlight possibilities to be avoided or seized upon. Allegories, in other words, merely foreground the fact that we can know the Third World woman, as we can know the First World woman, only through signs. Spivak violently jumps out of the allegorical frame in the conclusion of 'French Feminism in an International Frame' (1987). The essay makes a startling juxtaposition of accounts of clitoridectomy with the master texts of capitalism and those of 'micro' liberal feminism (Margaret Drabble's *The Waterfall*). Here Spivak puts her finger on precisely what characterises deconstruction: its disbelief in 'objective' reality/representation. The essay introduces French feminist thought and Spivak positions herself as a mediator between the more abstract ideas she finds in that writing and feminism's more immediate need to undermine patriarchal practices such as clitoridectomy. Spivak portrays the effacement of the clitoris, not in some French feminist *écriture* way by describing the linguistic effacement of female sexual iconography, but by facing up to the harsh and very real physical effacement of the clitoris in Sudanese practices of clitoridectomy. At the same time, Spivak argues that clitoridectomy is a metonymy for patriarchy's general assault on women. Clitoridectomy is both a real, harsh sexual practice brutal to women and a symbolic representation of the 'cutting' attacks on women's writing. Spivak's stance is one of refusal – a refusal to speak *about* the Third World or *for* the Third World – but it is not one of negativity. Silvia Tandeciarz in 'Reading Gayatri Spivak's "French Feminism . . ." ' disagrees and argues that Spivak 'avoids' difficulties 'by imposing the presumption of French feminist theorizing over the veiled bodies of the women of the Sudan' (Tandeciarz, 1991, p. 78). But although Spivak's address is clearly to a reader conversant with critical theory, perhaps even to a specific academic group, she equally clearly asserts the reality of a world beyond the academic. Her deconstructive welding of theories of social psychology and Marxism with the specific cultural/literary situations constructed by imperialism is quite breathtaking. For example, she describes the place of widow sacrifice as an unacknowledged imperial metaphor in *Jane Eyre* (Spivak, 1990, p. 73). But what signals an exciting and crucial way in which deconstruction changes as it emerges into feminism is Spivak's constant use of autobiography in her essays. While political/literary allegories emerge as Spivak's recurrent theme, I am also struck by how many of these essays inevitably come around to the question of place, specifically the place of the post-colonial critic, as the singular and pointed title of a collection of her interviews betrays. An unarticulated relation between her own domination/dominating role as a metropolitan Bengali woman in the Western academy seems to motivate each piece. As she puts it in an early essay ('Finding Feminist Readings: Dante–Yeats', 1980) 'women must tell each other's stories, not because they are simpleminded creatures, but because they must call into question the model of criticism as neutral theorem or science' (Spivak, 1987, p. 15). Already here Spivak has moved away from Derrida's idea that 'myself' and 'woman' can be 'no more than textual ruses', and instead often prefers to make an ethnographic account of the *moment* of her own reading, including the setting, and descriptions of the students she teaches. Like Adrienne Rich, Spivak regards all readings as irreducibly marked by the subject who reads and hence she makes interruptions and 'cross-hatchings' by continually quoting herself and allowing the reader to refer to her own representative space (Spivak, 1990, p. 38).

How do these moments sit with traditional literary criticism's view that the autobiography of the critic is merely incidental to a reading? Spivak follows Derrida's claim that criticism must step outside its traditional frame particularly because the interests of white and Black women lie outside the academy. The narrator 'Spivak' is the key. Like Zora Neale Hurston in *Mules and Men*, Spivak – particularly in her reading of Mahasweta Devi's short story 'Breast-Giver' – provides us with a deconstructive mixture of readings: as an academic, as a subaltern herself, and as a Marxist historian. As Diana Fuss points out 'if we read from multiple subject positions the very act of reading becomes a force for dislocating our belief in stable subjects and essential meanings', or patriarchal imperialism (see Fuss, 1989, p. 35). Feminist deconstruction, in other words, can provide an answer to some of the objections to deconstruction: its inaccessibility; its ignorance of actual social practices and its privileging of the producer/text at the expense of consumer/text (see Boyne and Rattansi, 1990).

POSTMODERNISM

Poststructuralism and deconstruction prepared the ground for *postmodernism* which is now a huge cultural phenomenon. Current postmodernism includes the arts along with critiques of philosophy and economics, and the term is often used to describe the whole of contemporary culture. In the arts, architecture and literature, postmodernists take delight in parodying history, mixing genres and claiming to be intimately involved in popular culture and the media. Cultural critics return repeatedly to the idea of postmodernity because its theories help to explain changes in late twentieth-century cultural practices. Hence the attempts to represent postmodernism as a coherent whole have inspired a plethora of writing including the now classic definitions of Jean-François Lyotard (1984) and Fredric Jameson (1984) as well as historical surveys by Andreas Huyssen (1986) and the literary grids of Linda Hutcheon (1988) and other feminist critics.

Like poststructuralism and deconstruction, postmodernism questions universal certainties and accepts, and indeed celebrates, the end of totalising literary narratives such as humanism and realism. But unlike poststructuralism and deconstruction, postmodernism often effaces the frontier between speech and writing, between literary and visual representations – a frontier that plays a crucial role in deconstruction and particularly in the writings of Jacques Derrida. One example of this difference is the often cited art work 'Post Partum Document' by Mary Kelly which mixes written texts, family history and photographs in a collage of styles. Another and equally key difference between postmodernism and poststructuralism is that poststructuralism is primarily a theory about *structures*, deep or superficial, within culture and literature and argues that we must look beyond (or post) these structures to social formations behind. Postmodernism, on the other hand, problematises the distinctions between culture, history and representations. What is different about postmodernism is its comprehensiveness. The major success of postmodernism, among its other achievements, is its radical break from modernist periodising. Postmodernists argue that history does not fit into neat period sections: the dominant characteristics of any period might include remnants of the past and plans for the future. Indeed, postmodernism challenges standard notions of history altogether. Arthur Kroker, in *The Postmodern Scene* (1988), dates postmodernism from the fourth century with the 'Augustinian subversion of embodied power', while Roy Boyne and Ali Rattansi, in *Postmodernism and Society* (1990), more conservatively ascribe its genesis to the Spanish writer Frederico de Onis in the 1930s, who first used the term in his *Antologia de la poesia espaniola e hispanoamerican* (1934).

Postmodernism first gained currency in America in the 1950s and 1960s in the work of the literary critics Irving Howe, Leslie Fiedler and Ihab Hassan. In 'Mapping the Postmodern' (1986), Andreas Huyssen argues that these critics, in texts as diverse as Fiedler's *Waiting for the End* and Irving Howe's *Decline of the New*, made an iconoclastic attack on the establishments of art and literature. These critics also made vigorous attempts to celebrate popular culture as much as the literary canon and projected a powerful sense of literary change and new frontiers, as the title of Fiedler's book suggests. For example, Leslie Fiedler claims that the detective story and the Western are important forms of literature and argues that postmodern fiction bridges high art and popular culture (for example, E. H. Doctorow's inclusion of Western motifs in *Welcome to Hard Times*). Postmodern fiction is characterised by a knowing play with genres, a scepticism about the values of high art and a disenchantment with any claim of realism. Indeed 'hyperreality' became a common theme in the postmodern art and architectural criticism of Charles Jencks and Hal Foster in the 1980s. In *The Language of Post-Modern Architecture* (1977), Charles Jencks adopts the term 'double-coded' from communication studies to describe how post-modernism represents different languages or codes including the styles of many cultural groups. Attempts to specify as equally postmodernist features of contemporary culture – buildings, the TV music channel MTV, and the consumer iconography of Disneyland, as well as fiction (the metafiction, or invented history novel, *Book of Daniel*) – involved critics in one major recognition. This was the idea that, although culture was a multiple collection of many different genres and forms, culture could be read, or understood, as surface.

A stress on *surface*, rather than on *structure* by the leading postmodernists, Baudrillard, Lyotard and Jameson, is the most obvious change from poststructuralism to postmodernism. Lyotard's *The Postmodern Condition* (1984) is regarded as the key text of postmodernism. It gives economic and cultural explanations for the new dissolution of boundaries between high and low culture and for the way in which culture is apparently endlessly able to synthesise and reconstitute art forms. Lyotard's central claim is that the grand narratives, or theories, of Marxism and humanism have ceased to work because 'metanarratives' do not help us to understand these constant revisions. Indeed, Lyotard chooses an incredulity to meta-narratives, or single, causal explanations of culture, as the key feature of postmodernism. Lyotard and other critics, such as Baudrillard, replace metanarratives with an examination of cultural *contexts*. That is to say, they argue that the meaning of culture derives both from its processes, like canon formation, and from the social contexts in which these processes take place. Just as deconstruction debunked the aesthetic choices of modernism, so postmodernists have to get on without what John Fekete calls the 'Good-God-Gold Standards, one and all, indeed without any capitalised standards' (Fekete, 1988, p. xi).

But however much postmodernism devotes itself to new features of contemporary culture, it is clear that in a variety of ways postmodernism does resemble modernism. The crucial features of modernity – chosen by Marx, Baudelaire and Benjamin – are that modernity is transitory; that modernity challenges the notion of evolutionary progress; and that modernity is urban. In *One-Way Street* (1979), Walter Benjamin called the arcades of Berlin a vanguard example of modernity; in 'The Painter of Modern Life' Baudelaire made a study of fashion; and Marx's *Das Kapital* above all, is devoted to a theory of commodities. Yet what unites critics of modernity and sets them apart from postmodernists is their Eurocentrism and their position as 'strangers in their own society' (Frisby, 1985). A notable feature of postmodernism is its celebration of the consumer culture which it inhabits.

In *A Poetics of Postmodernism* (1988) Linda Hutcheon offers a schematic account of postmodernism and a comprehensive timetabling of its artistic forms to date. She draws attention to the plurality of disciplines and institutions involved in post-modernism from the media to universities and she suggests that all institutions are currently interrogating their own borders, artistic conventions and histories. The notion of separate academic disciplines such as philosophy, literature and art is in any case of very recent date. Disciplines were created only a hundred years ago. Disciplines are themselves part and product of the languages they use. What interests Hutcheon in postmodernism is the way in which literary identity is often asserted through a parodic intertextual relation to traditions.

One example might be Toni Morrison's Utopian women's household in *Song of Solomon* which parodies William Faulkner's *Absalom, Absalom!*. Postmodernism challenges the singularity of master narratives, like the concept of linear history, in the name of multiplicity and difference. We see this vividly in Gayle Jones's novel *Corregidora* where the narrator has to contest the racism of her own incestuous history in which Corregidora, the slave owner, fathered both her mother and grandmother. Hutcheon hints at, but does not explore, postmodernism's appeal to feminists in her analogy between postmodernism and 'ex-centrics': Blacks, women and others on the margins of culture.

How has postmodernism as theory and practice been deployed by feminists? How has it informed feminist criticism? Both feminists and postmodernists attack the notion that art is a separate and superior realm from life. Both argue that social institutions construct 'values' as much as they reflect 'truths' and in any case represent white Western masculine thought and experience. The first considered analysis of women's role in postmodernism was in the visual arts. Rosalind Krauss, in 'The Originality of the Avant-Garde: A Postmodernist Repetition' (1981), first hinted at the radical implications postmodernism might have for women by describing how postmodernism questions the concept of origin, of masculine individualism. Indeed, in 'The Discourse of Others: Feminists and Postmodernism' (1983), Craig Owens went on to argue that postmodernism would have a radical future only if it listened to 'the feminist voice' and if postmodern art practice was better informed by feminist politics.

It is not only the arts which have witnessed important debates about disciplinary boundaries. Feminists have utilised postmodernist strategies to challenge many disciplines. American feminists working in the natural sciences (for example, Evelyn Fox Keller and Donna Haraway) attack the false rationality of contemporary science. By straddling the borderline between discourse analysis, social psychology and science, Evelyn Fox Keller, in 'Feminism and Science' (1982), is able to propose a new perspective, a way of knowing the world that is a truer 'standpoint' than existing scientific paradigms. Evelyn Fox

Keller, Sandra Harding and Dorothy Smith are among the feminist writers often labelled feminist standpoint theorists. While standpoint theory cannot be *reconciled* with postmodernism, it similarly confronts and contests the notion that science is dedicated to an objective pursuit of the truth. Science, these critics show, is obsessed by binaries: mind (masculine) and nature (feminine). They point to the invasive exploration of the natural world undertaken by Francis Bacon which continues in the bifurcation scientists make today between subjectivity and objectivity. Science, they claim, has worked with a limited notion of rationality from the seventeenth century to the present – one which is biased against women and the natural world which scientists equate imagistically. Feminist scientists and feminist literary critics share an opposition to disciplinary boundaries and a postmodern perception that the interweaving of history, psychology and representation can challenge political certainties. Both share a radical intent to destabilise historic givens. For example, Alice Walker's *In The Temple of My Familiar* is a postmodern rethinking of history. In the novel Walker takes individual histories to include the possibility of many previous incarnations, both human and animal. Similarly feminism is itself a mixture of contradictory languages; on the one hand, adopting the language of liberal humanism with its notions of individual freedom and self-determination for women, while, on the other, praising the 'imaginary', irrational, fluid pre-symbolic speech of mothering. One example of this epistemological multiplicity is Toni Morrison's *Tar Baby* which links gender difference to questions of language and authority at the heart of postmodernism. Morrison parodies the notion of an essential 'feminine' by giving the male character, Son, a feminine 'fluid' identity.

Just as Spivak utilises deconstruction to challenge the power of colonial languages, so postmodernists (for example, Alice Jardine, Meaghan Morris and Rachel Blau DuPlessis) are attracted to postmodernism's democratic and accessible mixture of languages both academic and non-academic. Not only does postmodernism refuse to give essential or single explanations for cultural representations but it bursts through the one key boundary which has contained and limited women throughout history – the divide between public and private. The distinction between the domestic and the public, so crucial to modernism and so antagonistic to women has been shot through by postmodernism's interest in consumerism (see Wolff, 1990).

ALICE JARDINE

Alice Jardine's theory of gynesis describes and explains the place of woman in Western thinking. In her book of that name, *Gynesis* (1988), Jardine applies the term to a process she discovers in French modernism where figures of 'women' are frequently utilised by male writers when attacking society. What Jardine analyses in her book is a breakdown in the master narratives of realism and Marxism. This breakdown has happened in relation to postmodernism, or what Jardine calls denaturalisation; that is, the proof offered by Derrida and Foucault that ideology is based on naturalised categories. What is specific to feminism, and what interests me, is that Jardine points out that this breakdown has been accompanied by a huge increase in the writing of theory and fiction by women about women. One of Jardine's strengths is her compelling mapping of the feminine as a sign of excess in male texts. For example, she argues that male artists frequently describe their opposition to bourgeois society in feminine terms. For Jardine any rethinking or reconceptualisation of difference 'will be gendered as female' (Jardine, 1988a, p. 60). An equally compelling feature of Jardine's current writing is her playing and punning with words. Jardine believes we must move into a 'fiction' of woman which she does convincingly herself in 'In the name of the modern: feminist questions *d'après gynesis*' (1988). The piece is a play to be performed by women and men alternatively reading and turning to tape. The piece questions fundamental aspects of masculine and feminine, presence and absence in post-modernism. Jardine does this, like Irigaray, by juxtaposing and punning with the voices of male postmodernists from the perspective of French feminism. The piece ends in a Utopian swerve as Jardine predicts that 'if the same "changed" . . . all the history, all the stories would be here to retell differently; the future would be incalculable' (Jardine, 1988b, p. 182).

MEAGHAN MORRIS

Other feminist postmodernists, such as the Australian critic Meaghan Morris, focus on more contemporary women and their cultural practices. Morris is interested in the way in which women have actively participated in the modernisation of social and cultural life since the Second World War. Beginning with *Michel Foucault: Power, Truth, Strategy* which she co-edited with Paul Patton in 1979, through to her current interest in consumerism ('Things To Do With Shopping Centres', 1988), Morris utilises Foucault's notions of knowledge/power and discursive fields and applies these to the ways in which 'women' are constructed in discursive and nondiscursive locations such as shopping centres, movies and in feminist and postmodernist theory. Morris argues that the management of change to which feminist criticism needs to address itself will involve a scrutiny of practices *throughout* patriarchy – 'leisure centres, unemployment activity' – as well as the sociology of consumerism. Fashion and shopping are particularly crucial topics for feminist criticism because, as Morris argues, both turn women into *consumers* and *objects* of knowledge. Morris points out that women also *enjoy* fashion and shopping, and frequently consume in order to transform their everyday lives, and that women are quite capable of resisting cultural stereotypes. It was Foucault above all, in *The History of Sexuality* (1976), who characterised power as a multiplicity of discursive fields with multiple resistances. Extending her Foucauldian techniques into postmodernism, Morris argues that gender identity can be understood only in terms of the complex and contradictory ways in which consumerism, pleasure and power and cultural languages are produced and institutionalised and then subverted and discredited in many 'fields', including shopping centres. Morris concludes that postmodernism is double coded. That is, the material which postmodernism absorbs from popular culture might help its message to reach a wider audience outside the academy while simultaneously postmodernism's parodic use of historical forms (in art, architecture and writing) appeal to the trained academic. It is ironic, of course, that a watered-down postmodern aesthetic has been appropriated most of all in shopping centres. While postmodern theory and postmodern practice need to be distinguished in some ways, the pink facades and curved arches of Californian malls mark capitalism's recuperation of the postmodern where artistic interest is turned into promotional concerns. Finally, then, postmodernism should not be characterised only by its formal, stylistic features but also in terms of its effect. As the critic Susan Suleiman argues, postmodernism is controversial not because of what it *is* but because of what it does. In other words it makes artistic interventions not just art objects (see Suleiman, 1990).

RACHEL BLAU DUPLESSIS

Postmodern criticism is marked most of all by 'self-reflexivity', by the interweaving of autobiography and theory. Rachel Blau DuPlessis is a spectacular exponent of this postmodern technique. In her essays DuPlessis makes daring combinations of her poetry and extracts from her daily diary together with literary criticism, history and psychoanalysis. *The Pink Guitar: Writing as Feminist Practice* (1990) contains her early and startlingly postmodern essay 'For the Etruscans' (1980). What is extraordinary about 'For the Etruscans' is its heterogeneity. Deliberately disorganised in structure (superficially) the text races over most of contemporary feminism's main concerns – discrimination in education, women's psychosocial difference from men and from each other, and the power of women's language. DuPlessis wrote the essay in 1979, collectively with her students, rather than as a 'masterful' author, and since then she has continually, and self-reflexively, rewritten the piece.

DuPlessis adopts postmodern techniques – of juxtaposition, de-centred subjects and an open, fluid surface – in order to enable the process of writing to be part of the content of writing. This skewers any modernist notion of a 'pure' isolated art object. The essay juxtaposes entries from her diary together with literary criticism about Virginia Woolf and memories of her graduate life, extracts from Freud and Etruscan history. The Etruscans come to stand as a grand metaphor for the exclusion of women's meaning-making from the literary canon. The Etruscan script, like women's writing, is *known* in the sense that its vocabulary has been translated but we lack knowledge about the social and private *contexts* in which the Etruscan language was spoken and written.

'For the Etruscans' is not written in the form of an essay or critical argument, but rather as a collage of speculations. DuPlessis uses no single consistent, literary genre nor does she privilege any single gender explanation whether from history or psychoanalysis. Indeed, 'For the Etruscans' exposes the discrepancies *between* psychoanalysis and history in its autobiographical digressions. Although the essay has been criticised for conflating the notion of a feminist aesthetic with modernist and postmodernist art (Felski, 1989, p. 47), DuPlessis does deliberately create a form of feminist postmodernism – a fluid, collective mixing of literary genres – so that she can talk about the place of the female in culture. *The Pink Guitar* as a whole takes up these themes. DuPlessis examines the writers H. D., Virginia Woolf and the contemporary poets Susan Howe and Beverly Dahlen. These women are all, like DuPlessis herself, authors inspired by modernism but constrained by the limitations of its gender iconography.

DuPlessis's voice is characteristically postmodern. She makes a very precise use of key postmodern strategies. The title of her book is itself a parodic punning on Wallace Stevens' famous poem 'The Man With the Blue Guitar', another reference to modernism and Picasso's equally famous painting. The project, as DuPlessis sees it, is to replace Stevens' (and Pound's and Eliot's) desperate masculine need for aesthetic control and artistic order with a collage of diaries, poems and aphorisms. DuPlessis also deftly attacks the binaries of structuralism in, for example, the title of her essay 'OtherHow: Poetry and Gender'. If there is one continuous trope in DuPlessis's writing it is her constant, witty and 'casual' punning (close to Mary Daly's *Gyn/Ecology*), as in 'Anyway. Any way' (DuPlessis, 1990, p. 112). Adopting a postmodernist open and discontinuous structure for many of her essays, DuPlessis makes a direct analogy between this structure and the discontinuous subjectivity of women: How could women above all fail to 'neglect to invent a form which produces this incessant, critical, splitting motion. To invent this form. To invent the theory for this form' (DuPlessis, 1990, p. 8).

The essays are open narratives. That is to say, they have no obvious beginning, middle or end; but in addition DuPlessis often designs an open *page*, utilising the margins of the text and changing its graphic design. It is now generally agreed that postmodernism welds theory to fiction, high with low culture. DuPlessis pursues this idea of convergence, introducing, for example, the theories of Julia Kristeva by means of her own daughter's 'semiotic' babblings: 'Week of 1 – 6 July, 17 months, Words: mur mur mur (more); caow; m/MMoo; DIRty; WWWride (ride); RRweh (wet); Bluhh (blueberries)' (DuPlessis, 1990, p. 99).

The essays feel thoroughly postmodern, as exemplified in the way in which DuPlessis takes a circular journey through the novels of Virginia Woolf and the history of the Etruscans *en route* to her lunch of 'pear, eight strawberries, now did I add some cottage cheese' (DuPlessis, 1990, p. 4). Like much of post-modern art (for example, Barbara Kruger and Jenny Holzer's billboards) DuPlessis exposes the links between aesthetics and consumer commodity production: she describes *The Golden Notebook* suggestively as 'the first Tampax in world literature' (DuPlessis, 1990). Because DuPlessis combines feminism with postmodernism she can question issues of gendered authority and meaning that are at the heart of contemporary culture. As she says, her essays are written in response to the 'Law, the Main, the Center' where 'Diffusions of power are defined' (DuPlessis, 1990, p. 3). And she attacks postmodernism's inattention to the historical specificities of race and gender. As a way out of the problematic of centres and power, DuPlessis includes autobiography, interweaving her account of H.D. with that of her own student career; and she values the margins, acknowledging the significance of Afro-American literary criti-cism and Utopias. Referring to the work of the American anthropologist James Clifford, DuPlessis creates an aesthetic of 'calibanization', plotting through the possibilities of a 'multi-poly-mishuganah set of discourses' (DuPlessis, 1990, p. 155). Postmodern ethnography and contemporary feminism have much in common. Both are attempting to tear the mask from disciplinary claims to objectivity, and both make clear that accounts of different cultures and genders cannot be purely factual but must always be cultural constructions. As the feminist ethnographer Judith Stacey argues, writing will always be 'a construction of the self as well as of the other' (Stacey, 1991, p. 115). Both wish their subjects and readers to collaborate in a shared process of meaning-making, one which is never fully controlled by either ethnographer or author. For example, DuPlessis has a recurring aim 'not to tell you what to do' and to write in a voice 'that does not seek authority of tone or stasis of position' because 'listener could be teacher' (DuPlessis, 1990, pp. 153; 13; 6). DuPlessis stresses the *content* of a critical reading, paying close attention not only to the text she observes but also to the observant reader.

DuPlessis's constant mixing of rhetorical levels and making the enunciative situation part of each essay, makes her writing clearly postmodern, but she also challenges postmodernism's frequent *lack* of meaning. She demands we bring the semiotic *into* meaning, 'how to put rhythm, pulse, humming space into meaning' (DuPlessis, 1990, p. 93). A crucial part of 'Language Acquisition' is DuPlessis's extended account of her daughter's speech development. This is not distanced by being reported but has its own dramatised space. DuPlessis creates a magnificent *texte de semiotic* by repeatedly demonstrating how women's reading pleasure (or *jouissance*) occurs with a falling away of fixed categories of public and private. Her erasure of the boundary between public and private languages helps to bring the work of literature into the real world of her reader.

SUMMARY

There are problems in identifying postmodernism too closely with feminism. There are many feminist issues not represented in postmodernism. One key issue is feminism's commitment to collectivity, to communities. To date, postmodernism has clearly been a very masculine enterprise. It overvalues the visual, with its 'scopic gaze' and metaphors of seeing, rather than the aural/semiotic. For example, in *Seduction* Baudrillard describes his fear of quadrophonics. He calls listening devices a sign of evil. Another limitation is Lyotard's fond belief that entry into critical knowledge is merely an issue of *access* and *adjustment* to new technologies 'public access to memory and data banks' (Lyotard, 1984, p. 6). Feminists know that entry into anything is an issue of patriarchal power and authority. Lyotard's descriptions of polytheistic media language games are devoid of any contact with the *ownership* of media production. These language games could never delegitimise gender power in the way in which, for example, Zora Neale Hurston's female narrators do in Eatonville. And I think it highly significant that the architect Charles Jencks should date postmodernism from the destruction of a *domestic* environment – the dynamiting of St Louis Pruitt-Igoe Housing.

The point of postmodernism, like any theory, is to present itself as complete so that it can be read. It often answers to post-Fordism by marketing past architecture and dead artists. But language is not a static entity that can be divided into building lots and summarily demolished. Language attends to power. It will alter its form depending on who is speaking. Postmodernism's call for experimentation, for language games, is often cut off from actual *agency*, from actual social reforms and social institutions.

Postmodernism often ignores the crucial instabilities of ethnicity and homosexuality as historically constituted and in living speakers. Woman's body is absent in some postmodernist writing which makes no serious consideration of women's subjective and social experiences of mothering; nor of the emancipatory needs of different ethnic groups; nor of the inequalities of difference and the need of women, Black and white, for agency and historical truth. As Nancy Hartsock argues, 'postmodern theories . . . deny marginalised people the right to participate in defining the terms of interaction with people in the mainstream' (Hartsock, 1987, p. 191).

However, there is little doubt that *feminist* postmodernism marks a new direction. It is clear from the extraordinarily supple writing of Spivak, Spillers and DuPlessis that the intersection of poststructuralist, deconstructive and postmodernist strategies with feminism provides these writers with exciting critical practices. All texts struggle with meaning – in particular, with the meaning of 'woman'; and all three critics offer new ways of representing women.

Most critics accepting the label poststructuralist agree that literature, like language, is controlled by social power and that by pluralising meanings we can open up fixed, binary terms (man = civilisation), understand the political determinants of these terms and move beyond them. I have tried to describe in this chapter the history and techniques of feminism and poststructuralism, as well as the work of its prominent writers. These critics speak urgently about ideology, about culture and about women.

SELECTED READING

Basic texts

Barthes, R. (1974) *SZ*, New York: Hill & Wang

Derrida, J. (1976) *Of Grammatology*, Baltimore: Johns Hopkins University Press

Derrida, J. (1986) 'Racism's last word', in H. Gates (ed.), *'Race', Writing and Difference*, Chicago: University of Chicago Press

DuPlessis, R. B. (1985) *Writing Beyond the Ending: Narrative strategies of twentieth-century women writers*, Bloomington: Indiana University Press

DuPlessis, R.B. (1990) *The Pink Guitar: Writing as feminist practice*, London: Routledge

Foucault, M. (1970) *The Order of Things*, New York: Pantheon

Foucault, M. (1977) *Language, Counter-Memory, Practice: Selected essays and interviews*, (ed.) D. F. Bouchard, Oxford: Blackwell

Jameson, F. (1984) 'Postmodernism, or the cultural logic of late capital', *New Left Review*, 146, pp. 53–92

Jardine, A. (1988a) *Gynesis: Configurations of woman and modernity*, Ithaca: Cornell University Press

Jardine, A. (1988b) 'In the name of the modern: feminist questions d'après gynesis' in S. Sheridan (ed.), *Grafts*, London: Verso

Krauss, R. (1981) 'The originality of the avant-garde: a postmodernist repetition', *October*, 18 (Fall) pp. 47–66

Lyotard, J. J. (1984) *The Postmodern Condition: A report on knowledge*, trans. G. Bennington and B. Massumi, Minneapolis: University of Minnesota Press

Morris, M. (1988a) *The Pirate's Fiancée: Feminism, reading postmodernism*, London: Verso

Morris, M. (1988b) 'Things to do with shopping centres', in S. Sheridan (ed.), *Grafts*, London: Verso

Owens, C. (1983) 'The discourse of others: feminists and postmodernism', in H. Foster (ed.), *The Anti-Aesthetic: Essays on postmodern culture*, Port Townsend, Wash.: Bay Press, pp. 57–82

Spillers, H. (1984) 'Interstices: a small drama of words', in C. S. Vance (ed.), *Pleasure and Danger*, London: Routledge & Kegan Paul

Spillers, H. (1987) 'Notes on an alternative model: Neither/Nor', in Davis, M., Marable, M., Pfeil, F. and Sprinker, M. (eds), *The Year Left 2*, London: Verso

Spillers, H. (1990) ' "An Order of Constancy": notes on Brooks and the feminine', in H. Gates (ed.), *Reading Black, Reading Feminist*, London: Penguin

Spillers, H. (1991) 'Who cuts the border? Some readings on "America" ', in H. Spillers (ed.), *Comparative American Identities*, London: Routledge

Spivak, G. (1987) *In Other Worlds: Essays in cultural politics*, London: Methuen

Spivak, G. (1989) 'Feminism and deconstruction, again: negotiating with unacknowledged masculinism', in T. Brennan (ed.), *Between Feminism and Psychoanalysis*, London: Routledge

Spivak, G. (1990) *The Post-Colonial Critic: Interviews, strategies, dialogues*, London: Routledge

Introductions

Boyne, R. and Rattansi, A. (1990) *Postmodernism and Society*, London: Macmillan

Brooker, P. (1992) *Modernism/Postmodernism*, London: Longmans

Docherty, T. (1992) *Postmodernism: A reader*, Hemel Hempstead: Harvester Wheatsheaf

Fekete, J. (ed.) (1988) *Life After Postmodernism*, London: Macmillan

Foster, H. (ed.) (1985) *Postmodern Culture*, London: Pluto

Hutcheon, L. (1988) *A Poetics of Postmodernism*, London: Routledge

Huyssen, A. (1986) *After the Great Divide: Modernism, mass culture, postmodernism*, Bloomington: Indiana University Press

Kroker, A. and Cook, D. (1988) *The Postmodern Scene*, London: Macmillan

Nicholson, L. J. (ed.) (1990) *Feminism/Postmodernism*, London: Routledge

Theory, Culture and Society: Special Issue on Postmodernism, 5: 2/3

Waugh, P. (ed.) (1992) *A Reader in Postmodernism*, London: Edward Arnold

Further reading

Carby, H. (1987) *Reconstructing Womanhood: The emergence of the Afro-American woman novelist*, New York: Oxford University Press

Christian, B. (1989) 'The race for theory' in L. Kauffman (ed.), *Gender and Theory*, Oxford: Blackwell

Coward, R. (1984) *Female Desire: Women's sexuality today*, London: Paladin

Di Stefano, C. and Benhabib, S. (1989) 'Contemporary feminist theory', *Dissent*, 36, pp. 366–70

Felman, S. (ed.) (1977) *Literature and Psychoanalysis*, special issue of *Yale French Studies*, 55/56

Felski, R. (1989) *Beyond Feminist Aesthetics: Feminist literature and social change*, Cambridge, Mass: Harvard University Press

Fox Keller, E. (1982) 'Feminism and science', in N. O. Keohane (ed.), *Feminist Theory*, Hemel Hempstead: Harvester Wheatsheaf

Freire, P. (1972) *The Pedagogy of the Oppressed*, London: Penguin

Frisby, D. (1985) *Fragments of Modernity*, Cambridge: Polity Press

Fuss, D. (1989) *Essentially Speaking*, London: Routledge

Hartsock, N. (1987) 'Rethinking modernisms: minority vs. majority theories', *Cultural Critique*, 7, pp. 187–206

Jackson, R. (1981) *Fantasy: The literature of subversion*, London: Methuen

King, K. (1990), 'Producing sex, theory and culture', in M. Hirsch and E. Fox Keller (eds), *Conflicts in Feminism*, London: Routledge

Kingston, M. H. (1976) *The Woman Warrior*, New York: Alfred A. Knopf, Inc

Morrison, T (1987) 'Site of memory', in W. Zinsser (ed.), *Inventing the Truth*, Boston: Houghton Mifflin

Smith, V. (1987) *Narrative Authority in Twentieth-Century Afro-American Fiction*, Cambridge, Mass.: Harvard University Press

Soyinka, W. (1976) *Myth, Literature and the African World*, Cambridge: Cambridge University Press

Stacey, J. (1991) 'Can there be a feminist ethnography?', in *Women's Words* (eds) S. B. Gluck and D. Patani, London: Routledge

Suleiman, S. (1990) *Subversive Intent: Gender, politics and the avant-garde*, Cambridge, Mass.: Harvard University Press

Tandeciarz, S. (1991) 'Reading Gayatri Spivak's "French Feminism in an International Frame": a problem for theory', *Genders*, 10, (Spring) pp. 75–91

Todorov, T. (1984) *The Conquest of America*, New York: Harper & Row

Waugh, P. (1989) *Feminine Fictions: Revisiting the postmodern*, London: Routledge

Weedon, C. (1987) *Feminist Practice and Post-structuralism*, Oxford: Blackwell

Wolff, J. (1990) *Feminine Sentences: Essays on women and culture*, Cambridge: Polity Press

7   Black feminisms: the African diaspora

INTRODUCTION

Black feminist criticism has attacked the misogyny of early Black studies (for example, Robert Bone's *The Negro Novel in America*) and the misrepresentations of white feminist critics (for example, Ellen Moers's *Literary Women*), yet it is hard not to fear when naming a territory 'Black criticism' that the very naming is a dangerous ghettoising. Will giving space to Black interests in a separate section suggest that the concerns of this feminism might be seen as 'marginal' rather than politically central to the feminist agenda? By implication, will the 'real' world of feminist criticism still be a more mainstream area like psychoanalysis? This is why each chapter so far has emphasised the contribution of Black critics in transforming *all* critical productions. In arguing, however, that most contemporary feminist criticism does not adequately attend to Black writing, we also have to acknowledge that this is not a simple question of its absence in college courses; and the task is not only one of rendering Black writing visible. The process of analysing the historical and contemporary position of Black writing, in itself, challenges some of the central categories and assumptions of mainstream criticism.

In *Inessential Woman: Problems of Exclusion in Feminist Thought* (1988) the white feminist critic Elizabeth Spelman argues that additive criticism, which she calls the ampersand problem in feminist thought, simply adds race to gender and ignores the interrelations of oppression (Spelman, 1988, p. 14). Ampersand thinking ignores how Black experience and culture, rural *and* urban, fundamentally *transform* the experience of living a gender. For example, Hazel Carby draws attention to the way in which Zora Neale Hurston is often called the 'mother' of contemporary Black women writers in order to valorise Black *folk* women at the expense of a more complex analysis of the multirelations of class, race, sexuality and urban experience.

Hence, while it is crucial to place a *separate* term Black feminist criticism into every feminist literary map, feminist criticism also has to emphasise the *overlapping* of ethnicities in *all* forms of criticism. It is clear, for example, that Gayatri Spivak and Hortense Spillers are major contemporary poststructuralist critics.

When writing about contemporary Black feminist criticism, however, it is also important to remember that the existence of feminist studies was itself an essential precondition for growth. While many Black critics have attacked the elitism and homophobia of much white feminist writing, it remains true that Black criticism has developed from the space created by the study of (white) women's literature and culture, and African feminist criticism grew from Afra-American feminist criticism. Of course, there is no single definitive or *exclusive* Black criticism. Regional, national and class differences within each culture are immense.

AFRA-AMERICAN FEMINIST CRITICISM

Afra-American feminist criticism could be said to begin in 1974 with two events: the publication of a special issue of *Black World* containing essays by June Jordan and Mary Helen Washington which carried on its cover a photograph of Zora Neale Hurston; and the publication of Alice Walker's 'In Search of Our Mothers' Gardens' in *MS* magazine (see Christian, 1989a).

It was the burgeoning visibility of Black women writers in the 1960s and 1970s which brought about this critical interest. The more 'established' novelist Gwendolyn Brooks and playwright Lorraine Hansbery were joined by the poets Audre Lorde and

Nikki Giovanni and the first novels of Toni Morrison (*The Bluest Eye*) and Alice Walker (*The Third Life of George Copeland*).

Until the 1970s Black women were misrepresented or marginalised in most critical texts. Even as late as 1979, anthologies either did not mention the work of Black women at all or casually dismissed writers like Zora Neale Hurston from an exclusively male hegemony in letters stemming from W. E. B. Du Bois. The writings of Afra-American women are simply absent in the Black literary histories written by men. In *Toward a Black Feminist Criticism* Barbara Smith describes what she calls the 'white racist pseudoscholarship' of Robert Bone's *The Negro Novel in America* (Smith, 1977, p. 4). Writers like Bone, she points out, not only do not address Black women's experience but frequently pretend that Black women writers do not exist. The effect has been twofold. Black women critics have had to spend valuable time reconstructing the Afro-American literary tradition to include women writers. Reclamation criticism includes Deborah McDowell's Black Women writers series for Beacon Press which reprinted Ann Petry and Alice Childress among others. This enabled Black feminist critics to reconceptualise the literary tradition to include a greater range of Black women's writing. A secondary task was to investigate and eradicate stereotypes of Black femininity and myths about Black women's roles.

The climate has changed. Audre Lorde, Alice Walker, Barbara Smith, and Barbara Christian, together with Valerie Smith, Mary Helen Washington and Gloria T. Hull and Toni Cade Bambara, among others, are undertaking a total reassessment of Black literature and literary history centring on Black women writers. In their research they are also discovering the differences and multiplicities of Black women's aesthetics. Alice Walker in 'In Search of Our Mothers' Gardens' (1984) sought out the autobiographies of Black women, revealing these to be rich and crucial texts and enlarging the field of Black literature. Slave and religious conversion narratives were investigated by Mary Washington (1980) in a pioneering essay about Black female identity. Faced with the demands of traditional literary critics for a 'universal' Black writing, Audre Lorde (1984) describes alternative, more 'intuitive', forms of criticism. This criticism is characterised by a transformation of conventional critical techniques as Lorde returns to the myths of Black community women. Barbara Smith (1977) attends both to the aesthetics and to the politics of Black women in her account of Black lesbian criticism.

But the first task for Black women critics was to prepare bibliographies. A literary history of Black women could not be created without a search for all available expressions of Black female identity. In *Black Lesbians: An Annotated Bibliography* (1981) J. R. Roberts gathers many hidden, and hitherto scattered, Black writings into one collection. She collects these materials both to encourage a holistic approach to teaching and to understand Black lesbian culture but also to make this culture at last accessible for feminist readers. To this end Roberts brought her materials to the attention of women's studies instructors by publishing interim selections in *Radical Teacher* and other key periodicals. She divides her text into subject sections – literature and criticism, lives, oppression, periodicals and music – in order to enlarge definitions of what might constitute Black lesbian writing. Roberts had found that the bibliographic situation mirrored the denial of Black lesbian experience in general. She sought primarily to make this culture visible rather than, as more formal criticism might do, to define and evaluate its content. But by struggling to reclaim a past, Roberts links contemporary Black writing with its cultural heritage. Other critics built on that work to challenge further the boundaries of literary history. In *Invented Lives: Narratives of Black Women (1860–1960)* (1987) Mary Helen Washington interweaves excerpts from Black women's writing with her own critical analysis. Washington, like Roberts, draws attention to writers who were hitherto unavailable in print and she gives a clear account of Black literary strategies, the misassumptions of traditional literary conventions and her own reading experiences.

BARBARA SMITH

The articulation of that more complex criticism came with Barbara Smith's pathbreaking essay *Toward A Black Feminist Criticism* (1977). In this much anthologised piece Smith set out to widen the contours of Black aesthetics. Smith *named* Black feminist criticism and gave it a direction. She makes several key points. The first is that feminist criticism must recognise the long-term literary history of Black women. Second, criticism must make an ideologically inspired reading of difference, as Smith herself demonstrates so effectively by reading Toni Morrison's *Sula* as a lesbian novel. Smith looks at how Black women's politics affects their art as well as examining the textual representation of politics; for example, in Morrison's use of visual imagery.

It could be argued that before Smith's essay appeared, Black lesbian studies did not exist. Smith argues that there are no 'inherent' lesbian features in writing, but that a Black lesbian reading is (in 1977) excluded from literary criticism altogether, just as Black writers were omitted from white feminist criticism and women writers by Black male critics. Smith starts her essay with the resonant sentences: 'I do not know where to begin. Long before I tried to write this I realised that I was attempting something unprecedented' (1977, p. 1).

The problem of audience is obviously a major one for the Black critic. Who is she writing for? Black academics, white academics, Black mothers, all women? By incorporating this issue as part of their analysis, Black critics help to explain the amazing achievement of a Black writer like Hurston in creating a literary voice of any sort. Naming therefore came first, but it was futile to name without creating a new analytic framework for the names of Black literature. Barbara Smith contends that only a new Black criticism can expose the full dimensions of many women's texts. If Smith, as Deborah McDowell points out, somewhat ignored the dreams and richness of Morrison's text (McDowell, 1989), her essay could be grounded in difference because of the body of literature established in bibliographies (Berry and McDaniels, 1980). Black feminist literary criticism parallels in its development the careers of Black writers also trying to create a literary identity in the midst of racial and sexual antagonism.

Smith went on to create the term 'simultaneity of discourse' to define Black feminist criticism. This is a way of reading which focuses on textual structure and in particular on the interrelation of structures of 'discourses' – of race, gender and sexuality.

Barbara Smith is a major theorist who has almost single-handedly created the field of Black feminist criticism with important anthologies of writing, criticism and Black women's studies. In *Home Girls* Smith defined a Black feminist standpoint as built on a notion of autonomy but not on separatism: 'Autonomy comes from a position of strength, separatism comes from a position of fear' (Smith, 1983, p. xi). Smith's choice of Black autonomy rather than separatism is freighted with magnetism for white feminist critics because Smith describes autonomy as incorporating dialogues between 'principled coalitions'. *All the Women Are White, All the Blacks Are Men, But Some of Us Are Brave: Black Women's Studies* (1982) co-edited with Gloria T. Hull and Patricia Bell Scott, marks a pivotal attempt to demystify the institutional parameters of literary criticism in the academy and to sketch out a new terrain of Black women's studies.

'The Truth that Never Hurts: Black Lesbians in Fiction in the 1980s' (1990) marks Smith's return to her pioneering essay of the 1970s. As she did over a decade before, Smith calls for a strategy of *naming* – for archives and histories; for political readings; the utility value of literary representations – and for *reflection*; 'to see our faces reflected in myriad cultural forms'. Smith points out that while Black feminism is more visible in 1990, Black lesbians are not.

The essay examines three 'autobiographies' – Gloria Naylor's *The Women of Brewster Place*, Alice Walker's *The Color Purple* and Audre Lorde's *Zami*. Through a detailed close reading Smith attacks Naylor's depiction of the lesbian as a 'victim' revealing how Naylor misrepresented lesbian characters by using motifs from much earlier literary periods. Smith calls *The Color Purple* a fable but also claims that the novel is a significant cultural statement. But only *Zami* Smith concludes, as we might expect, deals fully with the cultural and historical *location* of the Black lesbian. In conclusion, Smith argues that the political explications of Black lesbian feminist theory and practice have crucial implications for all women's potential liberation. While this claim is stated rather than substantiated in her essay, Smith, with eclectic intent, begins to open up that space with extended quotations from Black women's writing.

While Smith's main focus is on absence, other Black feminist critics, together with Smith, explore new configurations of race and gender in literary texts. The issue of difference is the pivot of Afra-American feminist criticism. For example, Black feminist critics prefer to discuss a common Black literary heritage rather than single, individual precursors in isolation. Toni Cade Bambara refuses the meritocratic frame of reference of traditional literary criticism. She says explicitly 'there is not *the* woman or *the* experience or *the* profile' (1979, p. 235). In 'What It Is I Think I'm Doing Anyhow?' Bambara refuses the 'mentorship' of white women writers such as Kate Chopin who 'hawk' alienation and suicide in the name of all protesting women. But equally she refuses to name an alternative and favoured Black writer or one who best 'captures' the Black experience. Bambara feels that these choices would come from a false frame of reference dominated by solo thinking. In order to do justice to the survival techniques (psychic, economic or literary) of Black community women, Black critics have to adopt an interdisciplinary approach, mixing songs, literature and oral history. Mary Helen Washington's *Invented Lives* is a good example of such hybridity and mixes critical essays with fiction and autobiography. Here Afra-American criticism represents a sustained attack on the 'neutrality' of 'universal' criticism.

Afra-American feminist criticism clearly challenges many of the assumptions of traditional literary criticism precisely because it is shaped by exclusion from that field, by its difference. Black feminist criticism is preoccupied by two closely related questions: first, what is the relationship between Black critics and writers and the majority of Black people and readers? Second, what is the relationship between Black feminist criticism and recent poststructuralism, postmodernism and academic theory in general? Both of these questions refer to issues of essentialism and difference. Hence, Black feminist criticism has two tasks, one concerned with cultural history and the other with language and new critical techniques.

Much of the energy of Hazel Carby's *Reconstructing Womanhood* is directed towards describing the *material* conditions impacting on nineteenth-century Afra-American writers including Harriet Jacobs and Anna Julia Cooper. Unlike the first stage of Afra-American feminist criticism which centred on Black women writers somewhat in isolation from their backgrounds, Carby demonstrates how, in the *antebellum* period of American history, Black women's writing is shaped by contemporary sexual practices and cultural history.

Black feminists opened up the critical agenda for another, and equally important, critical project to emerge: namely the creation of *ways* of reading, or the revivication of ways of reading that centre on Black linguistic practices. Barbara Christian's critique of the white academy in 'The Race for Theory' and her account of the different language motifs in which the writers Zora Neale Hurston and Alice Walker cast their stories suggest the direction such a project might take. Christian eschews white academic paradigms because these are incompatible with the modes of call and response and hieroglyphics long extant in Black writing. Black feminist cultural/ materialist readings and readings of language difference alike are grounded in the concerns of the Black community and in a continuing dialogue between literature and sexual politics. For example, often the literary text in a curious way calls a culture into question. The controversy among some Black Americans about Ntozake Shange's choreo poem *For Colored Girls* shows how much the Black community thinks of literature *as* sexual politics (Smith, 1983, p. 290). The play sparked debates in the Black community on issues of masculinity and femininity just as *The Color Purple* was to do much later.

If the field of Black feminist criticism is charted by Roberts, its principles described by Smith, and its innovative techniques are outlined by Christian, writers such as Audre Lorde and Alice Walker as well as these critics go on to develop its themes. The study of the Black woman in literature, to Lorde and Walker, is much better seen as part of a larger study of expression in Black culture. Black feminist criticism requires, they insist, a radical examination of how language operates in Black women's history, and how Black women create and support through language what becomes, for them, a flourishing culture.

AUDRE LORDE

Audre Lorde was a poet/critic and self-proclaimed 'Black lesbian feminist socialist mother of two' (Lorde, 1984, p. 114) who first published poetry in 1968 (*The First Cities*). The run-on of terms in this quotation, without commas or slashes, is deliberately instructive pointing to the value of dialogue, where racism and homophobia would privilege one term only. Lorde believes that concepts of difference in much of white feminist criticism trivialise the power and creativity in 'the chaos of knowledge' (Lorde, 1984, p. 111). As the title of her essays *Sister Outsider* makes clear, Lorde believes we should juxtapose and celebrate differences not deny these, if we are to begin to name ourselves. Neither in her poems nor in her essays does Lorde adopt a racially 'separate' idiom or vocabulary. If we adopt a course plotted by Lorde following analogies and differences, we discover a feminist criticism that is more imaginative than descriptive, a third process, embodied in images.

One good example of this vitality is Audre Lorde's *A Burst of Light* where she uses the image of light to point to certain celebratory identifications. At the Sapphires Sapphos a table laden with food is transmuted into a 'dreamlike fullness of women sharing color and food and warmth and light – Zami come true' (Lorde, 1988, p. 51). Lorde immediately juxtaposes this image with the violence of medicine using the word 'light' colloquially 'In the light of all the reading I've been doing these past weeks . . . I've made up my mind not to have a liver biopsy'. The juxtaposition of different tones, different diction is a key to Lorde's technique. The meaning of light here is not incompatible with its earlier usage but jars us into tears at Lorde's courage, and tears too at the absence of light which she needs to describe her body in order to save it. Without light 'cancer survivors are invisible to each other and we begin to be invisible to ourselves' (Lorde, 1988, p. 127). Similarly there is no 'light' at a women's writing conference she attended in Melbourne because Lorde could not 'see' the daughters of Black Aboriginal women in her audience. Racism is not a matter of contrasting racial groups but an internalised view that one race's culture is superior to (an)other. Lorde's use of an imagery of light, her attention to the very different experiences of Afra-American and Australian Aboriginal women suggest that a Black feminist critique can have global implications. Lorde's book is a very good example of what bell hooks calls the Black 'performative'. This is a form of writing/speaking which 'performs' with style and creativity the 'underclass experience that is devalued in academia' (Childers and hooks, 1990, p. 78).

In her much quoted essay 'His Master's Tools' Lorde explores the issues of critical languages and institutions and their ability to misshape Black representations in particular. The resonant title points to the heart of a Black feminist critique which is that only non-patriarchal, non-racist forms of thinking and writing can empower Black and white women. Lorde's critical practice is a sustained effort to create that empowerment. For example, she insisted that the book *Wild Women in the Whirlwind* must not go to press without including an essay on Black lesbian literature (by Barbara Smith). Lorde mixes genres. Her autobiography *Zami* mixes the fluidity of poetry with Carriacou history, matriarchal myth and contemporary politics. Disciplinary juxtapositions are a key feature of Black feminist criticism. For example, Audre Lorde argues that the issue of the representation of Black matriarchy as a 'social disease' diverted attention in the 1960s from the source of Black women's strength. In conversation with Adrienne Rich Lorde stresses the value of nonverbal communication which she argues is an energising force beneath language (Lorde, 1984). This source of energy Lorde locates in the semiotic – in mother-bonding. While many of her poems explore divisions and hatred between mothers and daughters, in 'The Woman Thing' Lorde describes her mother's strength as a specifically racial strength.

Lorde radically reforms the boundaries of criticism. Black feminist criticism does not involve rejecting white criticism but rejecting the limitations of ethnocentric white criticism. Indeed, the point of her 'An Open Letter to Mary Daly' is to attack what she considers as Daly's narrow 'ecology' since Daly restricts herself in the main to white, Judaeo-Christian imagery. One good example of the validity of Lorde's attack is Elaine Showalter's introduction to Barbara Smith in Showalter's collection *The New Feminist Criticism*. Showalter claims that Black feminist scholarship to date, and Smith's work in particular, is 'practical' rather than theoretic. Apart from the fact that Smith is a major Black theorist, this binary division carries with it connotations of Black practical/white intellectual; Black emotional/white rational. Showalter attacks Smith's claim to a 'specifically Black female language' yet Adrienne Rich's dream of a 'common language' has never suffered a similar attack.

Although valuing difference as a dynamic focus for criticism, Lorde is very concerned that white feminists should teach Black studies; but this is dependent on the methods of feminist criticism changing. Since Black poems *subtly* formulate the hidden features of Black women's lives, that formulation, Lorde suggests, will be understood critically only in hidden 'bubbles' rather than in the linear step-by-step approach of traditional criticism. So, for example, Lorde describes grammar as a 'process', where tenses are a way of 'ordering the chaos around time' (1984, p. 95). Lorde's first work of prose 'Poetry is not a Luxury' (1977) argues that the psychic history of Black women writers should have a particular significance for critics because Black writers have consistently chosen to appear in their own texts in particular ways. When reading slave narratives, for example, we have to deal with their multi-functional nature since these are neither solely literary nor solely history. The writings of Anna J. Cooper, as in 'A Voice from the South by a Black Woman of the South' (1892), and the slave stories of Sylvia DuBois and Sojourner Truth are best read in this way, working on figurative as well as on historical levels. In her very original essay 'Uses of the Erotic: The Erotic as Power' Lorde looks at the connections between power and sexuality and redefines the role of the erotic in literature in opposition to abusive pornography. The erotic, to Lorde, is a life-giving force which can be a source of power, change and creativity, as well as being a space of pleasurable exploration. It is our silences, Lorde says, which immobilise us, not our differences. This, conceptually, is not far removed from the easy generalisations of much post-war Reichian and libertarian writing. But, for Lorde, the way to speak is not sociologically. While conscious that feminists (including Adrienne Rich) are suspicious of this apparent return to a place of total intuition to 'the Black mother in each of us', Lorde fears that sociology can only *analyse* perceptions not create them. She prefers to use anthropology in her search for the intuitive voices and alternative cultures of Black women.

Was it feasible for Black women writers to assert another kind of consciousness? Does the search for 'intuition' imply a substitution of 'private' psychological needs over the social and historical? The accusation reflects a radical misunderstanding of contemporary Black criticism. There is indeed a real problem of how the history and oppression of Black women, like that of white women, is related to psychology, and one point of Lorde's writings is to make it possible for us to think through that relation in cultural terms. What Lorde is producing indeed is an alternative psycho/literary critique which helps to eradicate the victim model of Black women produced in the 1960s.

For many Black feminist critics, that critique depends on defining an Afracentric feminist point of view. Black feminist critics suggest that Afracentrism functions in opposition to Western forms of thinking (see Collins, 1990, p. 26). Afracentrism draws on African religions, on the values and language of Black communities, on an interdependence of orality, culture and community activities and in particular on the cultural significance of mothering. Alice Walker uses the term 'womanist' in distinction from 'feminist' to celebrate Afracentrism and allow a wider picture of Black womanhood to emerge: 'Womanist is to feminist as purple is to lavender' (Walker, 1984, p. xii).

Mother myths have great power and are a continuing part of many African cultures where motherhood is traditionally venerated. In criticism the focus permits a writer such as Walker to introduce her autobiography into the critical text, in an exploration of Black women's community experiences, which helps to eradicate concepts like the 'black exotic' which engender no such live negotiations for American Black women.

ALICE WALKER

Walker's criticism highlights the way in which Black critics can name and control their *own* critical 'stories'. Alice Walker was born into a Georgian sharecropping family, studied at Spelman College and was active in the Civil Rights Movement. Recognised as one of America's leading writers, she received both the American Book Award and the Pulitzer Prize in 1983. All Walker's writing – her novels as well as her critical essays – explore key critical issues: the role of Black women artists; the connection between artists and Black communities and Black history; and the significance, and richness, of myth and Black culture.

Some of the most important critical writing by Black women emerges in creative texts. Alice Walker's writing seems to me a particularly pertinent model of the way in which fiction can foreground different political/theoretical arguments by juxtaposing different forms of language. For example, *In The Temple of My Familiar* is a complex story which mixes the spiritual narratives of people speaking in tongues, with historical accounts, autobiography and dreams, refusing to represent women's bodies, heterosexual practices and racial and sexual violence from any single perspective.

Alice Walker's knowledge-claim in 'Saving the Life' is that Afra-American 'call and response', or testifying dialogue, is a very special interactive epistemology of connectedness with deep roots in African culture. Walker argues that the oral stories told by her female ancestors have equal value with a written Black heritage. Many of Walker's pivotal images of women are drawn from African oral literature and myth. For example, 'Womanist' has links with the Yorùbá deity Òsun – a strong fertile woman. Alice Walker argues that oral myths and images provide models of critical thinking. In 'Our Mothers' Gardens' (1984) Walker is both a storyteller and moral philosopher. She describes her position as a 'mediator' between contemporary culture and Afra-American belief systems. Her role as narrator therefore is a crucial one both in her essays and in her creative work. For example, in *In The Temple of My Familiar* Alice Walker describes her spirituality as a move 'away from sociology, away from the writing of explanations and statistics and further into mystery, into poetry and into prophecy' (Walker, 1989, p. 8). Her heroine Lissie has existed in past lives as a white man and as a lion and Walker's theme is one of 'parent knowledge', of listening to ancestral voices rather than formal education. So Fanny, for example, resigns from women's studies to become a masseuse believing that physical, more than intellectual, contact is a source of healing. By the end of the novel male, as well as female, characters succeed in re-entering traditional modes of thought. Since Walker's message is that prehistorical African spirituality survives and is perpetuated in the culture of women, her work is a powerful feminist theology.

Walker's novels demonstrate that the opposition between critical and creative discourses is a meaningless opposition. In *The Color Purple*, Celie's liberation is part of her spiritual freedom from traditional Christianity. It is Celie's friendship with a bisexual, economically independent Black woman which leads to 'spiritual experience'. Walker makes explicit in the novel the notion that women best change our theories about experience by bonding sexually with other women. Shug tells Celie that God loves all their sexual feelings, and Celie's transformed notion of God recognises the divinity as neither male nor female but as an androgynous spirit. This spirituality, which Walker suggests is buried within us, is realised by attention to the natural world. *The Color Purple* describes a version of animism 'Dear God, dear stars, dear trees' (Walker, 1983, p. 249).

All Walker's work is intertextual. In her essays the responsibility for change is always given to women artists, weavers and musicians not to academic thinkers, and in 'In Search of Our Mothers' Gardens' Walker enlarges definitions of art to include quiltmaking, baking and gardening. Walker's landmark essay sets out to answer the question, 'What is a Black literary tradition?' by revalidating Black women's community arts. Castigated by bell hooks in particular for refusing to tie racial and gender exploitation directly to patriarchy, Walker *does* write suggestively of the many ways in which Black women's literary/artistic development was stultified by the very *material* conditions of their lives. Her view is that Black women have always been great artists and thinkers skilled in cultural production precisely because slavery and a racist *postbellum* society denied Black women access to conventional learning: the process of quiltmaking is a clear model of the critical task. Walker made a celebratory rediscovery of Black women writers. In her essay 'Zora Neale Hurston: A Cautionary Tale and a Partisan View' Walker describes what reading about Hurston taught her of her own cultural inheritance. Walker undertook a heroic battle to create an Afra-American literary canon with Hurston as a key precursor figure.

By reading Black writers we can capture, Walker feels, all the stories Blacks had forgotten. More important for Walker was the positive picture of Blacks created by Hurston, as complex, undiminished human beings not as the 'victim' figures so often found in white criticism. It is all the sadder that Hurston's obscurity came as a direct result of a white critical preference for Richard Wright's 'protest' writing. One of Walker's critical techniques is the use of dialogue, exemplified in her testing out the value of Hurston's writing not only by assessing this against other Black or white writing but by reading Hurston aloud to her Southern kin. Hurston's accounts of Eatonville, Polk County and Haiti in *Mules and Men* similarly display the variety and diversity of dialect languages and demonstrate the inapplicability of white critical categories. That is to say, the polyphonic stories, proverbs and hybrid narratives told to Hurston create their own form and critical values. Against this Black flexibility, white feminist criticism appears somewhat racist and limited. In *'One* Child of One's Own' (Walker, 1984, p. 372) wittily deprecating the books of Patricia Meyer Spacks (author of *The Female Imagination* (1975) with whom Walker once shared an office) Walker wonders at Spacks's ignorance of Black writing. If the white 'female imagination' refuses to construct theories about (Black) experiences, how can Spacks, Walker ironically asks, theorise about the Brontës and nineteenth-century Yorkshire?

'*One* Child of One's Own' is an autobiographical account of Walker's entry into an identity as a Black woman professor and mother. By working openly on an emotional level, the piece prevents us from viewing racism as removed from ourselves or as a process in which we, Black or white, do not personally participate. The piece is about integrity and creative freedom in culture, language and in academic curriculae. Focusing on recurrent themes – the development of a Black woman artist/ writer – Alice Walker's essays are theoretical and pedagogical at the same time, written in a clear and concentrated style mixing dialect, puns and Black humour. The major differences between the Afra-American literary criticism of Alice Walker and that of white feminists is Walker's attention to dialogue, to the cultural and spiritual history of Black women and to global issues – to an African diaspora.

But although Alice Walker enlarges the terrain of Black feminist criticism by linking contemporary themes with slave narratives and by writing literary criticism as story and as autobiographical narrative, her criticism never rejects white aesthetics. For example, *The Color Purple* uses the schematic simplicity of Conrad's *Heart of Darkness* and marks Walker's reinvention of the eighteenth-century epistolary genre. The letters contain a variety of syntactical forms: internal dialogue, monologue, narrative, sadly unanswered interrogatives, jokes, dreams and philosophy. Similarly, Walker's essay techniques parallel those of white criticism in some ways. Walker has learnt her lessons of feminist criticism from Virginia Woolf. She continually 'rewrites' Woolf by substituting Black for white names in quotations from Woolf. Alice Walker has also edited a collection of Black autobiographies, written by Southern women during a Headstart programme, adding an introductory letter full of her own fears of writing about women which is very like Virginia Woolf's earlier introduction to the lives of members of the Women's Co-operative Guild (Walker, 1984, p. 22). The topics and forms of Walker's criticism also depend on other white forerunners. Her very beautiful account of her mother's garden, which names her mother as a Black artist, closely resembles Colette's famous paean to her mother. But if themes in Black criticism overlap themes present in the writings of white women critics, Walker has isolated the key Afra-American theme which is that of the Black woman as frustrated artist. Her strength comes perhaps less from her focus than from her stance, pithily summed up in a comment by C. L. R. James that Alice Walker is 'not seeking to impress white people at all' (James, 1979, p. 259).

What Smith, Lorde, Walker and other Black feminist critics discover is a way of putting aside the limited confines of white criticism and yet creating focuses and techniques that could serve the experiences and needs of all feminist women. Simply, Black women cannot be white women with colour.

BARBARA CHRISTIAN

Barbara Christian's essay 'The Race for Theory' illustrates this point. Christian's argument, as her title suggests, is that the critical world, by which she means the American academy, has been taken over by the 'race' of professional theory-creating critics, and this white academic hegemony has silenced women of colour, symbolised for Christian by the term 'minority discourse'. As she points out, Black women are central in much writing in the world not 'minor' (if not to the American academy). Christian turns from her critique of white academic theory to 'theorising' the creative writing of Black women poets

and novelists. Black women have continually speculated theoretically about the world, she argues, although for the most part
in stories, proverbs or what Christian calls 'hierogylphs' – forms
different from those of Western logic. Hence, Black theory has
not been recognised by the academy just as Black people are
often refused entry to its institutions.

Christian is not attacking theory simplistically. She is not
positing some intuitive, truthful, ultimate type, experience or
language against theory but rather argues that theory has been
'co-opted'. She refuses to diminish theory by corrupting theory
with method. Theory should not become mere coins in an
academic marketplace, of value only in its profitability in
reading literary texts: 'I am tired of being asked to produce a
black feminist literary theory as if I were a mechanical man'
(Christian, 1989a, p. 227).

'The Race for Theory' argues that just at the moment when
writing by Afra-American women and women of colour was
beginning to be more central in the discipline of literary
criticism, so a new language of literary criticism emerged, the
alienating language of theory. It is no accident, Christian claims,
that these two moments occurred together nor that the growth
of theory emerged at the same time as the 'death' of the author.

Barbara Christian was the first Black feminist critic to write a
book-length text about Black women's literary history, *Black
Women Novelists* (1980), and this was followed by *Black Feminist
Criticism* (1985) and her many other essays, including 'The Race
for Theory'. Christian's task is to articulate clearly an Afra-
American literary feminism. Features of this feminism, in as far
as it is represented, are threefold. First are its positive images of
Black womanhood. For example, Christian finds positive images
of mothering in Black slave narratives. Second, an Afracentric
feminism will stress the importance of self-knowledge, which
Christian argues is clear in Gwendolyn Brooks's *Maud Martha*.
Third, Christian draws attention to the need to widen representations of Black women's friendships, to which she herself
contributes with accounts of the buried stories of Black lesbians.

Christian focuses on images of mothering, for example, in her
account of Alice Walker's *Meridian* and Buchi Emecheta's *The
Joys of Motherhood*. She reveals her fascination with mothering
relationships in these texts and she uses the novels as pegs on

which to hang her particular view of the lived and written histories of Black women. What she tries to do is to trace Black women's sense of self-identity to mother and daughter relationships which are replicated, Christian argues, in the community culture created by Black women today.

Throughout her criticism Christian adopts a Black womanist perspective. 'The High and Lows of Black Feminist Criticism' (1990) is a good example of what this might involve. She looks at criticism through an autobiographical prism of her undergraduate and postgraduate experience. Citing her debt to her 'foremother' Alice Walker's inspirational literary redefinitions, Christian pursues a similar path by attending to everyday Black language and history – the 'lowground' of literature. This pursuit is a pressing event according to Christian precisely because the prescriptions of literary criticism had cast Black writing as too 'tainted' by sociology. Christian's term 'rememory' refers to the force of reconstruction and her interest in the *historical* context of her chosen subjects.

In 'But What Do We Think We're Doing Anyway?' (1989) Christian claims that the kernel of Black feminist literary criticism is 'dialogue' both with foremothers and with 'ordinary' Black women. Hairdressers and typists are frequently more knowledgeable about contemporary Black writing, Christian claims, than the academy. This is because, throughout the twentieth century, Black thinking has involved *two* processes – the practical and the ideal ways of behaving. It was W. E. B. Du Bois who first named this awareness 'double consciousness'. Alongside a new audience Christian proposes a new *form* for Black feminist criticism. Just as Christian widens 'literature' to include letters and diaries, so she widens the discipline of literary criticism by describing it as an *open process*. For example, the essay ends interrogatively in a series of direct questions to the reader.

Christian's criticism is essentially an ideologically inspired criticism. An ideological criticism is one in which literature is understood to signify historical ideas as part of the internal practices of the text. Christian emphasises the historical and cultural specificities of Black women writers and the literary techniques available to them. In her 1986 essay, 'We Are the Ones . . .', an analysis of Alice Walker's 'political' novels,

Christian stresses how Walker's politics can be read as a politics of community in which writing becomes an act of group survival. As if in sympathy with Marxist criticism, Christian argues that it is Walker's attention to George Copeland's *history* which enables Walker to focus on Black *resistance* as well as on Black repression.

One of the central problems of ideological criticism is evident in Christian's essay – a too tight analogy between literary form and literary *effect*. Yet Christian does recuperate and celebrate Black cultural forms, whether low (gardens, hairdressing) or high (Black women writers).

SUMMARY: AFRA-AMERICAN

Lorde, Smith, Walker and Christian all address the significant issues of Black feminist criticism. They revivify non-canonical texts and explore the new methods of criticism such texts demand. Most importantly, all these critics extend Black 'literature' into community art and into African spirituality and question the conventions of literary criticism and literary history. Black feminist criticism's account of Black women empowered by spirituality provides criticism with a major new trope. H. L. Gates describes this as the trope of the 'talking book' – a double-voiced discourse of Black vernacular/white literary rhetoric (see Gates, 1990). Black studies provide prisms through which we can question white heterosexual academia about its literary categories, about its literary techniques and, in particular, about the meaning of the institution of literature itself in its relation to women, Black and white.

AFRICAN FEMINIST CRITICISM

Currently African, like Afra-American feminist criticism has a complex interdisciplinarity. Critics frequently draw on ethnography, history, politics and white feminist theory as well as on traditional literary criticism. The criticism of Nigerians, for example Molara Ogundipe-Leslie, is matched by the Afra-American collection edited by Cheryl Wall, *Changing Our Own Words* (1989). The last decades have witnessed some important challenges to the traditional conventions of academic writing. For example, many feminist anthologies focus on oral literature and open up criticism to include autobiography and historical analysis, just as many Black American fiction writers have turned to oral literature – Toni Morrison and Alice Walker among others. As a white feminist it is difficult to summarise such a large area of work, not only because of the obvious dangers of reductionism and misrepresentation but also because it is impossible and undesirable to describe African feminist criticism as a unified single project.

The most obvious complexity which feminist criticism has to address is the number of languages utilised by African women writers. For example, there are Anglophone writers of fiction from both East and West Africa (Buchi Emecheta, Ama Ata Aidoo and Florence Nwapa), and South Africa (Bessie Head). Nwapa herself mixes Igbo and English. There are Francophone writers (for example, Mariama Bâ and Clémentine Faïk-Nzuji) and Egyptian writers (for example, Nawal el-Sa'dawi and Andrée Chedid) as well as Algerian women (Assia Djebar). In addition, many African women writers challenge the exclusions and inclusions of academic literary map-making by writing poetry, plays, novels and autobiographies as well as children's books alongside criticism. For example, Andrée Chedid has published short stories, over sixteen books of poetry, novels and four plays.

Many African writers challenge specialist genres and engage easily with autobiography and a wide demography in a complex understanding of African culture and history. Indeed, it is the opposition to a unified Black identity, characteristic of this writing, which challenges the category 'Black woman' beloved by white criticism. The intellectual space that in the West is filled by critics and theoreticians is often the province of African women writers. For example, Bessie Head's novels are replete with sociology and theory. There is less differentiation between genres in African writing. The Nigerian critics, for example Molara Ogundipe-Leslie, are key poets as well as academics. Ogundipe-Leslie's narrative poem 'The Nigerian Literary Scene' discusses the state of criticism in Nigeria and its opposing camps of Leavisites and Marxists in the manner of Pope's heroic couplets (Ogundipe-Leslie, 1980).

The attention to African orality (for example, the use of proverbs) undermines one of the major assumptions of literary criticism because this disrupts a notion of progressive linear literary history. In Zaire, Clémentine Faïk-Nzuji has spent much of her life collecting Luba folk lore and Claire Farrer made a rich collection of traditional heritage in *Women and Folklore* (1975) (see James, 1990). Gay Wilentz's *Binding Cultures* (1992) attests to the ties between orality and contemporary writing. In 1984 Bessie Head incorporated interviews and historiography into her multigeneric novel *A Bewitched Crossroad: An African Saga* (1984). Many autobiographies by African women challenge Western notions of subjectivity. For example, Ellen Kuzweyo's *Call Me Woman* (1985) interweaves sociology, political speeches, private moments and letters to create a new kind of feminist testimonial.

The critical texts include Evelyne Accad's *Veil of Shame: The Role of Women in Contemporary Fiction of North Africa and the Arab World* (1990); Carole Boyce Davies and Anne Adams Graves, *Ngambika: Studies of Women in African Literature* (1986); Charlotte H. Bruner's *Unwinding Threads: Writing by Women in Africa* (1983); Mineke Schipper's *Unheard Words: Women and Literature in Africa, the Arab World, Asia, the Caribbean and Latin America* (1985); Lloyd Brown's *Women Writers in Black Africa* (1981); and the essays by Molara Ogundipe-Leslie (1980; 1984) and Lauretta Ngcobo (1984a; 1987; 1988). There are special editions of *Research in African Literatures*, the British journal *Wasafari* as well as *Kunapipi* devoted to women writers. All attest to the increasing significance of African feminist writing. This work is not only a growing part of feminist criticism but African writing is also recognised internationally (see Busby, 1992). Aminata Sow-Fall from Senegal won the Grand Prix Littéraire d'Afrique Noire (1980) for her novel *La grève des bàttu ou les déchets humains* (1979) and the first Noma Award was won by Mariama Bâ for her novel *Une si longue lettre* (1979). From 1978, Southern African Black women could publish in *Staffrider* magazine and in the mid-1980s Serita Sa Sechaba, a Black women's publishing company, was set up. One result of this international recognition is the founding of Black women's independent publishing presses; for example, in Britain, Maud Sulter's Urban Fox Press; and from Nigeria, Buchi Emecheta and Florence Nwapa founded

Ogwugwa Afor and Tana Press respectively (see Berrian, 1990). Ama Ata Aidoo, Ghana's former Minister of Culture and Education has been an active propagandist for women's culture in all her plays, stories and novels from *Our Sister Killjoy* (1979) onwards.

Yet despite this productivity and the remarkable number and diversity of African women's writings, Western *academic* recognition of African writing has been lacking. Certainly any attempt to analyse African writing in explicitly gendered terms is largely absent from those critical publications such as the *MLA* journal which are not explicitly devoted to cultural critiques. There have been some attempts in America and Britain to revise the traditional canon and address gender and ethnicity. For example, Toni Cade Bambara's story 'Gorilla, My Love' is now a standard text in American elementary schools and Jean Rhys's *Wide Sargasso Sea* is part of the British 'A' level English examination. Yet most Western higher academic literary agendas do not go so far as to include Black writing in any *central* or *basic* introduction to literary history. Some factors may help to explain the shocking differences between the total volume of Black writing and the inattention to Black writing in Western academic journals, abstracts and core courses. Even Afro-American writers are denied a *central* place in academic literary agendas, both in terms of their low representation in academic institutions (and thus lack of academic power) and in terms of a white failure to address the range of Black creativity as literary subjects. Historically, of course, throughout the 1930s and 1940s most American Blacks did not have access to higher education and segregation severely restricted their economic freedom to enjoy academic critical work. Until the late 1960s few Black students were admitted to graduate schools in America and currently Black enrolment in those schools is actually declining (see Moses, 1990).

Similarly in Africa, the more recent contribution to criticism by feminists reflects the larger numbers of women now able to receive university education and be active scholars. Feminist literary criticism in Southern Africa began in the late 1970s and 1980s and was visible at the AUETSA (Association of University Teachers of Southern Africa) conference in 1988 with papers organised by Margaret Lenta (see Lockett, 1992). Anne Roche and Marie-Blanche Tahon, writing in a special issue of *Research in African Literature* devoted to North African literature, argue that Algerian women's writing has been 'unrepresentable' precisely because women writers share an accurate but contradictory and fragmented vision of women's participation in combat and culture (see Roche, 1992).

In Africa *the* definitive and consistent feature of both colonial and independent governments has been censorship and the banning or imprisonment of writers. South Africa has witnessed decades of censorship which began to ameliorate only with the publication of Sipho Jepamin's novel *A Ride on the Whirlwind* (1981). A typical example is the banning of a key contemporary feminist novel, Lauretta Ngcobo's *Cross of Gold* (1981). Since her flight to Britain in 1963, Ngcobo has been an active lecturer, critic, writer and President of ATCAL (Association for the Teaching of Caribbean, African, Asian and Associated Literature). Ngcobo created the critical expression: 'internal and external exile' to describe this experience. Migration engenders both cultural displacement and a sense of cultural 'inferiority'. This censorship combined with a breakdown of cultural traditions also affects writers from 'democratic' countries. In Kenya, for example, the leading writer Ngugi wa Thiong'o was detained and his books removed from schools. Egypt's famous feminist writer and one-time government minister, Nawal el-Sa'dawi, was arrested in 1981 and Malawi's Dr. Banda created a censorship board which banned books for moral and religious issues as well as political reasons.

Hence, in a special issue of *Kunapipi*: 'An Altered Aesthetics' devoted to South African writing, Cherry Clayton and other critics attack the post-colonial view that hybridity is the gateway to a new culture. Rather, they argue that cultural flexibility comes only *after* battles of nationality and race, and that not all African writers regard the family as a patriarchal institution. Pamela Ryan endorses this view in her account of the very different sense of time and space enjoyed by Virginia Woolf and denied to Black women writers (see Ryan, 1992). While this widespread cultural censorship has the most profoundly negative effect on writers' independence, some critics feel that other, less direct, forms of censorship have been equally negative. For example, the late date of 1980 for Mariama Bâ's Noma award, and the recognition of Francophone African writing that this award represented, may be explained by the inhibiting effort of Muslim social and cultural mores in many areas of West Africa. Hence Africans (as well as Afro-Caribbeans and Afro-Americans) have to engage in a far more difficult struggle than white writers. In addition the African publishing industry is still small, and Asenath Odaga is not alone in having readers who assumed that her books were written by her husband.

Economic deprivation and self-censorship contribute further insecurities while the censorship of oral and indigenous folk cultures deprives Black writers of the security of their own history. From a feminist point of view, the critical recognition of African literature has further contradictory implications for women. The first African writers to be recognised in the West were male. As if colluding in the practice of colonial regimes to educate men rather than women, the academy did nothing to challenge this explicit sexism. Further, as Carole Boyce Davies points out, many independent African societies were shaped by sexist beliefs that Western education would affect women's futures as mothers, with negative consequences for girls' entry into higher education (see Davies, 1986).

The extent to which African women writers were taken seriously by critics was subject to a similar sexism. For example, Chinweizu's attack on Western ethnocentrism in *Toward the Decolonization of African Literature* (1983) is a very revealing model of gender blindness. Chinweizu argues that the founding of *The Horn* literary magazine by ex-Leeds University-trained émigrées which created the Nigerian Ibadan Nsukka School of Poetry, in turn created a hegemony of Euromodernism. Wittily, Chinweizu protests an agenda whose 'overall goal is to shepherd Nigerian poetry onto a Euromodernist wilderness pasture, covered with an imported, attenuated and mutilated version of Western modernism and there to graze it full of the Hopkins disease' (Chinweizu, 1983, p. 209). Chinweizu's focus is on the academic suspicion of orality and his view is that African literary criticism should be ultimately a branch of social criticism.

From a feminist perspective we can see how Euromodernism *as well as* Chinweizu's inattention to women's writing are profoundly masculinist since neither include women writers. In creative writing by African men (for example, in Ngugi's novels) just as in Chinweizu's criticism, women are frequently represented only as a cause of disruption or as a source of redemption. Yet Ngugi's *The Trial of Dedan Kimathi* (1976) was co-authored with Mìcere Gìthae Mūgo, the feminist critic. Like Ngugi, Mūgo was exiled from Kenya and now teaches at the University of Zimbabwe. Her book *Visions of Africa* (1981) contrasts the views of colonists and imperialists with the strong voices of activist women – Mau Mau officers, for example.

Misogyny has often been noted in Afro-American criticism. The question of the differential treatment of contemporary Black women writers is raised in Claudia Tate's *Black Women Writers at Work* (1983). Yet the bridge Chinweizu constructs between literary and social criticism in the wake of colonial departures offers possibilities for feminists. For example, the focus on proverbs and folk tales opens up an obvious space for non-literate women's autobiographies. Nevertheless, Chinweizu's reading of African literature obscures the specificity and significance of women's experiences. Focuses central to feminist critics (for example, polygamy) are not addressed if an African literary aesthetic is equated only with its oral roots. Further, the overwhelming interest male critics display in women characters who are prostitutes and city types, as, for example, in the critic Kenneth Little's 'The Sociology of Urban Woman's Image in African Literature' (1979), contribute further to the sexual objectification of African women.

Many African feminist critics and writers draw attention to the double bind experienced by African women writers when white feminist critics gloss over race and post-colonial critics (for example, Abdul Jan Mohamed) turn to allegory rather than to gender (see *Research in African Literatures*, 21:1, 1990). In 'To be an African Woman Writer', the Ghanaian writer/critic Ama Ata Aidoo graphically catalogues a long list of well-known critical studies of African literature which omit women writers (see Aidoo, 1988). Hence, the subversion of the contemporary male canon is a crucial step in the creation of an African feminist aesthetic: Florence Stratton, for example, brilliantly debunks Wole Soyinka's exploitation of female sexuality pointing to the more sophisticated treatment of prostitute figures by women writers who frequently depict prostitution not as a *women's* issue but as part of men's degradation under particular political systems (Stratton, 1990).

As these examples make clear, attention to the gender dimensions of Black writing is not a simple matter. In addition, critical analysis of Black writing depends in large part on addressing literatures with very different histories and cultures, an issue which has direct implications for the question of how to construct 'Black woman'. Feminist critics (for example, Carole Boyce Davies, Lauretta Ngcobo and the critics represented in the collections *Research in African Literatures* and *Women in Africa Today*) aim therefore to create a complex criticism which listens as much to the white feminist theory of Hélène Cixous, for example, as to differences between Black cultures, rather than constructing an artificially unified Black aesthetic. Carole Boyce Davies, for example, sutures feminist theory to postcolonial discourse in her studies. Perhaps inevitably women writers' collective use of folk culture is seen by critics and writers, for example, Buchi Emecheta, as of enormous significance. The critic Asenath Bole Odaga has drawn attention to the creative and intellectual importance of oral literature. Writing both in Luo and English, Odaga has published several studies of oral traditions including *Yesterday's Today: The Study of Oral Literature* (1984) and teaching materials for schools in Kenya, currently the only African country where oral literature is taught throughout the education system from school to university (see James, 1990).

African feminist criticism is extremely diverse: it ranges from Florence Stratton's focus on archetypes; Davies and Graves *Ngambika* which stakes out a range of African feminisms; Kirsten Holst Peterson and Anna Rutherford's *A Double Colonization* which includes essays by Agnes Sam and Lauretta Ngcobo on the tensions of exile; and the work of Ngcobo herself. These critiques pivot around two major concerns. One is a shared sense of the import of history, matched by the American Bernice Johnson Reagon's essays which describe historic diasporal links between women of African descent. The other is a refusal of any static, 'primitive' picture of Africa.

Ngugi wa Thiong'o puts this succinctly in 'Towards a National Culture': 'Contrary to the myth and fiction of our conquerors Africa was always in a turmoil of change, with empires rising and falling. African traditional structures and cultures then were neither static nor uniform' (Ngugi, 1972, p. 5). An historically rooted African aesthetic is one clear aim although this was undervalued during colonialisation. For example, Penina Muhando, the Tanzanian playwright has drawn attention to the significance of African traditional performance. Ogundipe-Leslie also argues that there is no *one* African aesthetic and that to study indigenous aesthetics we need to understand the aesthetic 'universes' of each community and culture (for example, in Nigeria: Yoruba, Tiv, Gikuyu and Tutsis cultures). Nigeria has witnessed the birth of an intertextual literary tradition. The 'confrontation' about prostitution between Flora Nwapa's *Efuru* (1966) and the male writer's Ekwensi's popular 1961 novel *Jagua Nana* continues in Buchi Emecheta's *The Joys of Motherhood* (1979) which starts with the last line of *Efuru* to rename and revise ideas of Igbo women's community and history. The critic Cecily Lockett applies a similar gynocritical perspective in her historical mapping of Southern African women's poetry, both Black *and* white, from the turn of the century (see Lockett, 1992). If we look at examples of how Black writers create their own discursive histories then the Belize writer Zee Edgell and the Nigerian writer Buchi Emecheta stand out. Zee Edgell's *Beka Lamb* (1982), written in the context of Belize's struggle for independence creates a fictional 'memory' to fill the absence of any independent Belize history in colonial education. Florence Stratton argues that Emecheta's writing is similarly marked by a strong historical sense. This takes, Stratton suggests, two different forms. On the one hand, Emecheta searches history for explanations about the social problems African women encounter. On the other hand, Emecheta often *creates* her own history by making symbolic analogies between the condition of her women characters and the condition of the country in which these women live. For example, *The Joys of Motherhood* anticipated Nigeria's independence from Britain and women's 'independence' from enforced polygamy. Similarly Mariama Bâ links the development of independence movements and changes in women's experience in *So Long a Letter* (1979).

These concerns suggest that criticism must be based on what one might call a simultaneity of response (cultural and artistic) to what, despite national differences, is a historical constant: the betrayal of nationalist ideals and the need for women to move beyond these. Rhonda Cobham and Chikwenye Ogunyemi examine the ways in which Black women's writing is in dialogue with history and myth. For example, in African literature men and women are frequently described not as individuals set into a wider social frame but as men and women set into a cosmic schema (see Cobham and Ogunyemi, 1988). Bessie Head's *Maru* (1971) derives its framework from several African myths. The rivalry between the two characters Maru and Moleka represents the polarised opposition of the twin deities of the sun and the moon. The Kenyan critic Rebeka Njau is a good example here. Njau draws her topics from myth: *Kenyan Women and their Mystical Powers* (1985) was written, Njau claims, in order to discover the strong mythical women of Kenyan history (see James, 1990).

African feminist criticism, then, stands at the crossroads of two critical directions – nationalism and the white feminist critique – neither of which can fully engage with African women's culture. An alternative path is a turn to myth. Florence Stratton focuses on archetypes and revisionary writing in order to reflect on doubles and madness in African literature. From this perspective, women writers can be linked cross-culturally: for example, she links the Botswana writer Bessie Head and the French feminist critic Hélène Cixous. Yet African feminism must also stand apart from contemporary white feminism. Fertility, for example, is an important constituent in fictional representations of African women and gives African women both a sense of identity and a social status. Many contemporary African women writers, like white writers, are unmarried but most have children. Filomina Steady's *The Black Woman Cross-Culturally* claims: 'The importance of motherhood and the evaluation of the childbearing capacity by African women is probably the most fundamental difference between the African woman and her Western counterpart' (Steady, 1981, p. 29). In addition, Steady argues that African childrearing practices are drawn from the oral tradition.

The connections between African and Afra-American feminism are less problematic. There are explicit overlaps and shared concerns. For example, Audre Lorde argues that African history is the history of Afra-Americans. Lorde's search for mythical archetypes such as the Amazon women of Dan matches the mythical African matriarchies of Buchi Emecheta. It is important to note that the first substantial feminist critique of African writing appeared in an American text: *Sturdy Black Bridges: Visions of Black Women in Literature* edited by Roseann P. Bell *et al.* (1979). The book collects essays and creative writing from America, Africa and the Caribbean and contains Andrea Benton Rushing's major study of women in African poetry. The idea of a universal Black feminine identity has been a central theme in much of Afra-American writing. For example, Alice Walker's term 'womanist', which she defines in 'In Search of Our Mothers' Gardens' as 'a woman who is a black feminist . . . who loves herself' is frequently cited as the basis of a Black feminist aesthetic. Yet Walker took the term directly from African and Caribbean culture. In *The Signifying Monkey* (1988) H. L. Gates describes this attention to the diaspora as a 'self-reflexive' criticism.

These ideas of Black subjectivity have been extensively developed by the South African writer, Bessie Head. Like Alice Walker, Head is attracted to a diverse range of images including women's gardens and the 'feminist' ideology which these images might represent. In Head's *A Question of Power* (1974) the main character Elizabeth survives by tending the land. Elizabeth's garden becomes 'magical' and enables her to acquire the magic of writing as she learns to note down farming methods. There is a wish shared by several Afra-American feminists to assert the unity Black American/Africa in order to replace the tacit universal white feminist woman with other moments of recognition.

This is visible, for instance, in the degree to which contemporary creative writing blurs with the writing of theory. Fiction is what theory is supposed to have vacated. But in Black writing the two genres are not distinct. Cobham (1987) points to the ways in which African women writers (and this would be true for men as well as for women) are thought of *as* theorists. African fiction is flooded with social and political ideas. It is often didactic and certainly it is often intensely moralistic. One good example here is the South African autobiography *Call Me Woman* (1985) by Ellen Kuzweyo which is scored through with social science 'reports' set into a history of unbridled and violent political aggression. The strength of this writing is that it grounds the creative; it makes literature more readily decipherable. Literature is never outside, or distant from, history. Similarly the intellectual space occupied by American writers such as Alice Walker, Audre Lorde and bell hooks is the customary province of theorists. That is to say, their creative writing contains vivid and truthful theories about Black medicine and Black cosmologies. So that despite certain culturally specific differences between Black American and Black African women there are similarities in their thinking. Both see themselves as massively defined by the notion of an African women's cultural diaspora while knowing that this vast cultural history is exactly marginalised by dominating national and white American cultures. These critics confront a similar ideological bind: in order to achieve status as writing women they are encouraged by the academy to renounce a 'folk' identity. In consequence, one of the primary aims of Black feminism is to bring together Africa and America in order to consider the significance of common cultures.

There are similar and recognisable common features which can be drawn out of the enormous variety of African languages and literary forms. The most obvious is that of a common oppression. Each language, each literature, each culture has at some point in history been subject to colonialisation. Each African culture has been misrepresented by white colonialism as an Other. Distancing often takes a gendered form as, for example, in the frightening yet seductive African female of Rider Haggard's *She*. Finally, African writing tends to represent collective and community concerns in opposition to a white Western faith in individualistic psychology. Despite their different geographical locations, most Black critics share the conviction that criticism must empower writers hitherto marginalised and excluded from white canons. In 'On the Abolition of the English Dept', the Kenyan writer Ngugi wa Thiong'o makes a spirited call:

> With Africa at the centre of things, not existing as an appendix or a satellite of other countries or literatures, things must be seen from the African perspective. The dominant object in that perspective is

African literature, the major branch of African culture. (Ngugi (1972) p. 150)

To be named as Black and culturally central is a precondition for Black criticism.

Feminist critics argue that we need to be very careful in applying Anglo-American or European critical paradigms to the assessment of African writing. For example, in her account of women ANC poets, Lynda Gilfillan suggests that, because of the ANC women's overt identification with the liberation movement, it may be more appropriate to evaluate their writing as resistance literature rather than as women's writing (see Gilfillan, 1992).

An important first stage in African criticism is the study of myths and archetypes. For example, Flora Nwapa, Nigeria's first woman novelist, makes an extensive use of folk tales and oral dialogues in *Edufa* (1969). Similarly Efua Sutherland created the Ghana Drama Studio and traditional oral drama to educate village communities. The criticism of Florence Stratton and Cecily Lockett is therefore gynocritical, attempting to develop an *awareness* of women's writing before positioning this theoretically.

MOLARA OGUNDIPE-LESLIE

One example of that more complex critique is the writing of the Nigerian critic, Ogundipe-Leslie. Her contribution to the critical milieu of African literature is extensive. The process of rediscovering lost or neglected African writers owes a debt to Ogundipe-Leslie's restoration of Amos Tutuola's writing to his place as a pioneering African realist.

Ogundipe-Leslie has taught in universities in Nigeria and America and her search for African feminist literary themes is matched by her critical articles on Chinua Achebe and Wole Soyinka as well as introductions to African aesthetics. As a Marxist critic Ogundipe-Leslie, in 'The Female Writer and Her Commitment', argues that criticism must have a teaching role and a vast canvas. Criticism should concern itself with the colonial past, the colonial experience as well as with feminist and alternative accounts of modernisation. Part of that canvas can be painted in, Ogundipe-Leslie suggests, through attention to a range of ideologies and social formations as well as through attention to a range of disciplinary materials (see Ogundipe-Leslie, 1987). An earlier essay 'African Women, Culture and Another Development' reflects her evolving understanding of culture, and the way in which criticism must make manifest culture's material as well as aesthetic features. Ogundipe-Leslie's Black feminist and materialist interrogation of the totalising language of nationalism replaces nationalism with a description of culture as 'the total product of a people's "being" and "consciousness" which emerges from their grappling with nature and living with other humans in a collective group' (Ogundipe-Leslie, 1984, p. 81).

CAROLE BOYCE DAVIES AND ANNE ADAMS GRAVES

Ngambika: Studies of Women in African Literature (1986) edited by Davies and Graves is the first collection of African feminist essays to deal fully with these issues. Davies is Professor of Afro-American Studies at the State University of New York having graduated from the University of Ibadan, Nigeria; and Graves is in the Africana Studies and Research Center at Cornell University. The focus of their research is women in African and Caribbean writing, including oral and written literature as well as feminist aesthetics and children's literature. *Ngambika* contains eighteen essays illustrating the range of contemporary African feminist criticism and includes studies of Hausa women's poetry (Mack), Igbo traditions (Fido) and the role of women in Gikuyu society (Nama). The primary aim of the book in bringing together the very diverse critiques of oral poetry, fiction and philosophy is precisely to consider the relationship between feminist criticism and Black aesthetics. The anthology does not offer any single perspective but it illustrates the strength and diversity of dialogue.

The editors' inclusion of accounts of multiple forms of 'literature' such as political testimonies and oral texts helps to contest the categories and conventions of traditional criticism. The questioning of genre categories by African feminist critics represents a significant challenge to Western conventions of literary history. In her well-documented and persuasive intro-ductory essay, Davies advocates an African feminist criticism which can contextualise women's culture within (but not necessarily only *from*) traditional African writing. Davies identi-fies the four main tasks of African feminist criticism:

> 1) Developing the canon of African women writers; 2) Examining stereotypical images of women in African literature; 3) Studying African women writers and the development of an African female aesthetic; and 4) examining women in oral traditional literature. (Davies (1986) pp. 13–14)

The first two of Davies' tasks draw their impetus from that general white feminist engagement with images and canons starting with Mary Ellmann's *Thinking About Women* (1968). Yet white Western feminist criticism went on to divide the theor-etical analysis of women's oppression from textual documenta-tion and deconstruction, locating the first part of this activity in economics and sociology and the second in literary criticism.

African literary feminism represents a considerable divergence of interest from this Western division of labour. *Ngambika's* feminist critics make a direct link between literature and politics in order to account for the political power of voice, gesture and orality. *Ngambika* follows Filomina Steady's pathbreaking analy-sis of African feminism in *The Black Woman Cross-Culturally* (1981), which argues that any definition of African feminism must include female autonomy *and* co-operation; must focus on the significance of mothering and kinship relations; and must validate African woman's linguistic subversions, such as their extensive use of ridicule. Thus, according to Davies, African feminist writers must share with African men a common celebration of ancient African societies while constantly examin-ing features of African writing that *limit* the representation of women. One good example of this balancing act is Buchi Emecheta's *The Joys of Motherhood* in which she suggests that polygamy works in many ways to benefit women. Yet on the other hand Emecheta is careful to show how a long-suffering barren woman loses status through polygamy when her husband turns to the younger wives. *Ngambika's* call for an

African feminist criticism which both addresses the problematic issues of indigenous cultures and yet lives in intimate association with traditional African orality is in marked opposition to the invisibility of folk cultures in Eurocentric critical traditions.

LAURETTA NGCOBO

A South African writer now in exile in Britain, Lauretta Ngcobo has made valuable contributions to the creation of a Black aesthetic. *Let It Be Told* which she edited in 1987, is an historic first collection of essays by Black women in Britain. Ngcobo's cogent introduction covers in broad outline the cultural experiences of Black women in Britain today (significantly *not* called Black British). She argues that literature is a crucial part of that culture because literature is the embodiment of heritage: 'In it is coded the compressed experience of the whole society, its beliefs, its progress and its values; in short the universal truth' (Ngcobo, 1987, p. 34). The title of the collection, with its anonymous 'It' and biblical command suggests that larger project. Ngcobo here, and in her other writing, attempts to describe a Black aesthetic in relation to social breakdowns in Britain today and the need of Black women for positive models. She argues that the *practices* of Africa might have been forgotten but that African *attitudes* still survive and need to be formally modelled for the next generation. The issue is urgent in Britain because, as Ngcobo claims, 'riot is the language of the unheard'. A Black aesthetic will be a 'rioting literature', one which makes a major critique of white culture. Ngcobo's examples of that more politicised criticism are the critiques of the Black lesbian writer Barbara Burford, the descriptions of intergenerational sexual violence in Joan Riley's autobiographical Caribbean novel *The Unbelonging* (1985) and Merle Collins's accounts of political and cultural changes in Grenada and Britain. Ngcobo refers to Britain as 'the lost society', setting in play resonances of impermanence, of 'unbelonging', and argues that poetry is a crucial source of Black identity because poetry can be multilinguistic, subjective, reflect a collective subject and (in the Caribbean) poetry is a performance act. New and important features of Black writing to which Ngcobo points are: the cross generational work inspired by the British Young Writers Award; and the strength of Black community culture enforced by exile. These features are flagged by Ngcobo's continuous use of the plural pronoun 'we'.

Her essay 'My Life and My Writing' in the volume *Double Colonization* (1986, Peterson and Rutherford (eds)) reveals a tension between material experience and cultural superstructure that is a marked feature of Black feminist writing. Unable to categorise her experiences conveniently into 'the city', 'the country', 'the exile', and 'the book', Ngcobo argues that criticism must take account of tensions, hybridity and the intertextualities offered by the mixed discourses of Black feminism. Describing a recent visit to South Africa (in *Kunapipi*, VXIII: 1/2, 1991) Ngcobo points to the unequal material differences between Black and white women which cast doubt on attempts to forge a sisterhood across a colour bar. In addition the new political situation in South Africa has created new class divisions among Black South African women. Ngcobo's critical focus here, as in her earlier essay 'African Motherhood – Myth and Reality' (1988), is on the connection between politics and literature. In that essay Ngcobo gives a critical overview of the role of women in traditional society and the marginalised images of women in South African society. As in 'Four African Women Writers' (1984), Ngcobo's constant call is for positive role models.

CARIBBEAN FEMINIST CRITICISM

The work of describing a women's literary tradition in the Caribbean has a similar shape to African criticism's account of African women's literary cultures. Caribbean critics similarly describe the Caribbean female tradition in broad terms in relation to Caribbean history and to consequent changes in women's self-expressions. Several recent texts have addressed the key issue that until recently the West Indian canon, like the African and European canons, has been male-dominated. This is the argument of Boyce Davies and Fido's text *Out of the Kumbla: Caribbean Women and Literature* (1990). The collection of essays focuses on the main themes: the importance of com-munity creativity rather than individual experiment; issues of exclusion and dispossession; and the creation of multigeneric writing. The issue of the female 'Other' that has alienated Caribbean women writers from Caribbean culture has a particular 'difference' from the 'Othering' of white European women. For example, if Western texts place the colonial as 'Other' whose role is simply to consolidate the self-image of the European master, what happens in the creation of a *female* colonial subject by a *female* Caribbean writer forced to write within patriarchal as well as imperialist traditions? This is the special focus of Evelyn O'Callaghan's subtle account of Erna Brodber's novel *Myal* in a special issue of *Kunapipi* devoted to Caribbean writing. O'Callaghan argues that Brodber's deliberate eschewing of any notion of a fixed unitary female subject offers a positive model of a Caribbean woman. In addition, the *speaking* voice in *Myal* is communal, mixing anecdotes, songs, spells, statistics, dreams and lyrical fantasies in an eclectic Creole discourse.

The major and significant collection is *Caribbean Women Writers: Essays from the First International Conference* edited by S. R. Cudjoe (1990). The book collects critical essays about familiar Caribbean writers such as Jean Rhys, together with autobiographical and critical musings by all the leading contemporary Caribbean women writers: Rosa Guy, Phyllis Allfrey, Merle Hodge, Grace Nichols, Michelle Cliff, Beryl Gilroy, Olive Senior and many others. In his overview introduction Cudjoe differentiates stages in Caribbean writing. The first stage ends with Sylvia Wynter's *The Hills of Hebron* (1966) which gives a public shape to the Caribbean self and which ushers in the second era characterised by Merle Hodge's *Crick Crack, Monkey* (1970) with its emphasis on a personal self. The main feminist essay 'Twentieth-Century Women' by Laura Niesen de Abruna counters Cudjoe's emphasis on progressive individualism with a more 'womanist' account drawn from her theoretical reading in the work of the American philosopher, Carol Gilligan and social psychologist, Nancy Chodorow. De Abruna argues, on the other hand, that Caribbean women's writing searches for an ethic of caring to be found in descriptions of personal relationships by Zee Edgell, Merle Hodge and Jamaica Kincaid in particular. The collection as a whole contains definitive bibliographies of the French-, Dutch- and Spanish-speaking

Caribbean which go some way to eradicate the negative images of women which dominate the Spanish Antilles as elsewhere. The notion of a communal voice, and of an ethic of caring as well as the cross-fertilisation of international Black feminism (for example, Michelle Cliff's American writings) mean that Caribbean writing has a unique and critical place in Black feminism.

SUMMARY

There are clear differences between Black feminist criticism in Africa, America, the Caribbean and Britain and white feminist criticism as well as between Black feminisms. In 'Feminism with a small f' Buchi Emecheta distances African feminism from European and American feminisms, arguing, for example, that Western women overemphasise the role of sexuality (Emecheta, 1988). In addition Jean O'Barr has drawn attention to the way in which Kenya's women writers are beginning to write about marriage debates, familiar internationally but not previously common to African literature (O'Barr, 1987).

African critics celebrate hybridity but not in any superficial way. Hybridity in African criticism represents the religious and cultural matrix which dates from prehistory. In addition African feminist criticism is dialogic. Texts betray little interest in private individual critiques but rather take the view that Black writers are historical agents participating in a collective enterprise. Efua Sutherland's plays, for example, chart social issues only within communal dramas.

Finally, African feminism argues that gender roles are shaped as much by matriarchy, Third World landscapes and very different cultures and kinships as by urban culture. In a pioneering account of images of women in Zimbabwean literature Rudo Gaidzanwa points out that the Zimbabwean women writers – Barbara Makhalisa, Stella Mandebvu and Eunice Mthethwa, among others – write in a very different way from Zimbabwean men – for example, women write non-judgementally about abortion – but that there are further moral and social differences between representations in Shona and Ndebele writing, and representations in English writing in

Africa (Gaidzanwa, 1985). African feminist criticism reconceptualises feminist aesthetics by expanding the terrain of literary criticism into a complex politics of gender, race and writing.

Afra-American feminist criticism

SELECTED READING

Basic texts

Bambara, T. C. (1979) 'Commitment: Tony Cade Bambara speaks', in Bell, R. P., Parker, B. J. and Guy-Sheftall, B. (eds), *Sturdy Black Bridges: Visions of black women in literature*, New York: Anchor Books

Berry, L. and McDaniels, J. (1980) 'Teaching contemporary black women writers', *Radical Teacher*, 17

Carby, H. (1987) *Reconstructing Womanhood: The emergence of the Afro-American woman novelist*, New York: Oxford University Press

Christian, B. (1980) *Black Women Novelists: The development of a tradition 1892–1976*, Westport, Conn.: Greenwood Press

Christian, B. (1986) 'We are the ones that we have been waiting for: political content in Alice Walker's novels', *Women's Studies International Forum*, 9:4, pp. 421–6

Christian, B. (1989a) 'The race for theory', in L. Kauffman (ed.) *Gender and Theory*, Oxford: Blackwell

Christian, B. (1989b) 'But what do we think we're doing anyway? The state of black feminist criticism(s) or my version of a little bit of history', in C. A. Wall (ed.), *Changing Our Own Words: Essays on criticism, theory and writing by black women*, New Brunswick: Rutgers University Press

Christian, B. (1990) 'The highs and lows of black feminist criticism', in H. L. Gates (ed.) *Reading Black: Reading feminist*, London: Penguin

hooks, b. (1991) *Yearning: Race, gender and cultural politics*, London: Turnaround

Hull, G. T., Scott, P. B. and Smith, B. (eds) (1982) *All the Women Are White, All the Blacks Are Men, But Some of Us Are Brave: Black women's studies*, New York: The Feminist Press

Lorde, A. (1984) *Sister Outsider*, Trumansburg, NY: Crossing Press

Lorde, A. (1988) *A Burst of Light*, London: Sheba

McDowell, D. (1989) 'Reading family matters', in C. A. Wall (ed.), *Changing Our Own Words*, New Brunswick: Rutgers University Press

Roberts, J. R. (1981) *Black Lesbians: An annotated bibliography*, Tallahassee, Fla: The Naiad Press

Smith, B. (1977) *Toward A Black Feminist Criticism*, Brooklyn, NY: Out & Out Books

Smith, B. (ed.) (1983) *Home Girls: A black feminist anthology*, New York: Kitchen Table Press

Smith, B. (1990) 'The truth that never hurts: black lesbians in fiction in the 1980s', in J. M. Braxton and A. N. McLaughlin (eds), *Wild Women in the Whirlwind: Afra-American culture and the contemporary literary renaissance*, London: Serpents Tail

Smith, V. (1987) *Narrative Authority in Twentieth Century Afro-American Fiction*, Cambridge, Mass.: Harvard University Press

Walker, A. (1983) *The Color Purple*, London: The Women's Press

Walker, A. (1984) *In Search of Our Mothers' Gardens*, London: The Women's Press

Walker, A. (1989) *In the Temple of My Familiar*, London: The Women's Press

Washington, M. H. (1980) 'These self-invented women: a theoretical framework for a literary history of black women', *Radical Teacher*, 17, pp. 3–7

Washington, M. H. (1987) *Invented Lives: Narratives of black women (1860–1960)*, New York: Anchor/Doubleday

Introductions

Braxton, J. M. and McLaughlin, A. N. (eds) (1990) *Wild Women in the Whirlwind: Afra-American culture and the contemporary literary renaissance*, London: Serpents Tail

Collins, P. H. (1990) *Black Feminist Thought: Knowledge, consciousness and the politics of empowerment*, London: Unwin Hyman

Evans, M. (1987) *Black Women Writers*, London: Pluto

Gates, H. L. (ed.) (1990) *Reading Black: Reading feminist*, Harmondsworth: Penguin

Pryse, M. and Spillers, H. J. (1985) *Conjuring: Black women, fiction and the literary tradition*, Bloomington: Indiana University Press

Russell, S. (1990) *Render Me My Song: African-American women writers from slavery to the present*, London: Pandora

Wall, C. A. (1989) *Changing Our Own Words: Essays on criticism, theory and writing by black women*, New Brunswick, NY: Rutgers University Press

Further reading

Childers, M. and hooks, b. (1990) 'A conversation about race and class', in M. Hirsch and E. Fox Keller (eds), *Conflicts in Feminism*, London: Routledge

Cooper, A. J. (1892) *A Voice from the South by a Black Woman of the South*, Xenio, Ohio: Aldine Printing House

Gates, H. L. (1984) *Black Literature and Literary Theory*, London: Methuen

James, C. L. R. (1979) 'Wisdom: an interview', in Bell, R. P., Parker, B. J. and Guy-Sheftall, B., (eds), *Sturdy Black Bridges: Visions of black women in literature*, New York: Anchor Books

Spacks, P. M. (1975) *The Female Imagination*, New York: Knopf

Spelman, E. (1988) *Inessential Woman: Problems of exclusion in feminist thought*, London: The Women's Press

Spillers, H. (1991) *Comparative American Identities: Race, sex and nationality in the modern text*, London: Routledge

African and Caribbean feminist criticism

SELECTED READING

Basic texts

Aidoo, A. A. (1988) 'To be an African woman writer: an overview and a detail', in K. H. Petersen (ed.), *Criticism and Ideology: Second African writers conference*, Uppsala: Scandinavian Institute of African Studies, pp. 155–73

Cobham, R. and Collins, M. (eds) (1987) *Watchers and Seekers: Creative writing by black women in Britain*, London: The Women's Press

Cudjoe, S. R. (ed.) (1990) *Caribbean Women Writers: Essays from the first international conference*, Wellesley, Mass.: Calaloux

Davies, C. B. and Fido, E. S. (eds) (1990) *Out of the Kumbla: Caribbean women and literature*, Trenton, NJ.: African World Press

Davies, C. B. and Graves, A. A. (eds) (1986) *Ngambika: Studies of women in African literature*, Trenton, NJ: Africa World Press

Emecheta, B. (1988) 'Feminism with a small f', in K. H. Petersen (ed.), *Criticism and Ideology: Second African writers conference*, Uppsala: Scandinavian Institute of African Studies, pp. 173–81

Gaidzanwa, R. B. (1985) *Images of Women in Zimbabwean Literature*, Harare: The College Press

James, A. (1990) *In their Own Voices*, London: James Curry

Lockett, C. (1992) 'Preface', *Tulsa Studies in Women's Literature: South African women writing*, 11:1 (Spring), pp. 47–9

Ngcobo, L. (1984a) 'Four African women writers', *South African Outlook*, May

Ngcobo, L. (1984b) 'Do books alter lives: an interview', *Wasafari*, 1:1 (Autumn) pp. 5–9

Ngcobo, L. (ed.) (1987) *Let It Be Told: Essays by black women in Britain*, London: Pluto

Ngcobo, L. (1988) 'African motherhood – myth and reality', in K. H. Petersen (ed.), *Criticism and Ideology: Second African writers conference*, Uppsala: Scandinavian Institute of African Studies

Ogundipe-Leslie, M. (1980) 'The Nigerian literary scene', *Kiabara*, 3:2, pp. 6–10

Ogundipe-Leslie, M. (1984) 'African women, culture and another development', *Journal of African Marxism*, 5, pp. 77–92

Ogundipe-Leslie, M. (1987) 'The female writer and her commitment', in Jones, E. D., Palmeri, E. and Jones, M. (eds), *Women in African Literature Today*, 15, London: James Curry

Peterson, K. H. and Rutherford, A. (eds) (1986) *A Double Colonization: Colonial and post-colonial women's writing*, Mundelstrup, Denmark: Dangaroo Press

Roche, A. (1992) 'Women's literature in Algeria', *Research in African Literatures: Special issue North African literature*, 23:2 (Summer) pp. 209–17

Rushing, A. B. (1979) 'Images of black women in modern African poetry: an overview' in Bell, R. P., Parker, B. J. and

Guy-Sheftall, B. (eds), *Sturdy Black Bridges: Visions of black women in literature*, Garden City, NY: Anchor Books

Stratton, F. (1990) ' "Periodic Embodiments": a ubiquitous trope in African men's writing' *Research in African Literatures: Special issue critical theory and African literatures*, 21:1 (Spring) pp. 111–26

Tahon, M. B. (1992) 'Women novelists and women in the struggle for Algeria's national liberation (1957–1980)', *Research in African Literatures*, 23:2 (Summer) pp. 39–51

Introductions

Accad, E. (1990) *Veil of Shame: The role of women in contemporary fiction of North Africa and the Arab world*, New York: New York University Press

Brown, L. (1981) *Women writers in black Africa*, Westport, Conn.: Greenwood

Bruner, C. H. (ed.) (1983) *Unwinding Threads: Writing by women in Africa*, London: Heinemann

Cobham, R. and Ogunyemi, C. O. (1988) *Research in African Literatures: Special issue women's writing*, 19:2 (Summer)

Gilroy, B. (1989) 'The woman writer and commitment: links between Caribbean and African literature, *Wasafari*, 10 (Summer) pp. 13–16

Jones, E. D. (ed.) (1987) *Women in African Literature Today*, London: James Curry

Kunapipi (1990) *Special Issue on Caribbean Writing*, XII: 3

Nasta, S. (ed.) (1991) *Motherlands: Black women's writing from Africa, the Caribbean and South Asia*, London: The Women's Press

Owomogela, O. (ed.) (1986) *African Literature in the Twentieth Century*, Nebraska: University of Nebraska Press

Saadawi, N. (1980) *The Hidden Face of Eve: Women in the Arab world*, Boston: Beacon Press

Schipper, M. (ed.) (1985) *Unheard Words: Women and literature in Africa, the Arab world, Asia, the Caribbean and Latin America*, London: Allison & Busby

Taiwo, O. (1984) *Female Novelists of Modern Africa*, New York: St Martins Press

Wasafari (1988) *Women's Issue*, 8 (Spring)

Further reading

Busby, M. (1992) *Daughters of Africa*, London: Jonathan Cape Ltd

Chinweizu, J. (1983) *Toward the Decolonization of African Literature*, Washington, DC: Howard University Press

Clayton, C. (1991) 'Post-colonial, Post-apartheid, Post-feminist: Family and state in prison narratives by South African Women' *Kunapipi: Special issue an altered aesthetic*, xIII: 1/2, pp. 136–65

de Abruna, L. N. (1990) 'Twentieth century women: writers from the English-speaking Caribbean', in *Caribbean Women Writers: Essays from the first international conference*, Wellesley, Mass.: Calaloux

Gilfillan, L. (1992) 'Black women poets in exile', *Tulsa Studies in Women's Literature*, 11:1 (Spring) pp. 79–95

Kuzweyo, E. (1985) *Call Me Woman*, London: The Women's Press

Little, K. (1979) 'The sociology of urban woman's image in African literature', *West Africa*, 3, 10 and 17 (September)

Moses, Y. (1990) '. . . but some of us are (still) brave', *The Women's Review of Books*, vII: 5 (February) pp. 31–2

Mūgo, M. G. (1978) *Visions of Africa: The fiction of Chinua Achebe, Margaret Lawrence, Elspeth Huxley, Ngugi wa Thiong'o*, Nairobi: Kenyan Literature Bureau

Ngugi, W. T. (1972) *Homecoming*, London: Heinemann

O'Barr, J. (1987) 'Feminist issues in the fiction of Kenya's women writers', in Jones, E. (ed.), *Women in African Literature Today*, 5, London: James Curry

O'Callaghan, E. (1990) 'Engineering the female subject: Erna Brodber's *Myal*', *Kunapipi*, xII: 3, pp. 93–103

Ryan, P. (1992) 'Black women do not have time to dream: the politics of time and space', *Tulsa Studies in Women's Literature*, 11:1 (Spring) pp. 95–102

Steady, F. (1981) *The Black Woman Cross-Culturally*, Cambridge, Mass.: Schenkman

Tate, C. (1983) *Black Women Writers at Work*, New York: Continuum

8   Lesbian feminist criticism

'We straddle the fence that says we cannot be uplifters of the race and lesbians at the same time' (Gomez and Smith, 1990, p. 54). Jewelle Gomez points to the difficulty faced by Black lesbians in claiming an identity when representations of race and sexuality are split and contradictory. Lesbian identities are further problematised socially, by the denial to lesbian women of an accredited public self, and critically by poststructuralist ideas of fragmented selves. In addition, social construction theory questions the idea of any biological, essential or universal identity as in, for example, 'the lesbian woman'. As Gomez argues, the construction of an entity 'Black lesbian' needs a believable cultural context. Central to this issue are questions of difference. Is lesbianism about content/style or the author/reader? In any case, is there a specific lesbian style of writing? If so, what are its characteristics and is it similar to, or different from, writing by heterosexual women or, indeed, writing by heterosexual and gay men?

The exploration of lesbianism is not straight forward (sic) but beset by contradictions. For example, the term 'homosexuality' itself was not available, at least in the English language, until the nineteenth century. According to Jonathan Katz 'homosexuality' was coined in 1865 by the German sodomy law reformer Karl Maria Kertbeny (see Katz, 1990). Thus, from the beginning 'homosexuality' was a term of legal and later medical classification too prescriptive to accommodate the often fantastic, Utopian world of non-heterosexual writing.

Should nineteenth-century women writers' private eroticism and public heterosexuality be labelled homosocial or 'lesbian'?

And is the term 'lesbian' applicable to a particular group of women or to all women-identified women? Currently, lesbian criticism includes sharply competing ideas of what lesbianism means, ranging from Adrienne Rich's concept of an all women-identified 'lesbian continuum' to a belief that lesbian writing must be distinctly different from writing by heterosexuals. In some ways, the experience of lesbianism, at a primary level, must give a particular and different writing and reading viewpoint. I am not suggesting that sexuality unilaterally constructs identity, since one of the important achievements of feminist criticism is to show how sexuality and gender identity are distinct social and analytical categories. But the underlying fact of one's sexual preference, whether conscious or unconscious, must affect one's cultural expectations and choices although the gender of the sexual object is not a sole definer of any individual identity.

This sets up the interesting question: can 'straights' be lesbian readers? There is, of course, no *single* lesbian reading style. Reading as a Black lesbian is not the same as reading as a white lesbian. Lesbian criticism offers several approaches, some closer to essentialism, or a belief in an innate lesbian identity, others offering a double perspective equally available to straights or lesbians. Adrienne Rich's early criticism (particularly her essay 'Vesuvius at Home: The Power of Emily Dickinson', 1975) assumes a close correspondence between lesbian identity and lesbian poetry and might be said to be a version of 'essentialism'. In the essay, Rich shows that Dickinson's life structures her art. 'Encodement approaches' – for example, those of Catharine Stimpson (see below) – describe language codes and masks in the writings of Gertrude Stein and other authors, codes which *depend* on a lesbian reader who can share that author's experience.

Other critics, notably Bonnie Zimmerman, have moved away from biographical and encodement approaches to a use of 'double vision' drawn from the dual perception of minorities in mainstream culture. Here it is possible for straights to read as lesbians if, as Zimmerman claims, lesbian identities are notional; dependent on an historical perception of self. Zimmerman's work (discussed below) offers, in addition, a rethinking of the gap between essentialism and social construction, if self-representations can simultaneously foreground positive images of women *and* discuss the fictionality of these images as, for example, Jeanette Winterson does in *Oranges Are Not The Only Fruit* (1985). My own view is close to that described by Biddy Martin – 'Lesbianism is a position from which to speak' (Martin, 1988, p. 113). Identifying and giving articulate expression to these concerns is the work of contemporary lesbian criticism.

Creative writing is a very positive feature of lesbian criticism. The first encounter with lesbian fiction is frequently a key moment in lesbian 'coming out' stories. First person fictions are a significant part of lesbian feminist writing. Such fictions usually attack the horrific stereotypes of lesbian identity created by heterosexist society and simultaneously attack traditional ideas of what is and what is not of literary value. And lesbian writings themselves, due to the dearth of *visual* models of lesbianism culturally available, carry particular significance in the formation of a lesbian identity. With richness and some sense of novelty, lesbian creative writers often address the literary tradition. For example, expressing the inexpressible is the aim of Susan Griffin. 'Thoughts on Writing' is in diary form and is a critique about her own 'literature'. Griffin begins the day wondering if the voice of the 'Other' in society (lesbian or Black) takes on in literary form 'the meaning of the voice of poetry' (Griffin, 1980, p. 115). In other words, lesbians, as outsiders, have some privileged perception (Griffin calls this 'synchronisities'), a larger knowledge not available to those working in traditional modes. Explicit in this argument is the idea that literary vocabulary does not mirror reality but can provide an alternative system of signification.

In addition, lesbian critics had to find a lesbian literary tradition before they could create lesbian critical techniques. The perplexing question this task immediately encounters is what is lesbianism? Addressing this issue the lesbian writer Valerie Miner argues 'this raises the touchy question: What is a lesbian novel?', that a lesbian novel must proceed from the 'term woman-identified' (Miner, 1990, p. 20). This central idea – that the *object* of sexuality in some way shapes the *choice* of sexuality – also marks Virginia Woolf's *Orlando*, which subverts a heterosexual fetish for specific identity by having the central character change gender, centuries and fictional styles. Woolf's novel requires a reader to focus on shifting situations as much as identify with a stable character.

While Miner's definition *recuperates* a range of lesbian experience, it is in danger of losing specificity. Griffin, in particular, has claimed that the disruption of the literary tradition that representations of sexual difference entail are symbolic disruptions rather than specific challenges. The notion that 'lesbian' was not simply a metaphor but an ideological *position* came from another direction. Lesbian literary criticism owes a great deal to lesbian theorists as well as to lesbian writers of fiction.

In the early 1970s lesbian theorists Grace Atkinson and Charlotte Bunch were arguing that lesbians were the radicals of feminism. A lesbian was a woman who believed in the primacy of women. 'Lesbian' was a source of an alternative model of female identity. More than that, as women-identified women, lesbians represented the *norm* of female experience and heterosexism represented an abnormal form of oppression. The logic of this radical theory was clear. Only lesbians could provide a fully adequate women-centred analysis. The 'reality' of lesbian experience in literature needed to be uncovered and made part of all women's history.

While such an isomorphism of object choice and literary outcome obviously suggest affinities and similarities among different texts, it still leaves open the nature of a lesbian identity. In her essay on lesbian film, Teresa de Lauretis makes a useful distinction between films which change representations and what *can* be represented and those which are sympathetic to lesbianism but do not put forward any new lesbian representations (see de Lauretis in Fuss, 1991). However similar works of literature may be, differences nevertheless obtain and these differences will carry the impress of the heterosexual and patriarchal contexts which exert suppressive pressures. Hence, in their attempts to define a lesbian aesthetic, many critics explore ways in which lesbian experience is affected by cultural constructions. For example, Bonnie Zimmerman, in 'Exiting from Patriarchy' (1983), characterises a text as lesbian by focusing attention on historical and cultural differences in lesbian representations, while also claiming 'lesbian' to involve a belief in non-violence combined with strong female role models.

One key task facing lesbian criticism is how to evaluate writing that pre-dates second-wave 'coming out' literature. Here lesbian criticism is much in debt to sexual historians, in particular to the subtle and overarching explanations provided by Michel Foucault. Foucault's *History of Sexuality* (1978) was a landmark study, offering many suggestive insights about the historical construction of sexuality in the West. Foucault points out that writings (discourses) about sexuality grew in great volume during the nineteenth and twentieth centuries. He suggests that as sexuality chose to signify 'the truth' about an individual, 'sexuality' became enmeshed in a huge range of medical, anthropological, biological and pedagogical discourses. But rather than this range indicating a *liberalisation* of thinking and an openness about sexuality, such discourses created new classifications of sexual practices which limited sexuality to particular norms. In turn society came to believe that these constructions were inherent characteristics of individuals. In addition, Foucault argues that discourses of sexuality actually *produce* sexuality. Any exploration of representations of sexual difference in literature will therefore be inseparable from the forms, concepts and vocabulary which are culturally available.

Foucault's critique helped lesbian criticism to move beyond an essentialist or naturalising way of thinking about sexuality (for example, the third sex or Uranian concept of lesbianism in Radclyffe Hall's *The Well of Loneliness*, 1928) to questions about cultural contexts, the interaction between these and literary subjectivity and even the possibility of a 'reverse' discourse or self-representation. So that, lesbian criticism has often been generated from outside the academy; for example, the writings of Audre Lorde. Katie King in 'Producing Sex, Theory and Culture' describes a range of lesbian criticisms including 'sex radical productions of gay culture' such as AIDS activism. King argues that in the 1990s lesbian scholarship which once played a significant role in feminist thought has 'now been displaced in the academy' (King, 1990, p. 88). Yet historically it was academic feminist criticism which initially succoured lesbian criticism. It was in second-wave feminism, along with the growth of a gay liberation movement, that lesbian criticism began to emerge. Without a feminist critique of the literary canon and phallic literary traditions, the notion of a separate or continuous, lesbian criticism was difficult to envision. As Biddy Martin points out in 'Lesbian Identity and Autobiographical Difference(s)' (1988), it was the feminist creation of a history of women-identified women and a celebration of women's friendships which gave lesbian criticism a solid foundation.

In the 1970s a reconfiguration of feminist criticism took place which insisted on the important literary contributions made by lesbian women. One of the first, and most influential, lesbian-feminist essays was Adrienne Rich's 'When We Dead Awaken: Writing as Re-Vision' (1971). The piece forcefully insists on addressing issues of visibility and invisibility; of seeing with fresh eyes; and on the need for a new literary tradition intimately intertwined with subjective/physical experience. The need to find literary self-reflections was of pressing moment in lesbian criticism. That self-conscious critique supported by a zealous widening of feminist criticism emerged in the lesbian caucus of the National Women's Studies Association (1977). The lesbian challenge to heterosexual presumptions was profound. A more significant challenge to white *and* heterosexist racism came in Barbara Smith's pioneering essay 'Toward a Black Feminist Criticism' (1977) with its transgressive lesbian reading of Toni Morrison's *Sula*. Among other pioneering critiques are Ann Shockley's 'The Black Lesbian in American Literature: An Overview' (1979) and literary and biographical research about Black lesbian writers: for example, Gloria T. Hull's work on Alice Dunbar Nelson (1982) and bibliographies by J. R. Roberts (1981) and Barbara Greir (1981).

A major theme in lesbian criticism is the tension between identifying the 'real' nature of lesbian writing which gets bound up with identifying a history of (real) lesbian women. As Elly Bulkin argues in her introduction to *Lesbian Fiction* (1981) the initial task was to discover a history of lesbian women as much as to find lesbian writers. Academic scholarship in other disciplines (particularly anthropology, sociology, history and psychology) demanded respect for lesbian issues, and supported the work of lesbian literary criticism. For example, Dolores Klaich's *Woman Plus Woman: Attitudes Toward Lesbianism* was published contemporaneously with Carroll Smith-Rosenberg's 'The Female World of Love and Ritual' (1975).

Smith-Rosenberg's amazingly influential essay opened the first issue of *Signs* and surveyed patterns in women's friendships in the nineteenth century. In that essay Smith-Rosenberg anticipated Adrienne Rich's 'Compulsory Heterosexuality and Lesbian Existence' (1980) by arguing against the concept of a fixed sexual identity or even fixed sexual choices, in favour of a continuum or spectrum of sexuality.

Bibliographies provided pioneering collections of crucial value to lesbians researching literary history and wanting to create an alternative canon. Barbara Greir's *The Lesbian in Literature: A Bibliography* (1981) provided the first major contemporary resource for lesbian scholars and readers. Greir was book reviewer for the lesbian periodical *The Ladder* and it was in this and the other feminist journals, *Sinister Wisdom*, *Chrysalis*, *Conditions* and *Signs* that introductions to lesbian literature began to appear. *Conditions* published the first interviews with Adrienne Rich who (as we shall see later) offers the most expansive definition of lesbianism as 'woman-identified experience'.

The primary job of lesbian criticism was to establish a lesbian literary tradition. But, as with Black feminism, when this task was accomplished, other focuses began to emerge. That development can best be illustrated through an account of representations of lesbianism in *The Ladder*. Appearing from 1956 to 1972 this periodical was the most explicit, and often the only available, commentary on lesbian culture of the period. As the key outlet for lesbian criticism and philosophy it provides a crucial indicator of the way lesbian criticism became more theoretical as it became more feminist.

At first, contributors to *The Ladder* avoided specifically feminist concerns. Authors typically used male pronouns and assumed that male and female homosexuality were subject to the same cultural and social constraints. The growing commitment of many lesbians to feminism led to redefinitions and changes in its lesbian criticism (Brown, 1970). Feminism provided a vocabulary of choice. If sexuality could be freely or unconsciously 'chosen', so too the critical text could move from identifying lesbian in relation to a male world (and therefore a male literary tradition) to a more problematic and exciting account of literary creativity. Lesbian critics were able to attack the language and culture of patriarchal criticism with overtly politicised alternatives.

Lesbian studies made its first priority the exploration of lesbian literary history. Elly Bulkin in her collections *Lesbian Fiction* (1981) and *Lesbian Poetry* (1981) described a long tradition of lesbian writing starting with Octave Thanet in the 1880s. Bulkin's texts are good accounts of the cultural contexts and political climates of particular decades like the 1930s. She describes the development of lesbian writing as a linear history. This begins with the deconstruction of negative literary images of lesbian women; moves to celebrating positive lesbian role models; and grows to an exacting and absorbing attention to diversity. Bulkin, like many other lesbian critics, had experienced this process first hand with a career trajectory which began with an admiration for, and identification with, positive role models before a sense of her own context and history emerged.

The history of lesbianism received its most extensive overview, however, with Lillian Faderman's *Surpassing the Love of Men: Romantic Friendship and Love Between Women from the Renaissance to the Present* (1981). As her title suggests, Faderman recounts the history of four hundred years of lesbian literature. She 'rescues' many women writers such as Mary Wollstonecraft and Anna Seward from heterosexuality and ranges across fiction and poetry to include popular magazine stories of the early twentieth century. *Odd Girls and Twilight Lovers: A History of Lesbian Life in Twentieth-Century America* (1991) builds on her earlier text in a detailed social history of lesbian life and culture.

Faderman's work earned her many admirers but also a great deal of criticism. The attacks focus on Faderman's view of history which suggests that 'lesbianism' is a modern phenomenon and on Faderman's wish to detach lesbian culture from the more contemporary definition of lesbianism which centralises the importance of sexual experience. Sonja Ruehl and others wanted Faderman to articulate what was specific about the experience and oppression of lesbians which, to Ruehl and others, was in the main sexual practice (Ruehl, 1982). Faderman tends to equate lesbian representations with lesbian social reality. But not only does Faderman create a lesbian tradition by reclaiming past writers, she also enlarges the domain of lesbianism as a sexual practice by making lesbian literary history respectable, which makes it possible for more women to think imaginatively about lesbianism. To write lesbian literary history at all requires an exploration of meanings and definitions of a more expansive lesbianism. Margaret Cruikshank built on these critiques in the safe space of burgeoning women's studies programmes with an extensive collection of teaching materials, *Lesbian Studies* (1982). The book is an anthology of lesbian perspectives on psychology, sociology and history as well as literature. She demonstrates the range of academic work in lesbian studies but also contextualises that range by describing the connections many contributors made between their lives and work. A common theme in many of the essays is the need for a multilevel perspective. To Cruikshank the feminist curriculum had challenged the sexist myth of 'woman as Other' but left underexamined the idea of the 'lesbian as Other'. Literature and literary criticism are Cruikshank's main focus because, as she explains, nearly all the sample syllabuses sent to her were for literature courses. The humanities, and hence literary criticism, have therefore played an important role in lesbian thinking. The special urgency of *Lesbian Studies* stems from the destruction of so much past lesbian writing and history which Cruikshank continues to document (see Cruikshank, 1992).

Monique Wittig's argument that 'lesbians are not women' challenges the relation between gender and sexuality created by heterosexuality. Since women occupy a fixed position in the heterosexual social order, then if one does not occupy that position, one is not a woman. Lesbians are therefore not women (see Wittig, 1980). In *Lesbian Peoples: Materials for a Dictionary* (1979) Wittig describes the sensitivity to lesbian readers displayed in lesbian texts. Lesbian writers often evocatively describe sexual capacities in order to heighten the reader's awareness of sexuality. The analogies lesbian writers frequently make between the shape of language (textuality) and the shape of women's bodies and sexual experience (sexuality) opens up criticism and literature to a more multilayered, complex model of writing and reading. Wittig, for example, subverts conventional genres with an extensive use of symbols and matriarchal myths. She carries her twinning of textuality and sexuality to elaborate lengths by allowing pronouns and characters to mingle and fuse, as in her key device, a 'j/e'.

All literature, for lesbian critics, is continually threatening to break down into sub-text and escape any single meaning which criticism wishes to impose. Lesbian criticism depends for its existence on rejecting the notion of a single, static interpretation. By making 'lesbian' a literary construct, criticism could serve as a convenient centre around which to gravitate a series of contradictory but potentially metonymic ideas about women. For example, just as some lesbian writers like Gertrude Stein use cryptic codes to create allegorical meanings, so lesbian criticism can mix dreams and journalism to subvert homophobic vocabulary, as Jill Johnston shows in *Lesbian Nation* (1973).

ESSENTIALISM AND CONSTRUCTION

The major issues still remain: is a lesbian reading 'essentially' different or can it be 'chosen' and constructed, and how do we evaluate differences *between* lesbian cultures? Straight feminist theory has perhaps for too long taken for granted the *sameness* of lesbian culture. As Barbara Smith argues, the 'survival' of a lesbian culture depends on our ability 'to see our faces reflected in myriad cultural forms' (Smith, 1990, p. 220). A lesbian reading must therefore offer several challenges. First, it can create a space for identifications as, for example, in Elly Bulkin's vivid introduction to *Lesbian Fiction*. Her essay starts with the resonating 'I have burned many a book of lesbian fiction' (Bulkin, 1981, p. xi). In the late 1950s and early 1960s, Bulkin claims, lesbians bought books stealthily:

> I smuggled them into the house . . . working my way through a quarter pound of chocolate filbert patties, hoping no one would knock, no one force me to slide my book under my pillow. I always read my books in the evening, always finished them in a single sitting, always burned them before going to sleep. (Bulkin (1981) p. xi)

The 'adolescent' images of transgression, of forbidden pleasure, and the marrying of textual pleasure to bodily pleasure and consumption, matches lesbian theory's current evaluation of female desire and sexual textuality (see, for example, the works of Luce Irigaray).

Second, the notion of constructionism can help us understand how lesbian writing changes and is shaped by differing historical periods while celebrating a separate, even 'essential', lesbian tradition. Of course, as Paulina Palmer has pointedly argued, 'there are many different versions of essentialism which themselves are socially constructed from different circumstances and events' (Palmer, 1989, p. 102).

Lesbian criticism takes its cue from these issues, sometimes focusing on the undermining of realism (posited as masculine) by lesbian utopianists such as Joanna Russ; sometimes focusing on the 'realities' of lesbian autobiographies and Bildungsromans to describe a lesbian experience hitherto marginalised or banished from literary history. There is a continuing view that lesbian writing *practices* create a space in which reader and author create 'lesbian'. For example, 'scenes of sisterhood' (Zimmerman, 1983) and the blurring of boundaries between self and other emerge as key lesbian tropes.

It was precisely the refusal of patriarchy by lesbian writers which, Faderman argues, forced writers to try stylistic experiments for which she and other critics had provided a more sophisticated criticism. The analysis by lesbian critics of alternative narrative techniques in lesbian literature was suggested by the idea that idiosyncratic or chosen modes of sexuality would need new prototypes or paradigms. Fantasies, particular kinds of imagery (for example, phallic 'substitutes') and modes of writing, such as allegories and utopias, could now be identified as lesbian without their authors having written explicitly about lesbianism at all. What Faderman, Cruikshank and others were demonstrating very successfully was the existence of literary configurations which could provide a lesbian typology. Lesbian literary histories were establishing the key texts of lesbian culture and paying particular attention to the intermixing of the popular with the avant-garde; a lesbian discourse was being defined as having a specific and different relation to conventional language.

If the 'coming out' story is the lesbian myth of origins, then salient fiction genres such as the novel of development take on a new importance. The descriptions by Cruikshank and others of the way in which lesbian writers were using the gothic to escape some of the restrictions of linear novel forms assumes that lesbians were 'choosing' to be literary lesbians as they were 'choosing' lesbian sexuality in contemporary life.

One of the most striking observations made by lesbian critics is the perception that heterosexual feminist criticism's view of traditional literary history as a masculine agenda, as an occupying power ruling over the passive, invisible woman writer, is itself a critical simile of heterosexuality. Lesbian accounts of the intimate links between style and sexuality would clearly need an alternative to this heterosexual model. Lesbian critics often attend to new languages. Catharine Stimpson sees lesbian creativity as rooted in an attention to objects, the use of silences and the alteration of syntax to admit women's breath (see Stimpson, 1988). Monique Wittig, for example, incorporates new symbolic objects from contemporary technology to revise her narrative form. Much of Black lesbian writing radically transforms the field of literary studies by incorporating material from Blues and spirituality, as, for instance, in the poetry of Audre Lorde. There are many earlier examples of lesbian linguistic invention: for example, Sylvia Townsend Warner's amazing *The Cat's Cradle Book* (1960) turns cat into a metaphor for lesbian writing because cat is not a recognised language. Warner created the languages of witches and cats as minority languages precisely to highlight the need for new literary grammars and syntax. The lesson to be drawn from these examples is that one overriding function of lesbian criticism must be to displace existing oppositions between major and minor in order to constitute a lesbian literary identity; for example, by deliberately confusing animal/spiritual/human as Wittig and Warner so deftly do.

MODERNISM

A crucial task of lesbian criticism is the construction of a fuller intellectual history of lesbian writing. Lesbian critics writing about literary periods have focused on modernism in order to reject the idea that the lesbian writer is an isolated self. Their goal is to disrupt processes of canonisation in which James Joyce, Ezra Pound and T. S. Eliot are the only masters of modernism (with a fleeting nod to Virginia Woolf's 'stream of consciousness') by exposing the androcentricity of what has become a 'universal' tradition. History matters to lesbian critics because by restoring lesbian writers to history and mapping the conceptual organisations which first excluded lesbian writers, critics can help us understand the difficulties writers experienced trying to represent 'lesbian' in periods when such experience lacked a language. For example, Gertrude Stein's use of codes points to the fact that lesbian representations always depend on new structures and figures. In addition, whether writing is pre- or post-Freud needs clearly pinpointing historically. For example, Sonja Ruehl's 'Inverts and Experts: Radclyffe Hall and the Lesbian Identity' (1982) reveals the limited range of categories which were historically available to Radclyffe Hall. Ruehl shows how Hall's definitions of lesbian as a 'congenital invert' – as a separate sexual group – were drawn from contemporary medical discourse.

Modernism is a period in which lesbian women were prominent both as writers, and as patrons of other writers. Americans such as Gertrude Stein, Djuna Barnes and Sylvia Beach played a crucial role in the development of modernism in Paris both by supporting the careers of James Joyce and Ernest Hemingway and also by themselves creating rich and experimental literary forms; for example, Barnes's *Nightwood* (1936). Lesbian criticism starts from the position that the literary history of modernism needs to be reconceptualised. For instance, lesbian modernist writers such as Natalie Barney deliberately drew on decadent and symbolist poetry of the 1890s – a recognisably *homosexual* culture – in order to create a lesbian writing rather than attending to abstraction or avant-garde forms then current (see Elliott and Wallace, 1992).

While lesbian critics reconceptualise artistic periods and movements, other lesbian critics work to retrieve a mythical matriarchal, lesbian past. For example, the Black lesbian poet, Audre Lorde, sets her work into what she calls a 'time tension' with African myths, particularly with those of her *ancestral* 'home', Dahomey. Further examples of other lesbian critical themes are an attention to family histories. In 'Lesbian Identity and Autobiographical Difference(s)' (1988) Biddy Martin draws attention to the complex and critical ways in which families figure in lesbian life histories. For psychoanalytic and historical reasons, mothering and the reproduction of mothering create more permeable ego boundaries in women than men. The French feminist theorist, Luce Irigaray, sheds light on why a complex pattern of mother/daughter relations might act as a metaphor for and inform lesbian relations. She argues that the representation of lesbian relations and desires expresses a fundamental rebellion to masculine descriptions and therefore expresses an undeniable contrast to heterosexuality. For example, lesbian poetry often involves a return to the mother. As Adrienne Rich shows in 'Twenty-One Love Poems' the bonds between mothers and daughters are reproduced in the erotic passion of women-identified women. Lesbian writers described how this creative, mothering nexus permeates contemporary lesbian thought. Audre Lorde has invented a new critical term for this kind of metaphorical autobiography – 'biomythography'. What biomythography describes are the composite mother/daughter relations and myths and fantasies which blur the binary between 'fact' and 'fiction'. In *Zami*, for example, Lorde both connects with and deconstructs a mothering 'ethic'.

BONNIE ZIMMERMAN

The task of thinking through how lesbian criticism might incorporate ideas about women's body, language and sexuality into cultural criticism has been aided immeasurably by Bonnie Zimmerman's work. In two extensive essays 'Exiting from Patriarchy: The Lesbian Novel of Development' (1983) and 'What Has Never Been: An Overview of Lesbian Feminist Criticism' (1985) and the book *The Safe Sea of Women: Lesbian Fiction 1969–1989* (1991), Zimmerman brought renewed attention to lesbian culture. Rather than focusing on any single feature of lesbianism, Zimmerman studies lesbians' contribution to literature as part of a collective growing into awareness. 'What Has Never Been' shows how the denial of lesbian artistic and aesthetic expression and the suppression of lesbian literary history has been as much a part of some contemporary feminist criticism as a feature of traditional literary studies. Lesbian efforts to name and describe a literary culture have met with much resistance. 'Lesbian' writing is itself a disputed genre. There is tremendous difficulty, Zimmerman acknowledges, in defining a 'lesbian' style since many women writers cannot be identified as lesbian. That is, lesbian criticism could be said to start from the negative lack of knowledge of who *are* all the lesbian writing women as well as being in some critical doubt as to the nature of a lesbian style.

Zimmerman describes lesbian writing as narratives bound by differing cultural and historical traditions. *Safe Sea* restores lesbian women's texts to literary history and describes the conceptual categories this new literary agenda will need. Zimmerman makes a strong case for a tradition of lesbian writing with its own patterns of images, preferred genres and themes as a starting-point from which all feminist criticism can challenge the heterosexist assumptions of literary studies. For example, Zimmerman describes the particular uses of tropes and metaphors of sight and sensation in lesbian texts. She replaces traditional literary periods with the more important stages in *lesbian* literary history, stages which construct a different story of a growth into consciousness. For example, the 1970s represent a prolonged phase of 'coming out' writing, what might be called the lesbian Bildungsroman, which describes powerful bonds between lesbian women.

Lesbian criticism, like the favoured lesbian genre of utopias, is a vision of the future. In the next phase, fiction writers Alice B. Sheldon (pseudonym James Tiptree Jr) in 'With Delicate Mad Hands' (1981) and Joanna Russ in *The Female Man* (1975) created new forms of sexuality, in fantasies of all-female worlds.

In the 1980s women of colour played a key role in challenging a unified and universal lesbian identity, in texts such as *This Bridge Called My Back* (1981) edited by Cherrie Moraga and Gloria Anzaldúa. *This Bridge* attacked literary racism: the assumption that lesbian experience was similar (usually that of white middle-class lesbians). The important aim of this critique is to create a more flexible lesbian literary identity (for example, 'the new mestiza'), one able to include connections between lesbian women of different cultures and ethnicities; between lesbian and gay fiction; and one open to innovative and experimental techniques, exemplified in Bertha Harris's vanguard novel, *Lover* (1976). These phases, Zimmerman argues, correspond to social and political changes; for example, the hostile debates in the 1970s between lesbian radicals and heterosexual feminists. Accordingly Zimmerman attends to the political and social implications of *claiming* a lesbian identity: for some lesbian writers (such as contributors to coming out stories) lesbian writing grew out of feminism and therefore represents a political choice; and metaphors of space and position now dominate lesbian criticism, revealing a switch in focus from essential experience to historical/social contexts.

Zimmerman's paradigm, while useful for lesbian literary history, is one of a range of possible critical options. Zimmerman herself tends to measure her writers against an ideal of lesbian community and self-development belonging to the 1970s, and there are other, and theoretical, lesbian methodologies.

QUEER THEORY AND EVE KOSOFSKY SEDGWICK

Currently gender studies includes work on gay, or queer theory. Eve Kosofsky Sedgwick's *Between Men* (1989) and *The Epistemology of the Closet* (1990) offer some challenges to lesbian criticism's generalisations about non-heterosexual experience. In these texts Sedgwick describes the literary histories of homophobia and misogyny but does not address lesbian experience directly. 'Lesbian' is a marked absence in both texts but Sedgwick claims that this is due to the fact that the term 'homosocial' used to describe women's friendships, need not be dichotomised against homosexual (Sedgwick, 1990, p. 3). Instead, homosexual textuality is opposed to heterosexual textuality. As Sedgwick argues 'the tensions implicit in the male-male bond are spatially connected . . . while the tensions of the male-female bond are temporally connected' (Sedgwick, 1990, p. 45).

There are similarities between Adrienne Rich's notion of a lesbian continuum and Sedgwick's characterisation of a homosocial continuum. Sedgwick is also in debt to Nancy Chodorow,

Dorothy Dinnerstein and Luce Irigaray's differing accounts of the relationship between social/cultural power and gender. *Between Men* wends its way from Shakespeare's sonnets, Wycherley's *The Country Wife*, Sterne's *A Sentimental Journey*, the Gothic to the Victorians, Tennyson and Dickens. *Epistemology of the Closet* follows chronologically to examine late nineteenth- and early twentieth-century writers including Melville, James and Proust. Both books describe the 'hidden' topic of literature which is male bonding. Sedgwick argues that cultural constructions of homophobia occur in organisational binaries such as innocence/initiation; sincerity/sentimentality, as well as in the more obvious binaries of growth/decadence. One result of Sedgwick's claim is a shift in attention from individual writers to *processes* of knowing in Western culture. As Sedgwick traces these binaries she utilises diverse techniques from deconstruction to a focus on key words, much like Paulo Freire's use of 'generative themes' in his pedagogy. For example, Sedgwick argues that the phrase 'a man's home is his castle' is a condensed ideological construction, and as the title of her second book suggests, Sedgwick analyses 'closet' as a key metaphor of cultural control. Sedgwick, together with other queer theorists, aims to take gay criticism beyond essentialist and social constructionist explanations. For instance, queer theory studies literary 'perversions' in the Renaissance, not only as a cultural phenomenon, but as constituting a linguistic transgression of heterosexual norms. Yet it must be noted that Sedgwick's inattention to the specificities of lesbian culture make her work of value more for its deconstruction of phallic and feminine imagery than for its *construction* of an identifiable lesbian criticism. The texts lack the autobiographic perceptions which brighten lesbian criticism, nor does Sedgwick have the historical reach of Faderman and other earlier critics.

JANE RULE

The first book to describe a lesbian literary tradition was Jane Rule's *Lesbian Images* (1975). Rule's book is a landmark text. As Bonnie Zimmerman points out 'it took five years for another complete book – Faderman's – to appear' (Zimmerman, 1991, p.

188). *Lesbian Images* describes the writing careers and relationships of Gertrude Stein, Ivy Compton-Burnett, Violette Leduc, May Sarton and Maureen Duffy, among others. The book has an evolutionary perspective, tracing the gradual emergence of lesbian writing from the constraints of patriarchy. But *Lesbian Images* is itself a vivid early example of that more multigeneric criticism which has since transformed lesbian studies and challenges the major discourses of Western thought. Rule prefaces her literary criticism with three key chapters: her autobiography; a historical account of homosexuality and its suppression by different religions; and the adoption of 'religious' homophobia by medicine and psychiatry. Each subsequent chapter offers a full survey of a writer's career interspersed with pointed quotations from secondary sources including autobiographies and letters. If the title of the book places it firmly in its moment when women's studies was devoted to 'images of women' courses, and Rule believes too firmly in the individuality of each positive image, Rule's preface marks out a larger intent.

Rule begins with a witty account of her own growing sense of sexual preference, her 'gauche' six-foot adolescent body and her outrage that this shape 'if a boy's', would be considered graceful. Rule's aim, like Virginia Woolf's, is to create 'a common reader or not so uncommon reader' hinting at a more inclusive lesbian audience. But there is more at work in these introductory chapters. It is no accident that Rule starts with autobiography. By this time, the 'coming out' story had become a standard introduction to many lesbian texts. But Rule includes the 'common' reader with direct questions, jokes and asides: 'Roasted Freud is by now as common and cheaper than hamburger and, when served, in danger of dulling the appetite for any subject' (Rule, 1975, p. 35).

Jane Rule is a well-known Canadian novelist as well as a critic. Her fiction incorporates many of her critical techniques. For example, *Contract with the World* (1980) is an open-ended narrative which deliberately refuses positive lesbian role models. Indeed, Rule took the unusual step, before publication, of announcing in her column in the gay press her reasons for avoiding simplistic, positive heroines, because she wanted to carry collectively her 'common' readers with her.

The first chapters of *Lesbian Images* set the agenda. It is as if Rule can tackle lesbian literary criticism only if supported by irrefutable evidence of homophobia and therefore the need for a lesbian politics. But these chapters are remarkably prophetic of lesbian critical concerns to come. 'Myth and Morality' describes homosexual practices in ancient Greece, the Middle East and the relation between laws, language and cultural practices; for example, the dialectic between Israelite laws and nomadism. Like Mary Daly, Rule points to the rigid gender roles at the centre of phallocratic thinking. The problem, as Rule sees it, is that the symbol systems and conceptual apparatuses of Judaism and Christianity are masculine – a sexist and partial 'net of meanings'. The chief victims of religious homophobia are lesbians.

Chapter two is a vivid and pointed account of sexology from Freud to Helene Deutsch. Rule's *bête noire* is the contemporary sexologist Charlotte Wolff and her book *Love between Women* (1972), which Rule believes misuses biological and naturalisation theories. While Rule's imputation of psychiatric moralism to Freud is perhaps unfair, certainly psychiatry shares with Christianity an absurd and homophobic treatment of gays, at one time, for example, associating homosexuality with left-handedness. Gloria Anzaldúa beautifully ironised that absurdity into a 'reverse discourse' in *Borderlands* (1987) with her celebratory left-handed lesbian world.

Rule develops her interest in more fluid representations of gender in the essay 'The Practice of Writing' (1976). Like Cixous in 'The Character of "Character" ' Rule dislikes the idea that authors should own 'the sexualities' of their characters; 'The long tradition of fiction with a central character around whom all others must find their secondary place supports hierarchies I don't find interesting' (Rule, 1976, pp. 34–5). Similarly, Rule's novel *Against the Season* works to undo stereotypes of older lesbians.

In Rule's last chapter she consciously questions her own critical interest in individual writers, arguing that this focus may be an inadequate way of illustrating historical change. Describing contemporary nonfiction lesbian writing, Rule makes a strong plea for a *community* of interest and a toleration of diversity in the face of what she sees as the recent 'violence' of radical lesbians. For example, Rule praises Del Martin's and Phyllis Lyon's *Lesbian/Woman* for its willingness to describe diverse sexual practices. She has a generous concern for that 'larger' feminist movement. Her novel *The Young In One Another's Arms* (1977) describes voluntary outcasts for whom lesbianism is one part of self-identity but not a more privileged vision. Throughout her critical and in her creative work Rule insists on sexually inflecting questions of individual, historical and literary representations.

Ellen Moers's *Literary Women* (1977) was published immediately after *Lesbian Images*. The chronological juxtaposition of the two books marks out Rule's more interactive and distinctive criticism from her neighbouring American's narrow liberalisms. Like Rule, Moers is refreshingly multinational, juxtaposing George Sand with Jane Austen, Harriet Beecher Stowe with George Eliot. In addition, Moers's thematic organisation (for example, her focus on metaphors of monsters, travel, childhood and landscape) allows her to flag matrilineal connections between women writers like Stowe and Eliot.

Yet the exclusions of *Literary Women* raise vital questions for feminist criticism. Moers discusses a women's tradition without reference to the work of Black women and lesbian women, Black or white. She uses her 'master's tools' to canonise white heterosexual writers and, like the master, uses no modifiers in her title to indicate the absence of women of difference. As Barbara Smith points out 'Moers includes the names of four Black and one Puertoriqūena writer in her seventy pages of bibliographic notes and does not deal at all with Third World women' (Smith, 1977, p. 5). Moers's heterosexism has been described as 'glaring' by Elly Bulkin and Bonnie Zimmerman, among others. For example, Moers includes lesbians under the heading of 'Freaks'. Yet, despite its suspect value-ridden selections, it is Moers's *Literary Women*, not Rule's *Lesbian Images*, which is generally recognised as a 'foremother' text of second-wave feminist literary criticism.

Of course, like many women new to feminism I remember my delight when first reading Moers's earlier version of her Rossetti chapter in *The New York Review of Books* and my thankful pleasure that at last women's special experiences of sexual harassment could be discussed in relation to literary representations. Despite this, the fact that Moers's text, not Rule's *Lesbian Images*, is regarded as one of the first examples of second-wave feminist literary criticism, demands challenge here. *Literary Women* does not attempt that more fundamental reshaping of the literary canon undertaken by Jane Rule, by Adrienne Rich's pathbreaking essay 'When We Dead Awaken: Writing as Revision' and by other lesbian criticism.

CATHARINE STIMPSON

In 1975 Catharine Stimpson founded what became *the* major American journal of feminist criticism, *Signs*. Stimpson's essays over the intervening years are collected in *Where the Meanings Are* (1988). Stimpson's punning title refers to Maurice Sendak's irreverent and now classic children's book, *Where the Wild Things Are*, to suggest that a similar 'wildness' and utopianism mark lesbian feminist criticism. The multilevel quality of Stimpson's writing, her use of scientific with organic metaphors and images of monstrosity dramatise the mobility of lesbian readings.

Stimpson argues that feminist criticism should have four features. First, it should reinscribe 'the pain we inflict on each other'. Second, critics should calibrate how culture can transcend that path. Third, the literary text is autonomous only in the sense that a flower is autonomous 'after we have picked it'. Finally, criticism must polyphonously incorporate diverse voices. Languages are like the 'spirals of DNA' playing against differences but not with any *innate* meaning because, as Stimpson resonantly suggests, DNA may be 'the letter of the current law of molecular biology, but they are letters first' (Stimpson, 1988, p. xviii). Stimpson's scientific vocabulary signals a condensed battle with critical meanings. Part of her task, as she sees it, is to craft a transformed account of lesbian writing in an inventive effort to elude the restrictions of traditional literary criticism. Her early essay 'The Androgyne and the Homosexual' (1974) focuses on the given taxonomies of both figures and on the 'questionable logic' against which the

'New Feminism' has bred the political 'lesbian'. Stimpson may or may not be informed about British New Feminist debates of the 1930s but the term has an equivalent appropriateness in the way both 'New Feminisms' attempted to map out a specifically gendered identity for women. Stimpson looks to science fiction, to LeGuin's *The Left Hand of Darkness* (1969), for more speculative representations of sexual identity just as she looks psychoanalytically to 'interior space' as her introductory reference to *Where the Wild Things Are* reveals.

The 'Zero Degree Deviancy: Lesbian Novel in English' (1981) contains a fuller thinking through of that speculation. The title, drawn from Barthes' *Writing Degree Zero*, is inspired by the linguistic similarity of 'zero' and 'code'. The Arab *sifr* (empty space) leads into the English 'cipher', a metaphor for the way in which lesbian writers in hostile cultures often need to write obliquely in ciphers. The lesbian novels which Stimpson surveys and categorises are lesbian romanticism (*Orlando*), lesbian realism (*The Autobiography of Alice B. Toklas*) as well as novels by supposed heterosexuals (*The Group*) through to the confident picaresques, *Rubyfruit Jungle* and *Riverfinger Woman*. The particular theme Stimpson notes in all of these texts is the mother 'at the heart of the labyrinth'. Stimpson's constant references to the half-beast Minotaur, to the Wild Things, combined with a vocabulary drawn from monstrosity, myth, science and biology match stylistically her view of lesbian writers as literary outsiders. In the last essay which is about contemporary feminism Stimpson again uses a striking visual image, a then current feminist postcard which transposes Nancy and Ronald Reagan's features onto each other's bodies. Spreading luxuriously from this image Stimpson addresses accounts of women's difference by Carol Gilligan and Jean Baker Miller among others and concludes, in a beautiful circular gesture, that feminist criticism needs gender 'switch points' rather than essentialism. Stimpson's lively style is a vivid example of the 'difference' of lesbian criticism. As she argues, feminist criticism must come to terms with these notions of lesbian fluidity and 'monstrosity' rather than holding up 'the silver cross of tradition before the werewolf of new syllabi' (Stimpson, 1988, p. xx).

MARY DALY

The American critic closest to Hélène Cixous is Mary Daly, who in taking the male Logos back to its roots has similarly articulated a women's language and its linguistic possibilities.

Daly is a Professor of theology who in her first major work, *Beyond God the Father* (1973), argued that patriarchal culture operates a binary system of rigid masculine and feminine gender roles. One of the main ways in which patriarchy imposes this system is by creating a form of 'I–It' thinking in which males are I (or subjects) and women are It (or objects). It is Daly's stark rejection of the power of patriarchal language which directs her criticism, though she agrees that it is impossible to create an absolutely 'new' language.

Her books are lessons in how to find in patriarchal language images and signs of those matriarchal sources which patriarchy disguises. For example, Daly (1984) describes how patriarchal archetypes like the Virgin Mary are distorted versions of what she calls living moving 'Archimages' – which rhymes with 'rages'. Of course, there are problems in any insistence that there was a matriarchal and hence essentially feminine style. This perpetuates long-held stereotypes about women as natural and presocial. A single *écriture féminine* can flatten out the linguistic differences *between* women.

Daly's most sustained rejection of male discourse is in the astonishing *Gyn/Ecology* (1978) and its successor volume, *Pure Lust* (1984). *Gyn/Ecology* describes the sadistic practices suffered by women in patriarchy which include witch-burning and clitoridectomy. Daly makes clear the relevance of this institutional and personal sexual violence to language study. For these atrocities to succeed, she argues, they need to be performed with rituals and ceremonies. Daly argues that ritualistic sexual practices are cultural forms with a similar shape to the orderliness and rituals of patriarchal writings.

Finally, she moves outside male-centred, binary logic altogether into a new female syntax. *Gyn/Ecology* and *Pure Lust* are the most notable example of *écriture féminine* that we have to date, and the most exciting. Daly changes syntax, the whole process of language, not just vocabulary. We must, she claims, connect our language with our bodies to 're-member the dismembered body of our heritage' (1978, p. 23). Daly takes on the political implications of vocabulary change in a quest, like Adrienne Rich, for a common language of women. Her technique is to fragment standard language into its parts, 'departments which depart from departments' and replace it with the female continuity of the solidus (1978, p. xiv). It may seem paradoxical to want a holistic woman's world yet take a path to it by word-splitting and fragmentation, but Daly has politicised etymology. She expands the elements of a word both in form and sense. *Gyn/Ecology* itself, Daly claims, is a 'gynocentric manifestation of the Intransitive Verb' (Daly, 1978, p. 23). Changing nouns to verbs is more than a linguistic game: it emphasises the importance of action. Prefixes particularly interest her. She employs alternative meanings for prefixes as 're-cover actually says "cover again" ' (1978, p. 24). One characteristic of prefixes is, of course, that they act to intensify nouns. So by separating out prefixes from what Daly understands to be patriarchal nouns, she begins the disempowerment of male discourse.

Traditional dictionaries always divide vocabulary into racial groups – those words native to the speaker and those taken from foreign 'intruders'. Mary Daly uses dictionaries as semantic resources but proposes an alternative and feminist classification of language. *Gyn/Ecology*, for example, ends not only with a customary general index but adds to it an 'index of new words'. Language change is Daly's theme from beginning to end. One outstanding feature of her approach is her recognition of the value of many vowels normally obscure since unstressed, for example, 'a-mazing'. Again, hyphens enable Daly to create new double forms, like 'Crone-logical', highlighting differences of meaning since a hyphen can add clarity to, or emphasise, the function of the prefix.

Gyn/Ecology is nothing less than a fresh semantics. Daly is not, detective-like, simply collecting evidence of male linguistic crimes but conducting a full enquiry into language by analysing as far as she can some of the issues that are involved in language choices. In her enquiry Daly therefore focuses on words which relate to the central experiences of women, which involve our ideas and values, in order to attack the 'shared' meaning of words in general used by men. Hers is an attack on the possession of meaning by men, which is bound up with a certain way of seeing gender. To Daly, vocabulary control is the prime element of male power.

Critics who take an empirical approach to semantic change and linguistic history might object that Daly does not describe specific sites for her revolution. They could claim that Daly ignores the way feminist discourses still have to circulate through the gate-keeping academic world of men. Daly would retort that the aim of feminist criticism is to replace male power, not to make compromises with it.

Despite Daly's unique verbal richness, however, her books are primarily philological and etymological, with the effect that she is much better at dealing with linguistic variations than with making connections. But she is making a specialised analysis of what is involved in meaning. To pick out a word's own internal structure is a necessary start to understanding the larger system of language itself, especially if you believe, as Daly does, that patriarchal controls derive from the construction of language. The importance of naming patriarchy is that 'they–in effect– drop dead' in what she calls a criticism of 'Positive Spooking'. In other words, Daly is trying to make linguistic judgements be judgements about sexual politics: 'Exorcism requires naming this environment of spirit/mind rape, refusing to be receptacles for semantic semen' (Daly, 1978, p. 324). This is language as a sexual battleground. One of Daly's key strengths, it seems to me, is her refusal to be silenced, her refusal of absences. Daly shows how a language of the body can communicate, can serve women's interests. To use a sexualised semantics is not necessarily to 'surrender' to essentialism. Daly's is a mature style which adds the resources of language to her intensity and precision about women's experiences.

One example of how Daly's ideas might work in literary criticism is to use her account of gendered semantics to focus on textual slippages. Feminist criticism can speak out from the gaps in texts to subvert traditional ways of reading. For example, Jean Rhys deliberately disrupts her novels with ellipses to hint at the disrupted psyches of her heroines. We can read texts not so much for what happens but for what is not happening – in the background of textual language and the original meanings of vocabulary. The text becomes what can only be 'got at' sideways in the margins. For example, Virginia Woolf frequently constructs monologues where the speaker slips in and out of character, to point to the impossibility of speaking in single names.

Mary Daly unites the psychological with the physical in her concept of a 'Hagocentric psychic space' (1978, p. 341). She argues that feminist criticism will help us break out of our mental set through focusing on forms of meaning which differ from the cognitive. Glances, touch, the not-said in narrative and semiotic spaces can reveal women's psyche and multiple identities. Mary Daly suggests that a useful critical technique is to build absences by 'paring away the layers of false selves from the Self' (1978, p. 381). Eventually she opts for an entirely separate women's culture in the 'Otherworld' journey of *Pure Lust*.

Yet, although Daly argues that a women's language will develop from women's own meaning-making, only rarely does she herself engage in dialogue with other women, particularly non-white women. This inattention to difference is the very persuasive point of Audre Lorde's essay, 'An Open Letter to Mary Daly'. Here Lorde claims that Daly's *Gyn/Ecology* misrepresents Black women's culture by presenting Black women only as victims (for example, of genital mutilation) and not as warriors and goddesses. As Lorde points out, Black women are continually creating positive images of Black womanhood in proverbs and stories as well as in Black activism. From a different direction Rosi Braidotti argues that Daly re-names only at the level of lexicon, subverting the signs but not the codes (Braidotti, 1991, p. 207). Yet though arguably Daly's Eurocentrism is fraught with consequences, *Gyn/Ecology* does describe a way of claiming a language, a new female symbolic, a new culture and revivified forms of thinking and action ('Spinning' and 'Spooking'). Race, class and institutional analyses do not often emerge as issues in Daly's writing. As a result Daly may be in danger, as Braidotti claims, of leading women back into 'meta- and supra-terrestrial beliefs' (Braidotti, 1991, p. 207). Daly's elaboration of a discursive territory avoids concrete instances of contemporary racial difference, but it is by no means inattentive to history. For example, Daly describes instances of white complicity in the torture of Black slaves citing the case of Sarah M. Grimké (Daly, 1984, p. 376). She also insists on the need to understand the *connections* between language, the text in which language appears, and the *social context* which produces both language and text. For example, Daly claims that *The Second Sex* is a great feminist work precisely because 'it helped to generate atmosphere', because it 'partially broke the Terrible Taboo' (Daly, 1984, p. 374).

In her analyses, Daly draws on and refers to a long-term history of 'Be-Friending' and desire between women, as an alternative to, and even a replacement for, patriarchal sexuality. Her deconstructions of patriarchal sexual violence and reconstructions of women's desires are transuniversal but are an original lesbian critique. What future role a feminist language/ dictionary could have is not fully clear. But Daly's exposure of the assumptions behind textual processes and her account of women-identified women's 'spiralling' can help to create a 'transformation whose idea and reality, whose time has come' (Daly, 1984, p. 410).

ADRIENNE RICH

Adrienne Rich has a firm sense of her 'politics of location' in contemporary feminism. Her criticism contains a variety of feminist ideas which Rich calls her 'Re-vision', or rewriting, of patriarchal culture: about women's oppression, male violence and racism. The question of motherhood, in *Of Woman Born* (1976), has been an extraordinarily fruitful topic for Rich who argues that mothers are the repressed subject in patriarchy. In *On Lies, Secrets, Silence* (1980), in 'Blood, Bread and Poetry' (1983), and later essays in *Signs* and elsewhere, Rich takes that relation between reproduction and sexuality into a more radical definition of difference. She has developed complex arguments about the differences between women, as well as between women and men, and thus challenges many normative values even in contemporary feminism.

Affiliation with women stirs Rich more than any other experience (after childbirth). In the 1974 version of her *Selected Poems* she altered the pronouns of protagonists to women. She describes many different kinds of women's groups, from contemporary Cambridge women in *Of Woman Born* to the nineteenth-century friendship of Elizabeth Stanton and Susan B. Anthony in *On Lies, Secrets, Silence*. Rich describes these groups as an alternative feminist intellectual tradition based on friendship: 'to name and found a culture of our own means a real break from the passivity of the twentieth-century Western mind' (Rich, 1980b, p. 13). The creation of a women's culture is the only necessary antidote to individualism.

Rich's call for a separate, female-identified physical and semantic space brings her close to the feminism of writers like Mary Daly and Luce Irigaray. But although she describes that space as fundamental to feminism, it is not necessarily a singular constituent. For example, Rich, unlike Mary Daly, examines in detail the interrelationship between socialisation and psychical patterns. And Rich's plans for alternative social models are her best contribution to that more expansive feminist critique.

In 'Toward a Woman-Centered University' Rich outlines her idea of a women's community:

> If a truly universal and excellent network of childcare can begin to develop, if women in sufficient numbers pervade the University at all levels . . . there is a strong chance that in our own time we would begin to see some true 'universality' of values emerging from the inadequate and distorted corpus of patriarchal knowledge. (Rich (1980b) pp. 154–5)

Rich adopts Virginia Woolf's three main techniques – subvert from within, be selective and validate women's personal experience – but moves ahead of Woolf into strategic planning. The full account reads very like Catherine Beecher Stowe or Dolores Hayden's architectural models of women's communities. Rich is very close to anarcho-feminism in her ideas of local and organisational pluralism.

In a later review in *Ms* Adrienne Rich clarifies this anarchist impulse and ties her view of women's culture more closely to literature:

> This new culture, created and defined by women, is the great phenomenon of our century. I believe that in any genuinely human retrospect it will loom above two world wars, and several socialist

revolutions . . . Women's art, though created in solitude, wells up out of community . . . and, by its very existence, it strengthens the network of the community. (Rich (1977), p. 106)

To Rich, the art/politics matrix of women's networks will ultimately prove to be the most significant political and cultural form in our time.

Why writing is so important for women, Rich argues, is because it can act as a bridge between women. Literary criticism provides Rich with the opportunity to adopt a typical stance of the divinating American – a Whitmanesque critic as seer.

PROBLEMATISING OF HETEROSEXUALITY

When feminists first spoke of 'difference' it was of women's difference from men. The move to defining a 'different' and lesbian identity is the work of Rich's key essay 'Compulsory Heterosexuality and Lesbian Existence' (1980). Lesbian criticism problematised heterosexuality by *politicising* heterosexuality. If heterosexuality is constructed and not 'natural', then it is immediately open to political thinking and reform. As Rich suggests in her conversation with Marline Packwood, lesbian identity is a necessary part of radical feminism: 'I think it has to be about transformation. And that's where I see lesbianism and feminism having very common ground' (Rich, 1981b, p. 14). Up to this point, feminist writing about sexuality focused largely on the relation between reproduction and social controls. Rich's essay rethinks 'difference', taking the term away from male/ female binaries. Rich's lesbian criticism marks a significant problematising of heterosexuality in several ways. First, she begins from the position that 'masculine' and 'feminine' are only the constructed binary oppositions of modern sexuality. Second, she argues that women's bonding might release new forms of sexuality. Finally, she claims that literature and textuality offer spaces for the metaphoric reshaping of sexual identities. The representation, or discussion, of lesbian sexuality implicitly problematises heterosexuality by, as Luce Irigaray suggests, removing women from the commodity exchange, as well as challenging the ways in which sexuality and gender are traditionally tied together.

Adrienne Rich built on de Beauvoir's thesis that women are originally homosexual, but she moved on to focus on elements such as desire and fantasy, which would be the special contribution of lesbian criticism to feminism. She was stepping into an area riddled with contradictions. What enables her to talk about 'difference' with coherence is 'a kind of clarity that we get from being that extra degree an outsider' (Rich, 1981b, p. 14). Rich's account of 'lesbian' is both historical and literary:

> Lesbian existence suggests both the fact of the historical presence of lesbians and our continuing creation of the meaning of that existence. I mean the term 'lesbian continuum' to include a range – through each woman's life and throughout history – of woman-identified experience, not simply the fact that a woman has had or consciously desired genital sexual experience with another woman. (Rich (1980a) p. 156)

Rich believes that lesbianism is part of a general female experience. She does not condemn heterosexual relationships *per se*, since she believes that patriarchy has, for too long, imposed arbitrary and sexual dichotomies (lesbian *or* heterosexual) which have no meaning. The eradication of false dichotomies is, as usual, part of Rich's critical aim. She *inverts* our 'normal' way of thinking by asking the *faux naif* and very resonating question: 'If women are the earliest sources of emotional caring and physical nurture . . . why in fact women would ever redirect (to men)' (Rich, 1980a, p. 145). The future for feminist criticism, Rich concludes, is to delineate a lesbian continuum and to unveil and describe the cultural mystification of lesbianism.

This has important consequences for feminist analysis. When Rich talks about the construction of lesbianism she means a psychic and literary construction as well as a social one. The taking up of 'lesbian' or 'heterosexual' positions, she rightly sees, reproduces oppression. 'Lesbianism' depends on the ever-present heterosexual order of reality. But by greatly enlarging the categories of 'lesbianism', and hence redrawing its system of representation, Rich can set up contradictions and distinctions which may alter patriarchal ideology as well as heterosexuality.

'Compulsory Heterosexuality and Lesbian Existence' sought to give feminism a new dynamic. The redrawing of sexual maps has, of course, been a central project of cultural criticism from Michel Foucault on. Both Foucault and Rich write about images of male power and the way in which power operates. For both, sexuality is controlled and regulated by capitalism. For both, deconstructing sexuality is a key to unlocking power because sexuality links otherwise disparate discourses. Where Rich differs from Foucault is that she does not assume that the *main* characteristic of sexuality is the way patriarchy encouraged sexual confessions (psychoanalyis) to codify social practices. To Rich, the main characteristic of contemporary sexuality is male violence. Lesbianism, she feels, is especially hated in patriarchy and, therefore, unlike Foucault who understands 'homosexual difference' as a patriarchal construction, Rich believes that lesbians *do* need, intensely need, to create separate spaces of 'difference'.

The essay provoked a great deal of debate among feminists. For example, Cora Kaplan in 'Wild Nights: Pleasure/Sexuality/Feminism' (in *Formations of Pleasure*, 1983) usefully compares Wollstonecraft and Rich in an interesting essay about sexuality. However, Kaplan makes two unjustifiable attacks. She claims that Rich *totally* condemns heterosexuality and, second, that Rich presents only abstract women. The first claim, as I have demonstrated textually, is untrue. The second is particularly unfair since Rich 'enters' her text only via the texts of other writers, all carefully referenced, interspersing academic theories with quotations in her usual vivid accessible fashion.

Rich does not imply that *only* heterosexual relations are distorted by power differentials, an implication which would prevent a recognition that lesbian relations might equally be structured by power inequities. However, Rich does describe sexuality as a driving force constituting some 'essential' truth about the human individual. It is an odd jump for Rich to take, with her brilliant account of anthropology in *Of Woman Born*. Surely the central triumph of feminist anthropology has been to prove that 'human nature' is a cultural construct.

But in a heightened form Rich describes the cultural-linguistic struggle of lesbianism. For this reason Rich is sometimes verbally aggressive, since her situation, after all, is objectively violent. The essay is a clear statement about the meaning of language as social practice and the role of lesbian criticism.

Lesbian identity cannot have meaning without a sustaining culture. It is impossible to use the word 'lesbian' without also using imagery, definitions and concepts. So lesbian criticism is about the construction of a viable, cultural language. Lesbian criticism can concentrate on notions of masculinity and femininity and their representations in literature, and clarify the arbitrary assignation of gender; it can associate more directly with the languages of ethnic or minority groups; it can evoke a community whose vitality is genuinely erotic. Rich quotes another lesbian poet, Audre Lorde: 'as Audre Lorde has described it (the energy) omnipresent in "the sharing of joy, whether physical, emotional, psychic", and in the sharing of work; as the empowering joy' (Rich, 1980a, p. 158). Rich's addition of libidinal work to Lorde's libidinal leisure puts her into an anarchist line stretching from Fourier. It is a potent and productive notion of critical process.

It is also a major ideological advance in feminist criticism. Lesbian criticism grasped the point very early that sexism and racism are totally interdependent. Rich writes continually about the connection betwen sexism, racism and homophobia. In *Of Woman Born* she describes the continuum of Black and white women's lives:

> Neither the 'pure' nor the 'lascivious' woman, neither the so-called mistress nor the slave woman, neither the woman praised for reducing herself to a brood animal nor the woman scorned and penalized as an 'old maid' or a 'dyke', has had any real autonomy or selfhood to gain from this subversion of the female body (and hence of the female mind). (Rich (1976) p. 35)

What is being argued here is that the construction of sexual difference by male violence is into a series of dehumanised and meaningless definitions. That issue of language is the focus of Rich's essay 'What Does Separatism Mean?' Here Rich provides a model list of readings about separatism, all meticulously documented. Separatism is simultaneously a linguistic and a territorial event – a 'space' where women can '*bear witness*' to each other (Rich, 1981a, p. 88). All the italicised vocabulary, the most intense statements, are about writing style, voice and meaning. Rich's conclusion is not to conclude. The title of the essay is 'Notes . . .' and the volatility of separatism is coded in the *process* of language 'about how and when and with what kinds of conscious identity it is practised' (Rich, 1981a, p. 90).

In a *Spare Rib* interview, Rich argues that 'When we really begin to understand fully how race and sex are enmeshed we will understand things about both of them that we don't yet understand' (Rich, 1981b, p. 15). She understands that existing concepts of racism and sexism are inadequate. Only by examining the workings of particular practices in past and contemporary cultures can we get at the unexpected character of sexual difference. The difficult problem, for feminist criticism, is how to analyse the effects of difference in everything from social policy to artistic practices. Criticism has to be about sexual politics to be feminist and it has to be about culture: ' "A Woman Is Talking to Death" is both a political poem and a love poem. I mean, that it is a political poem to the extent that it is a love poem, and a love poem insofar as it is political' (Rich, 1980a, p. 251).

For Rich 'difference' is a source of eroticism and dialogue between women, and therefore of new ideas for criticism:

> If we conceive of feminism as more than a frivolous label, if we conceive of it as an ethics, a methodology, a more complex way of thinking about, thus more responsibly acting upon, the conditions of human life, we need a self-knowledge which can only develop through a steady, passionate attention to *all* female experience . . . If this is so, we cannot work alone. (Rich (1980a) p. 213)

All the themes are here. Knowledge is generated by a women-centred 'passionate' women's community. Feminism is not just an account of women's issues but 'a way of thinking'. Rich's criticism is a criticism about the origin of criticism. So she is not talking only about discrimination against women but about discrimination against women's knowledge and experience. For Rich, feminism means – depending on the direction it takes – two very different things: on the one hand, it is something very concrete – emotional sisterhood with contemporary women; on the other, it is an almost pantheistic celebration of female history.

The core of Rich's work – her notion that a miscarriage of the symbolic 'difference' of women inevitably aborts our social freedom – will bear comparison with the finest criticism.

SUMMARY

Just as there is no single definition of 'lesbian' so there is no single 'school' of lesbian criticism. Each critic is marked both by her moment and by the ways in which she comes to call herself lesbian. If one function of criticism is to explore and interpret the textually invisible then lesbian criticism has unique strengths to offer. A radical theme in lesbian criticism is the idea that feminist criticism should address how texts *internalise* heterosexism as well as addressing absences in the literary canon. In addition the issues raised by lesbian critics overlap with those raised by non-lesbians as well as by lesbian Third World feminists and others writing from outside the academy – in, for example, the startling and original collection, compiled by Moraga and Anzaldúa, *This Bridge Called My Back* (1981). Lesbian critics are changing the configurations of criticism. For example, lesbian critics focus on the instabilities in classic male-female-male triads and new erotic triangulations; and on the 'unspoken' in literary texts 'present' in ruptures, such as abrupt parenthesis or breaks in syntax. Lesbian criticism and queer theory provide textual strategies which subvert the norms of literary discourse as well as subverting everyday sexual stereotypes. Along with their new typologies lesbian critics have engendered a deep distrust of existing critical systems. Jane Rule, Monique Wittig, Catharine Stimpson, Mary Daly and Bonnie Zimmerman are writers who take very seriously the relation of politics and literature. Lesbian critics are concerned both with politics in texts and the politics and possibilities of the text itself. A separate lesbian identity provides feminist criticism with a cutting edge and innovatory techniques which enable it to move ahead.

As Judith Butler argues, *if* lesbian criticism frees itself from heterosexual models . . . '*if* it were not for the notion of the homosexual *as* copy, there would be no construct of heterosexuality *as* origin' (Butler, 1991, p. 22).

SELECTED READING

Basic texts

Brown, R. M. (1970) 'The woman-identified woman', *The Ladder* 14: 11/12, pp. 6–8
Bulkin, E. (ed.) (1981a) *Lesbian Fiction*, Watertown, Mass.: Persephone Press
Bulkin, E. (ed.) (1981b) *Lesbian Poetry*, Watertown, Mass: Persephone Press
Cruikshank, M. (ed.) (1982) *Lesbian Studies: Present and future*, New York: The Feminist Press
Daly, M. (1978) *Gyn/Ecology*, Boston: Beacon Press
Daly, M. (1984) *Pure Lust*, Boston: Beacon Press
Faderman, L. (1981) *Surpassing the Love of Men: Romantic friendship and love between women from the renaissance to the present*, New York: William Morrow
Faderman, L, (1991) *Odd Girls and Twilight Lovers: A history of lesbian life in twentieth-century America*, New York: Columbia University Press
Grier, B., Watson, J. and Jordan, R. (eds) (1981) *The Lesbian in Literature: A bibliography*, Tallahassee Fla.: The Naiad Press
Griffin, S. (1980) 'Thoughts on writing', in J. Sternburg (ed.), *The Writer on Her Work*, New York: Norton
Johnston, J. (1973) *Lesbian Nation*, New York: Simon & Schuster
Moraga, C. and Anzaldúa, G. (eds) (1981) *This Bridge Called My Back: Writings by radical women of color*, New York: Kitchen Table Press
Rich, A. (1976) *Of Woman Born*, New York: Norton
Rich, A. (1977) 'There is a fly in this house', *Ms*, February
Rich, A. (1980a) 'Compulsory heterosexuality and lesbian existence', *Signs* 5:4 (Summer), pp. 631–60
Rich, A. (1980b) 'When we dead awaken', in *On Lies, Secrets, Silence*, London: Virago
Rich, A. (1981a) 'Notes for a magazine: what does separatism mean?', *Sinister Wisdom*, 18, pp. 83–91
Rich, A. (1981b) 'Interview', *Spare Rib*, 103, pp. 14–16
Rich, A. (1983a) 'Blood, bread and poetry: the location of the poet', *The Massachusetts Review*, 24:3, pp. 521–41

Rich, A. (1983b) 'Compulsory heterosexuality and lesbian existence', in E. Abel and E. K. Abel (eds), *Women, Gender and Scholarship*, Chicago: University of Chicago Press

Roberts, J. R. (1981) *Black Lesbians: An annotated bibliography*, Tallahassee: The Naiad Press

Rule, J. (1975) *Lesbian Images*, Trumansburg, NY: Crossing Press

Rule, J. (1976) 'The practice of writing', *Canadian Women's Studies*, 1:3, pp. 34–5

Sedgwick, E. K. (1989) *Between Men: English literature and male homosocial desire*, Irvington, NY: Columbia University Press

Sedgwick, E. K. (1990) *Epistemology of the Closet*, Berkeley, Calif.: University of California Press; (1991) Hemel Hempstead: Harvester Wheatsheaf

Shockley, A. (1979) 'The black lesbian in American literature: an overview', *Conditions*, 5, repeated in *Home Girls* (below)

Smith, B. (1977) *Toward a Black Feminist Criticism*, New York: Out & Out Books

Smith, B. (1983) *Home Girls*, New York: Kitchen Table Press

Smith, B. (1990) 'The truth that never hurts: black lesbians in fiction in the 1980s', in J. M. Braxton and A. McLaughlin (eds), *Wild Women in the Whirlwind*, London: Serpents Tail

Smith-Rosenberg, C. (1975) 'The female world of love and ritual: relations between women in nineteenth-century America', *Signs*, 1 (Autumn) pp. 1–30

Stimpson, C. (1988) *Where the Meanings Are: Feminism and cultural spaces*, London: Routledge

Wittig, M. (1980) 'The straight mind', *Feminist Issues*, 1:1, pp. 103–11

Wittig, M. and Zeig, S. (1979) *Lesbian Peoples Materials for a Dictionary*, New York: Avon

Zimmerman, B. (1983) 'Exiting from patriarchy: the lesbian novel of development', in Abel, E., Hirsch, M. and Langland, E. (eds), *The Voyage In: Fictions of female development*, Dartmouth College, Hanover: University Press of New England

Zimmerman, B. (1985) 'What has never been: an overview of lesbian feminist criticism', in E. Showalter (ed.), *The New Feminist Criticism*, New York: Pantheon

Zimmerman, B. (1991) *The Safe Sea of Women: Lesbian fiction 1969–1989*, Boston: Beacon Press

Introductions

Benstock, S. (ed.) (1987) *Feminist Issues in Literary Scholarship*, Bloomington: Indiana University Press
Bristow, J. (ed.) (1990) 'Special issue on lesbian and gay cultures, theories and texts', *Textual Practice*, 4:2 (Summer)
Bristow, J. (ed.) (1992) *Sexual Sameness: Textual differences in lesbian and gay writing*, London: Routledge
Burke, C. G. (1986) 'Rethinking the maternal', in *The Future of Difference* (eds) H. Eisenstein and A. Jardine, Boston: G. K. Hall
Díaz-Diocaretz, M. (1985) *Translating Poetic Discourse: Questions on feminist strategies in Adrienne Rich*, Philadelphia: John Benjamins
Feminist Review (1990) *Special Issue on Perverse Politics: Lesbian Issues*, 34 (Spring)
Freedman, E. B., Gelp, B. C., Johnson, S. L. and Neston, K. M. (eds) (1985) *The Lesbian Issue*, Chicago: University of Chicago Press
Fuss, D. (ed.) (1991) *Inside/Out: Lesbian theories, gay theories*, London: Routledge
Gelpi, B. and Gelpi, A. (1975) *Adrienne Rich's Poetry*, New York: Norton
Jay, K. and Glasgow, J. (eds) (1990) *Lesbian Texts and Contexts: Radical revisions*, New York: New York University Press
Meese, E. A. (1990) *(Ex)Tensions: Re-figuring feminist criticism*, Urbana: University of Illinois Press
Munt, S. (ed.) (1992) *New Lesbian Criticism: Literary and cultural readings*, Hemel Hempstead: Harvester Wheatsheaf

Further reading

Braidotti, R. (1991) *Patterns of Dissonance*, Cambridge: Polity Press
Butler, J. (1991) 'Imitation and gender insubordination', in Fuss (1991) above
Cruikshank, M. (1992) *The Gay and Lesbian Liberation Movement*, New York: Routledge
Elliott, J. and Wallace, A. (1992) 'Fleurs du Mal or second-hand

roses, Natalie Barney, Romaine Brooks, and the originality of
the avant-garde', *Feminist Review*, 40, pp. 6–31

Foucault, M. (1978) *The History of Sexuality. Vol. 1: An introduction*, New York: Pantheon

Gomez, J. and Smith, B. (1990) 'Talking about it: homophobia in
the black community', *Feminist Review*, 34, pp. 47–55

Hull, G. T. (1982) 'Researching Alice Dunbar-Nelson: a personal
and literary perspective', in G. T. Hull, *et al.* (eds), *All the
Women are White, All the Blacks Are Men, But Some of Us are
Brave: Black women's studies*, New York: The Feminist Press

Kaplan, C. (1983) 'Wild nights: pleasure/sexuality/feminism', in
Formations of Pleasure, Formations Editorial Collective,
London: Routledge & Kegan Paul

Katz, J. (1990) 'The invention of heterosexuality', *Socialist
Review*, 21:1, pp. 7–34

King, K. (1990) 'Producing sex, theory and culture', in M. Hirsch
and E. Fox Keller (eds), *Conflicts in Feminism*, London:
Routledge

Klaich, D. (1974) *Woman Plus Woman: Attitudes toward lesbianism*,
New York: William Morrow

Martin, B. (1988) 'Lesbian identity and autobiographical difference(s)' in B. Brodski and C. Schenck (eds), *Life/Lines:
Theorizing women's autobiography*, Ithaca: Cornell University
Press

Martin, D. and Lyon, P. (1972) *Lesbian/Woman*, San Francisco:
Glide Publications

Miner, V. (1990) 'An imaginative collectivity of writers and
readers', in K. Jay and J. Glasgow (eds), *Lesbian Texts and
Contexts: Radical revisions*, New York: New York University
Press

Palmer, P. (1989) *Contemporary Women's Fiction: Narrative practice
and feminist theory*, Hemel Hempstead: Harvester Wheatsheaf

Ruehl, S. (1982) 'Inverts and experts: Radclyffe Hall and the
lesbian identity', in R. Brunt and C. Rowan (eds), *Feminism,
Culture and Politics*, London: Lawrence and Wishart

Ruehl, S. (1983) *Sex and Love*, London: The Women's Press

Wolff, C. (1972) *Love Between Women*, New York: Harper
Colophon Books

9 Third World feminist criticism: third wave and fifth gear

Until the 1980s there was a widespread and systematic neglect of Third World writing by traditional criticism in the West. This neglect took many forms. First, the academy excluded most Asian and Black theory, criticism and creative writing. Second, the issues raised by Third World critics are often simplified; and finally, a very few Third World critics have been appropriated into a largely unchanged literary agenda. This neglect is unsurprising given that, as Susan Hardy Aitken pertinently argues, 'During the same time that the traditional canon was taking shape, the major European nations were engaging in a colonising project unprecedented in scope since the Roman Empire' (Aitken, 1986, p.294).

This academic ethnocentricity is shaped by the use of Western concepts – for example, periodisation – and by an interest in social and cultural themes drawn only from Western society. Currently, dazzling and complex discussions of ethnocentrism and oppositional criticism are contained in the writings of Rosario Castellanos and the more recent writings of Chandra Mohanty, Gloria Anzaldúa, Rey Chow, Trin Minh-ha, Gayatri Spivak and Chela Sandoval, in particular. These writers are setting an agenda for feminist literary criticism for the 1990s and beyond.

Third World feminist criticism focuses on three major issues: on the politics of universalism; on cultural controls and misrepresentations; and on the homogeneity of the canon. A central concern is to create a feminist criticism which is neither universalist nor written only from the margins and which can attend to writing ignored by the canon. These critics seek to bring into literary studies particular forms of ethnic difference, genres and languages at present ignored by the West. Currently, Third World critics are identifying key writers; creating new representations and nonethnocentric critical languages; and analysing the politics of feminist criticism.

The groundwork for this new criticism has developed over several years in many collections of writing by Afra-American, Black British and Third World women. Anthologies, autobiographies and preface essays are the best evidence of Third World feminist criticism rather than single works. *Unheard Words: Women and Literature in Africa, the Arab World, Asia, the Caribbean and Latin America* (1985) edited by Mineke Schipper is a preliminary account of women's writing and culture. The groundbreaking book in America was *This Bridge Called My Back: Writings by Radical Women of Color* (1981) edited by Cherríe Moraga and Gloria Anzaldúa. By the second edition in 1983 Moraga and Anzaldúa could already claim that the *Bridge* was internationalist, 'bridging' the gap between American women of colour and Third World women. In the introduction to *Ngambika: Studies of Women in African Literature* (1986) the editors Carole Boyce Davies and Anne Adams Graves create an African feminist criticism (see chapter 7, Black feminisms). In India, the first collection of critical essays on women poets is *Studies in Contemporary Indo-English Verse I* (1984) edited by A. N. Dwivedi. In Britain, the first book of this kind is *Charting the Journey* (1988); edited by S. Grewel *et al.*, which explores issues of gender and race in terms of the concept 'Black British'.

A number of ideas which challenge literary traditions emerge in these books. Third World criticism focuses on the significance of memory and autobiography. Third World feminist critics argue that although there are other categories of exclusion in literary criticism (for example, working-class writing), ethnic authors have to date been more marginalised than other groups. Gloria Anzaldúa's theory of border writing (see below) casts doubt on the belief that writing can represent in any simple way a single group, class or ethnic voice. The feminist politician and writer Rosario Castellanos shows that women who emerge as culturally representative, (and her interest is in the Mayan figure, La Malinche) depend on a traditional macho culture. Rey Chow argues that Western criticism does not read Third World writing as a configuration of elements, some Western, some Eastern, but rather sees it as an exotic and isolated genre. Chela Sandoval set out definitions of 'oppositional consciousness'.

What is involved in naming an area of feminist criticism Third World? Questions of definition are not easy. There is an obstinate, even intractable, difficulty with the label 'Third World'. The term was first used in August 1952 when Alfred Savvy, a French demographer, wrote in *France Observateur* 'this Third World, ignored, scorned, exploited, as was the Third Estate, also wants to say something' (Harlow, 1987, p.5). But this notion of estates immediately suggests a hierarchy of representations. In addition, the term 'Third World' is frequently applied both to geographical entities and to oppressed 'underdeveloped' peoples. But clearly women in the Third World are not necessarily more 'underdeveloped' or oppressed than Western women, White or Black. The distinction between 'First' and 'Third' Worlds carries with it other problems: the issue of spatial barriers and the dangers of a binary – the West/ Others. Third World feminist critics draw attention to this difficulty and to the need to undermine a global patriarchal organisation. 'Post-colonial' is currently in fashion. However, a chapter titled 'Post-colonial' should include study of the effects of colonialism *on* writing, and, for this, this chapter has no space. In addition, and more significantly, 'Third World' *does* imply a political solidarity. Use of the term does not necessarily imply a fixed binary. For example, First and Third World feminist critics attack the traditionalism/modernism dichotomy characterising the rigid capitalist Third World/First World binary (see Chow, 1990).

How does Third World criticism relate to other critical movements of the 1980s such as postmodernism? Postmodernism's focus on popular culture is especially helpful to feminist critics trying to articulate a whole expanse of hitherto suppressed cultural representations. In some ways Third World critics could claim postmodernism, with its de-centring strategies, as an ally. On the other hand, many critics feel that postmodernism downplays the very real experiences of marginality in favour of some play of 'significations'. While both postmodernism and Third World criticism problematise the centrality of the white male author, often postmodernism seems very self-reflexive rather than culturally reflexive. For example, postmodernism's obsession with consumer culture, with TV advertising and pulp fiction has a limited politics. Postmodernism, as Carole Davies points out, simply plays 'on the entire conception of marginality' rather than making the outsider creatively central to any critical theory (Davies, 1991, p. 249). As Rey Chow makes clear, Western postmodernism transforms ethnicity into an abstract list of differences which fails to challenge the literary canon. One very good example of this Western denial comes in the two prefaces to Ellen Kuzweyo's *Call Me Woman*, one by the white South African Nadine Gordimer and the other by the Black South African Bessie Head. *Call Me Woman* is Ellen Kuzweyo's testimonial about her life, political activities and detention under the Terrorism Act in South Africa. Since control of the means of communication is so pronounced in South Africa, writing is in many ways a key means of political subversion available to Black South Africans.

The white Nadine Gordimer introduces *Call Me Woman* in these terms:

> Ellen Kuzweyo is history in the person of one woman. Fortunately, although she is not a writer, she has the memory and the gift of unselfconscious expression that enable her to tell her story as no-one else could. It is a story that will be both exotically revealing and revealingly familiar to readers. (Gordimer (1985) p. xi)

Nadine Gordimer is a liberal anti-apartheid writer yet even she here creates a hammeringly tendentious and crude stereotype. Kuzweyo's book is the work of 'one woman' (and therefore not threatening); she is not a writer but is 'unselfconscious' even 'exotic'. Gordimer actively repels the complex and sophisticated features of Kuzweyo's book. *Call Me Woman* is a book that is, in any terms, a dense interweaving of sociology, politics and history with autobiography. Gordimer subsumes Kuzwayo under a compulsory and racist 'exoticism'.

Bessie Head, the Black South African writer, is motivated by other concerns, and in contrast to Gordimer, she describes the political and social context of Kuzwayo's work, not its isolation:

> . . . finding it impossible to believe that people could endure such terrific suffering. The truth is the human physical frame cannot endure unnatural states of torture, unnatural states of detention. (Head (1985) p. xiv)

Head is clear-sighted on the main issue: that all Black writing in the colonial context is a form of protest. The clarity with which Head conveys this view stems from her understanding of the very real imaginative and physical energies in Kuzwayo's writing.

At the 1987 annual NWSA (National Women's Studies Association) meeting, Chela Sandoval offered a less contentious definition of 'Third World'. To be 'Third World' means three things: first, to have been de-centred from any point of power in order to be used as the negative pole against which the dominant powers can then define themselves; second, to be working politically to challenge the systems that keep power moving in its current patterns, thus shifting it onto new terrains; and third, such a name would work to underline the similarity between our oppression in the United States and that of our international sisters in Third World countries. All the main themes are here – the idea that 'de-centring' is a feature of Third World criticism, the importance of new 'terrains'; and the applicability of transnational critiques. Sandoval's ideas have been cited by Donna Haraway, Katie King and Teresa de Lauretis among others. The critical visibility of Sandoval is now more assured with the publication of her fine essay 'US Third World Feminism' in *Genders* (1991). In this essay Sandoval refines her earlier definition of Third World criticism. Assuaging a universal category, Sandoval offers 'a mobile unity, constantly weaving and interweaving an interaction of differences into coalition' (Sandoval, 1991, p. 18). Further on she offers the fascinating and novel paradigm of a car clutch, in which oppositional consciousness is like a group of 'differentials' which can be engaged or disengaged like car clutches with her own preferred gear being the 'fifth position' (Sandoval, 1991, p. 14).

Sandoval's essay makes a rich and dense engagement with ideas from First and Third Worlds, and the term 'fifth gear', of course, carries a sexual connotation of 'cruising', its more usual name. Other critics (for example, Chandra Mohanty and the other editors of *Third World Women and the Politics of Feminism*) prefer the term Third World to 'postcolonial or developing countries' (Mohanty, 1991, p. ix).

White feminist criticism and Third World feminist criticism have much in common then but are not reducibly similar. Historically some white feminist and Third World criticism emerged out of other forms of criticism; for example, from a 'masculine' Marxism or from nationalist agendas. In addition, the term feminism itself is sometimes refused by women suspicious of white imperialism; Alice Walker, for example, uses the term 'womanist'. The critics in this chapter are all concerned with feminist criticism not as a homogeneous field but as a set of multiple forms of 'oppositional consciousness'.

AREAS

India

Feminist criticism from and about India is highly self-conscious about the politics involved in any form of writing. The critical enterprise has two strands, the first concerned with the formulation and exploration of a female tradition. Critics such as Lakshmi Kannan, Roopali Chibber, Shirley Geok-lin Lim and the poets Charmayne d'Souza, Pratibha Bhat, and novelists Nayantara Sahgal and Anita Desai are exploring women's 'invisible' experiences and finding new forms and styles appropriate to that exploration. A more theoretical enterprise is using the tools of literary criticism to examine 'gendered subalterns' in a whole range of texts including literature. In the military world of the British Raj a subaltern was a native soldier who carried out the often racist decisions of his white superiors: in literary criticism 'subaltern' describes a cultural identity silenced by colonialism which critics are concerned to 'liberate' (see Spivak in the Deconstruction section of chapter 6). For example, in 'Shahbano' (1992) Zakia Pathak reads against the grain of Muslim laws and national narratives to examine subaltern representations.

Indian criticism has expanded its focus over the last ten years. It is a criticism which is consciously international. The growing number of women in higher education, and the establishment of writing workshops enabled women researching a female tradition to emphasise both the quantity and variety of women's writing. Meenakshi Mukherjee's *Realism and Reality* (1985) and Alladi Uma's *Woman and her Family: Indian and Afro-American: A Literary Perspective* (1989) resemble Ellen Moers's *Literary Women* and offer basic images of women's approach. For example, Uma considers in parallel the writers Anita Desai and Alice Walker largely in terms of typical female roles as the chapters of her book – 'Woman as Mother', 'Woman as Daughter' – reveal. Mukherjee addresses another dimension still to be fully explored – the locating of women's writing in the context of social reform movements such as the woman question debates of nineteenth-century Bengal. Currently women poets are creating new forms of writing in India. Literary magazines (*Indian Literature*) and small presses have sprung up which publish women's poetry. As Shamim Chowdhury's 'An Introduction to the Women Poets of Bangladesh' (1990) makes clear, good women poets are being recognised by feminist critics.

In the first collection of critical essays about women poets, *Studies in Contemporary Indo-English Verse* (1984), Lakshmi Kannan in her overview draws attention to the 'explosive' impact on India of de Beauvoir's *The Second Sex* and Germaine Greer's *The Female Eunuch*. The founding of the Writers Workshop in the late 1950s had led to a resurgence of poetry writing and there are large numbers of women poets writing in English making daring experiments in form and rhythm. In the same volume other critics (for example, Monika Varma) describe the cultural restrictions and traditional behaviours which often stifle sexual expression in particular. Kannan draws attention to additional problems: for example, that Tamil critical vocabulary is still in the process of formation and has to make free use of English terminology. Hence creative writing itself acts as a form of critical theory. For example, Roopali Chibber's 'Patriarchy and the Indian Woman Poet' (1990) surveys Indian women's poetry of the 1980s and reveals a sorority of urban post-Independence women boasting degrees in subjects as varied as law and molecular genetics. Strongly influenced by her readings of Moers and Gilbert and Gubar, Chibber describes the Indian idealisation of motherhood and the positive elements of domestic experience in Bhat's 'The Homescape' as well as the 'anti-feminist' poetry of Vijaya Goel and the lack of Indian attention to female sexuality. Themes specific to India are the tragic effect of communal violence as well as a multigeneric writing (for example, the poetry dictionary verse of d'Souza's 'A Spelling Guide to Women' (1990)). What makes the future of Indian writing exciting is its move from the typical, respectable workshop-influenced poetry (for example, that of Monika Varma or Kamala Das) to the exploration of new ways of making language resist genres (for example, d'Souza's dictionary verse).

Zakia Pathak's 'A Pedagogy for PostColonial Feminists' (1992) addresses at length the links between the 'contradictions of a textual practice . . . the multiplicity of subject positions' and political events in India. Her excellent essay together with the collection edited by Lola Chatterjee *Woman/Image/Text: Feminist Readings of Literary Texts* (1986) demonstrate an important move in Indian criticism which is to use revisionary readings for political and religious effect. Where 'Shahbano' describes Muslim law, the Shahbano case and Indian politics almost as 'novels' – that is to say, reading their discourses subversively to spoil the usual 'happy ending' of nationalism (a uniform civil code) – a 'Pedagogy' is more conventional literary criticism. Pathak describes teaching at Miranda House, a women's college at Delhi University, the *Book of Job*, *Murder in the Cathedral*, *Lord Jim* and *A Passage to India* together with the Mandir Masjid dispute (centring on the religious significance of a site claimed by both Hindu and Muslims). Pathak argues that disparate societies might use similar motifs set in similar constructions (for example, the theological insistence on Yahweh and Ram) as ways of manipulating cultures. Here Pathak draws on the theories of the Subaltern School (discussed in chapter 6, above) and on postmodernism. Pathak defines feminist criticism as a pedagogical politics which looks for hesitations, metaphors of East and West and gender affiliations across race. What links all

Pathak's 'texts' is a focus on women's subjectivity whether this is Adela's experience in the caves in *A Passage to India* or Shahbano's contestation of gender roles under Muslim law.

A number of points emerge here. First, Pathak favours a criticism informed by Western theory but created for an Indian pedagogical practice. Her 'position' as a teacher is crucial to the formation of 'oppositional consciousness' as it was for Florence Howe, Adrienne Rich and Audre Lorde in America in the early 1970s. Second, the distinction between popular culture, high art, history and law becomes blurred. Finally, and most importantly, the essay is supremely postmodernist. That is to say, Pathak, like Judith Butler in another context, stages, or restages, criticism as 'performance' acknowledging a multiplicity of subject positions rather than a 'composite "Indian" response' (see Pathak, 1992).

While respecting the cultural specificity of literature, Indian feminist criticism is radically committed to an affirmative 'political' criticism. For example, Naseem Khan focuses on the growing awareness of the constrictions and subversions of female mythic virtues in recent writing by Asian women in both the subcontinent and Britain. The work of Kamala Markandeya, Suniti Namjoshi, and Bapsi Sidhwa, she argues, marks out a new feminist shape which combines an imagery of deliberate physical impediment, a frequent first person singular and old storytelling traditions. Asian writing is now an integral part of both British and American mainstream literature and points to the need for a wider, more complex critical canvas (see Khan, 1992).

Latin America

A few words about the origin of Latin American criticism will provide a context for the detailed discussion of Castellanos to follow. Feminist writing and criticism have been very fertile in Latin America from the 1930s but seldom encountered in the Western academy until the last decades. The history of this movement is being written (for example, Susan Bassnett's exemplary collection *Knives and Angels: Women Writers in Latin America* (1990) which builds on Mineke Schipper's *Unheard Words*) and the movement is strongly international.

Given the diversity of countries as well as languages and histories of colonialism and post-colonialism, it would be absurd to define a single Latin American imagination. Many critics in Latin America, like many in India and Africa, have writing careers which encompass many genres – for example, creative writing as well as children's book writing – as does the Cuban critic, Mirta Aguirre. It is generally agreed that the founding of the literary journal *Sur* by the Argentinian critic Victoria Ocampo transformed Latin American culture. Gabriela Mistral's Nobel Prize for literature, as well as the recognition of Maria Luisa Bombal, Alejandra Pizarnik and Clarice Lispector represent a new cultural history.

Critics like Ocampo in *Sur* and Castellanos address issues of translation, of cultural provincialism, and they were themselves internationalists focusing on European writing and theory. For example, both Ocampo and Rosario Castellanos are strongly influenced by the writing of Virginia Woolf. Luisa Valenzuela argues that this criticism combined with women's participation in armed struggles generated testimonial writing and a more open use of language (see Valenzuela, 1986). Rosario Castellanos, for example, from the time of her student days, advocated an international, liberal feminism and her criticism is clearly shaped by major themes in European feminism, in particular its attention to education, the family and the sexual division of labour (see Castellanos, below).

Australia

Since 1970 Australian feminist criticism has shown increasing diversity, reflecting a growing sophistication about gender representations. In the main this criticism has focused on writing by Australian women. Critics have not only discovered and critiqued the work of white women writers previously ignored by mainstream criticism, but have also introduced into the academy and to the public, Aboriginal, migrant and ethnic writing and have explored the problematic issue of recuperation which this work raises.

Women's writing in Australia before 1970 largely drew upon existing narrative conventions (realism) and traditional poetic forms. It eschewed experimentation in favour of psychological realism. However, in *Exiles at Home* Drusilla Modjeska suggests that writers such as Zora Cross, Olga Masters, Miles Franklin and Mollie Skinner *did* explore new aspects of women's experience including such forbidden topics as illegitimacy (Modjeska, 1987). In 'A Writer's Friends and Associates' and 'Zora Cross's Entry into Australian Literature' both Julie Saunders and Michael Sharkey point out more importantly, that, Cross, for instance, prided herself on her friendships and knowledge of Aboriginal customs (Saunders, 1990; Sharkey, 1990).

This critical contribution to 'retrieval history' (see Spender, D, 1988 and Spender, L, 1988) has been matched by the development of other critical studies, notably introductions to contemporary women writers, both resident and expatriate. Examples include Carole Ferrier's (1990b) interview with Pearlie McNeill, founder of Women Write and author of *One of the Family* (1989), as well as her work on migrant and Aboriginal writing and culture (Ferrier, 1990a). Here, the major concerns centre on representations of dominant/marginal groups. The growth of non-mainstream writing and criticism in the last decades has been phenomenal. For example, in her survey of the teaching of Black women writers in 1988, Carole Ferrier concluded that, unlike today, the work of Black writers was extremely marginal in Australian educational institutions (Ferrier, 1988).

The development of feminist critical interest in Aboriginal writing is an outgrowth of a cultural revitalisation, initially indigenous, but highlighted during the Bicentenary (1988). Many Aborigines used that moment to publicise their minority economic status as well as their differing cultural experiences and needs from those officially designated to them by the dominant culture.

Although a single periodical cannot adequately represent the entire Australian feminist critical community, changes in the content of *Hecate: An Interdisciplinary Journal of Women's Liberation* are an interesting indicator of the fast growth of Australian theory and criticism. *Hecate*'s first issues offer examples of a feminist criticism in debt to European concerns, with a steady focus on American and European writing ('Sylvia Plath', 1, 2; 'Psychoanalysis and Surrealism', 2, 1). By volume 5, articles on pioneer women's autobiographies appear, followed by a consistent attention to Aboriginal and Black women's writing. This radical reshaping of Australian feminist criticism could be seen to reflect the greater interest in, and theoretical understanding of, Marxism shown by Australian feminists than, for instance, their American counterparts. The editor of *Hecate*, Carole Ferrier, one of Australia's major critics, identified herself in 1991 as an 'unreconstructed Marxist', and other key critics, such as Sneja Gunew, have also made deft use of Althusserian concepts to focus on the institutional processes necessarily involved in any cultural production.

The results of these enquiries enabled critics to support the work of migrant and Aboriginal writers and to develop appropriate and sophisticated critical models. In addition, Aboriginal and Maori critics themselves are now engaged in a defining drive. Like other Third World criticism, Maori criticism is fiercely political as well as literary: an example is the outstanding work of the Maori critic, Moaria Wahini (1993).

The major problem, as Diane Bell points out in 'Aboriginal Women, Separate Spaces and Feminism' is that Aborigines constitute 1.1 per cent of the Australian population, and 92 per cent live in communities of fewer than 400 persons. (Bell, 1991). A number of exciting feminist critiques address both the oral and cultural differences of Aboriginal autobiography. Aboriginal autobiographies, especially those testimonials notated by 'white fellas', highlight the paradox at the heart of all feminist criticism: is a non-patriarchal women's writing, in its very production, being co-opted? As feminist critics point out, Aboriginal autobiography reveals a fragmentation of self and culture which feminist critics respond to in the wake of postmodernism. Similarly, in her important work on migrant writing, Sneja Gunew draws attention to the welcome diversification of the Eurocentric literary canon, while stressing as a problem that this diversification is dependent on the first-person confessional. Her example is the writing of Antigone Kefala (Gunew, 1988b).

As in her earlier essay 'Home and Away: Nostalgia in Australian (Migrant) Writing' (1988a), Gunew's major concerns centre on the production of meaning by migrant writing for which she offers the persuasive model of *mimicry* or 'passing'. For example, she notes the non-realist, montage effect in much migrant writing, which resists narrative closure. Because the enunciating positions are outside and partial, subjectivity, Gunew feels, is continually being 'interpellated' (here Gunew draws on Althusser's concept: see chapter 3, Marxist/socialist-feminist criticism). Such writing, Gunew suggests, offers parodic readings of cultural and gendered certainties. Gunew's terms resemble Gloria Anzaldúa's 'masks' and Judith Butler's notion of gender performance (see below). Pursuing Gunew's themes, Efi Hatzimanolis, in 'The Politics of Nostalgia: Community and Difference in Migrant Writing' points out that it is only conservative patriarchy which sees migrant writing as a unified and essentialist product of nostalgia (Hatzimanolis, 1990). An important study that has intensified interest in Aboriginal autobiography, particularly the contemporary writers, Sally Morgan and Glenyse Ward (the first Aboriginal autobiographer published by the Aboriginal press, Magabala Books), is Diane Bell's *Daughters of the Dreaming* (1983). The book describes the relationship between orality and ritual as well as Aboriginal women's specific responsibility for the *kukurrpa* or 'dreaming'. Bell is a white anthropologist, but, because her book describes the group activity of story-telling in terms of the impact of audience on story content, as well as other communal aspects of oral culture – a refusal of linear chronology and an almost Kristeva-like quality of cyclical time – *Daughters of the Dreaming* was a source of alternative critical focuses. Aboriginal culture itself, as the Aboriginal feminist writer Jackie Huggins points out, has literary styles and oral modes in different genres from those of non-Aboriginal peoples. Huggins herself refuses the term 'Aborigines', which she feels has been co-opted, in favour of 'Aboriginals' (Huggins, 1991). The new autobiographies and adjacent criticism throw into question rules of autobiography and literary history constructed in the academy.

The question of authority and ownership is now a key question for Australian feminist critics. In a brief but deftly constructed answer, Carole Ferrier's 'Resisting Authority' describes the problem for a white critic of giving 'voice' to a 'different' cultural rhythm and chronology, as well as touching on the complex relations between autobiography, speaking positions and poststructualism. While her call 'to employ a range of strategies' might be characterised as a form of critical pluralism, the essay advocates a possible solution in a critical *balance* of voices and the development of self-reflexivity (Ferrier, 1990a). This brief outline aims to show that Australian feminist critics share a continued vital and vivid engagement with the politics and culture of literature.

TECHNIQUES

Taking a comprehensive sweep across Third World feminist criticism we can see critics subverting tradition by questioning the boundaries of genres, not only literary genres such as poetry/drama/fiction, but the genre of criticism itself in hybrid mixtures of autobiography/theory/poetry and narrative, as in Gloria Anzaldúa's *Borderlands*. This hybridity may be due in part to a lack of positive models. Anzaldúa has a special interest in place and displacement. Other techniques include a constant circling from present to past as with Castellanos's attention to women figures from Mayan and post-Columbian history. In addition many critics insist on the social role of the feminist critic, denying a Western non-feminist preoccupation with individual and isolated 'thinking'. For example, Anzaldúa often quotes her mother verbatim focusing on the interface between standard and vernacular speaking styles.

There are a number of elements crucial to Third World criticism. These include stressing the tight relation between writing and society; the importance of a matriarchal and communal consciousness created by storytelling; and the possibility that this consciousness might transform criticism. While language difference is not a feature of all Third World critics, Anzaldúa does use untranslated Chicana vocabulary. Other critics, particularly Rey Chow and Chandra Mohanty, focus more on European theory, particularly postmodernist theory, in order to articulate the distinctive features of Third World writing.

According to Gilles Deleuze and Félix Guattari, the three salient characteristics of minority literature are: its subversion of the territory of the majority through language; its fundamental concern with politics; and its urge to represent collective issues (Deleuze and Guattari, 1983). These ideas are visible throughout Third World feminist criticism from the 1970s to the present day. This tripartite sense of territory, politics and collectivity is reflected in the actual titles of many books written by Black Americans and women of colour: for example, *This Bridge Called My Back* (1981) and *Borderlands* (1987) both emphasise the crossing of territories, while *All the Women Are White, All the Blacks Are Men, But Some of Us Are Brave* (1982) draws attention to issues of collectivity and marginality.

In Third World feminist criticism it is a use of life histories (for example, Anzaldúa's use of mestiza memory) and the interaction between these and contemporary theory such as postmodernism which makes a major challenge to traditional literary criticism. Mestiza memory represents a plural history of Anglo and Mexican cultures leading to a mestiza or plural consciousness. Anzaldúa makes clear that life histories are an important means of reconstituting Chicana culture. Barbara Harlow draws attention to the importance of autobiography for groups who have 'historically been denied access' to literary or critical production (Harlow, 1987, p. 121). Gloria Anzaldúa and Rosario Castellanos's critical tone is often confessional and frequently set in a first-person narrative. Third World autobiography is markedly different from Western autobiography in two significant ways: first, it is less retrospective and more focused on a future, non-ethnocentric culture; second, when the past *is* discussed it is seen through a clear political lens. In the last decades, Western publishers have seized on autobiographies and experiential writing by Third World women. But, as Chandra Mohanty points out, this interest is part of the marketplace, not evidence in itself of any decentring of Western literary history (see Mohanty, 1991, p. 34). It is the way in which autobiography is understood and located institutionally which is of paramount importance.

Another technique, drawing on postmodernism, is the use of multiple forms of narrative. Anzaldúa mixes her own poetry with paraphrased historical stories, myth and fables about the Aztec past and almost quasijournalistic accounts of agricultural labour. The hybridity is not confusing but flags Anzaldúa's almost constant need to question the universals of knowledge and culture. This draws attention to the struggle for personal expression in any colonial and postcolonial context.

A third kind of critical innovation is the way in which Third World feminist critics directly engage their readers by soliciting a reader's active help in completing the critical story. *Testimonials* and autobiographical criticism are written usually to interpellate (or invite in) a reader. Third World *testimonials* have been given by working-class narrators to a reader who is usually an intellectual, as in *I, Rigoberta Menchú* (1984). What I am calling *testimonial* criticism is fundamentally about constructing relationships between an author and a reader in order to create shared experiences. Inevitably, given the publishing exigencies of having to sell to white Western audiences as well as to peer groups, Anzaldúa and other critics deliberately seek solidarity with women across all cultures by utilising humour and parody and turning the reader into an author/translator.

A fourth theme more visible in the work of Minh-ha, Mohanty and Castellanos is the technique of switching between media: for example, by referring back and forth between film and fiction or, in the case of Chow, between theory and popular Chinese romances.

This is oppositional criticism. That is to say, the fundamental aim of these critics is to find a way in which to oppose Western elites. How is this done? Most obviously perhaps by interweaving two languages – the oral everyday speech of the community with theory. This graphically exposes the tensions and oppositions between, for example, Chicana culture and the literary tradition. In addition, critics like Castellanos celebrate oppositional voices by invoking mythical figures. Castellanos transforms the history of La Malinche – the concubine of Cortés known for 'betraying' her people – into an allegory about colonialism. Like Castellanos herself, La Malinche was a major translator of Mexican culture to the West.

One of the most persistent problems with traditional literary criticism is its assumption that only certain kinds of writing can be called 'literature'. Therefore a key question for Third World feminist critics is how to extend 'the literary' to include many kinds of stories. For example, in her essay 'Incident at Yalenty', Castellanos tells the story of a peasant girl inspired by a travelling theatre group to apply to be taught at the National Institute. The essay draws out issues about the denial of education which women and all minorities experience: 'Her father answered that he was not going to turn his daughter over to strangers' (Ahern, 1988, p. 221). Castellanos sees this incident as an allegory of the cultural domination of all minority women.

A common theme, then, in Third World feminist criticism is the attempt to disengage with received critical notions and 'engage' in fifth gear to drive across a new landscape hewn out of history, and spotted with locations new to literary theory. Such a landscape would need to be explored with new methods, which Sandoval calls a 'science of oppositional ideology' and she describes, almost cinematographically, many different subject/ figures (Sandoval, 1991, p. 2).

Yet to point to new directions we must first know the nature of the past we leave behind. Modern feminism presents an especial difficulty for Third World critics. We cannot escape the fact that Western feminism grew out of the Enlightenment and therefore carries with it Enlightenment ideas that development and progress are evolutionary and that society will gradually bring women into the centre. As Trinh T. Minh-ha points out, African women do not see themselves as minors with little or no rights, little or no independence but as figures central to their cultures (Minh-ha, 1990).

In US 'Third World Feminism' Chela Sandoval makes a sharp critique of white Western feminist criticism and its desire to create a linear and (to Sandoval) a false history of the stages of feminism. Sandoval describes the feminist typologies which were created during the 1980s, which fast became the 'official' history of feminism. For example, Elaine Showalter's essay 'Towards a Feminist Poetics' (1979) outlines a three-phase story of feminist literary poetics which 'evolves' from feminine to feminist and then to female writing. In *The Future of Difference* (1985) Hester Eisenstein created four taxonomic categories to describe feminist thought and Alison Jagger in *Feminist Politics and Human Nature* (1983) claims that socialist feminism is the fourth and final stage. Other feminists (for example, Cora Kaplan in 'Pandora's Box', 1986) prefer to describe three forms of feminist criticism: liberal, Marxist and radical. According to Sandoval, all these alignments and re-alignments act as corrals, limiting the network of possibilities created by feminist women of colour. Sandoval's metaphor for feminist criticism – a fifth gear in a group of differentials – is therefore a bold stroke.

Gloria Anzaldúa shares Sandoval's anger and claims in 'La Prieta' (Moraga and Anzaldúa, 1981) that she lives 'between and among' cultures. The question she addresses is: is there, or can there ever be, a transnational feminism, given the need for Third World critics to tackle particular mythologies of nationalism and capitalist culture?

While white feminist criticism often seems to be merely swinging between one taxonomy or other and is often swamped by its categories, Third World feminist criticism pivots around other concerns. Barbara Harlow acutely points out that in many developing countries the absence of men whether 'through death, struggle, migration, or imprisonment' is critical to the emergence of new 'entities' of Third World women. It is not enough, Third World feminist critics argue, simply to make a celebratory identification of these women and bring them into the critical spotlight but to understand that women are repositories and transmitters of culture. If we take one example from Native American culture: it is women, not men, who are currently the myth makers of Native American literature. In *Words* the editor Laura Coltelli argues that women have always held important positions in Native American creation myths and tribal communities but currently, American Indian women's literary production covers 'a whole gamut of experiential and emotional landscapes: the interrelation between traditional values and new lifestyles' (Coltelli, 1990, p. 4).

Such all-embracing frameworks demand far more than one single critical method. There is a great deal of sophisticated debate in Third World feminist criticism at the present time which centres on the relation between cultural history and cultural mixtures and the inapplicability of white Western theory to explain this relation. Third World feminist criticism sees itself engaged in a double task: the work of retrieval combined with a constant critique of traditional literary institutions. In Third World feminist criticism the personal and experiential necessarily connect with larger political issues. When we reach the heart of white feminist criticism it is significant that white feminist criticism defines itself in terms of its theories and its history (first-wave and second-wave feminisms), whereas it addresses Third World writing often in terms only of 'experience specific to her group' (Showalter, 1985, p. 264). In other words, the picture being painted is one of an unambiguously progressive identity of feminist thought but present only in white feminist criticism and absent in Third World writing. This white stereotyping divides feminist criticism into those critics who *make* literary history (white) and those who add mere experience (Third World). The leading Native American poet, Paula Gunn Allen, describes this move very well in the similar context of anthropology which 'recruits Indians into the program to teach them to be sophisticated informants, but not to teach them to be sophisticated theoreticians' (Allen, 1990, p. 152). Not surprisingly many Third World feminist critics have come to recognise that their own collective tradition will be the only 'powerful response to the European philosophical subject: the logocentric I' (Coltelli, 1990, p. 208).

Clearly there are as many Third World feminisms as there are theorists. However the focus on place and displacement; the creation of a positive model of 'Otherness'; the rewriting of the 'record' in tension with European theory; the reading of history as if history is a language; the focus on myth, allegory and the use of untranslated words, footnotes or addresses to a reader; the refusal to create a hierarchy of texts – these are all features of Third World feminist criticism.

CHANDRA TALPADE MOHANTY AND COLONIAL DISCOURSE

A number of writers have made a particular study of concepts of 'Otherness' in traditional criticism. These critics call themselves colonial discourse critics and their work has become very influential in the last decade. In her widely cited essay 'Under Western Eyes: Feminist Scholarship and Colonial Discourses' (1985) Chandra Talpade Mohanty argues that Western criticism, both non-feminist and feminist, artificially constructs two entities: the coloniser and the colonised. Mohanty examines the political implications of this practice which allows the colonised only a 'language' permitted, or indeed constructed, by the coloniser. The essay analyses the 'monolith' of Third World woman in Western feminist texts and argues that this construction is predominantly discursive. To avoid constructing 'monoliths', Mohanty argues, criticism must accurately describe differences in cultures and create new words to express similarities and common ground (Mohanty, 1985, p. 333). Mohanty utilises the skills of literary criticism, giving examples of these monolithic images from literature: 'the veiled woman, the powerful mother, the chaste virgin, the obedient wife' (Mohanty, 1985, p. 352). And it is in these images, Mohanty argues, that Western feminists appropriate and colonise the complex literary, oral, and cultural productions of women of very different classes, races and castes in the Third World.

Two initial lessons are immediately clear: first, the student of Third World writing must go beyond the images and stereotypes that predominate in conventional literary history; and second, the study of Third World writing must situate literature in a more fluid context of material and social inequalities. One of Mohanty's achievements is her clear-sighted attack on the principles she sees at work in Western feminist criticism about the Third World. These principles are of three kinds, Mohanty claims. The first principle concerns the assumption, by the West, that Third World women are an identical group regardless of place or ethnicity. The second principle 'consists in the uncritical use of particular methodologies' involved in the first assumption. Mohanty cites here the way a critic isolates a religious or a kinship system in their analysis of writing. The third principle is the politics which both these frames of analysis create. This involves the self-representation of Western women in literature or other disciplines as modern women with some degree of control over their bodies and sexualities and Western feminists 're-presentation' of women in the Third World as domestic or uneducated victims (see Mohanty, 1985, p. 337).

The lesson for feminist criticism here is that Third World criticism cannot be added onto existing methods of literary criticism as an additional 'type' but involves understanding the connection between the particular ways in which inequalities are created and controlled in existing criticism; for example, Western concepts of periodisation or a Western 'appropriation' of modernism (see Chow below).

These theories of Mohanty and others are so significant because they show how literary representations relate to material aggression in a form of epistemic violence as Trinh T. Minh-ha succinctly shows in her superb summary (in *This Bridge Called My Back*, p. 372). What Third World feminist criticism gives us is a new definition of 'difference'. These critics do not talk about an intact and different 'subject', a unitary I, but of contradictory even parodoxical meanings. The message here is that post-colonial criticism should not simply *re*-present Third World women but set up contradictions and possibilities drawn from many disciplines.

ROSARIO CASTELLANOS

Arguably, in her essays about Mexican women's culture and writing, *Mujer que sabe latín* (1973), the novelist, poet, playwright and feminist critic Rosario Castellanos initiated Third World feminist criticism. Born in 1925, Castellanos was one of the 'Generation of 1950' – young Central American writers studying at the National University of Mexico. In 1971, after a prolific writing career and professorships in both America and Mexico, Castellanos was chosen by President Echeverría as the Mexican Ambassador to Israel where she suddenly died (see Ahern, 1988).

Castellanos's essays, particularly 'Woman and Her Image' (Ahern, 1988), 'Language as an Instrument of Domination', 'If Not Poetry, Then What?', all constitute a gendered history of Latin American writing and culture. A central focus in her work are the three powerful, archetypal figures of La Malinche, the Virgin of Guadalupe, and Sor Juana Inés de la Cruz. La Malinche (1500) was sold as a slave to the Spanish, becoming Cortes's concubine and translator. '*Malinchismo*' in contemporary Mexican culture is to be a traitor. The Virgin of Guadalupe (1531) is the Patroness of Mexico, and Sor Juana Inés de la Cruz (1648–1695) was a brilliant poet, philosopher, musician and astronomer. In broad terms these three women represent female sexuality and the 'prostitution' of Mexico to foreigners; virginity; and the intellect/spinster. Castellanos, taking the three women to be metaphors of contemporary issues affecting Mexican women, revitalised these patriarchal images in order to create a place for women in national culture.

The themes which Castellanos systematically explores in her essays are women-centred: language and repression; women's own shortcomings; the strengths of the domestic; women's history, and the function of motherhood.

As a contributor to the popular journals *Novedades*, *¡Siempre!* and *Excélsior*, she learnt to use materials from everyday life and her essays were very popular. Writing for the popular press encouraged Castellanos to attack literary hierarchies, to adopt ideas from popular forms (for example, *telenovelas* (soap operas)); and to make an ironic use of cliché and truisms. Addressing that non-academic audience made Castellanos conscious of the part played by the family, by myth and history in the construction of Mexican women's literature and identities. For example, in her essay *Mujer* (Ahern, 1988), she refuses to use a formal rhetoric. Instead she adopts a domestic imagery, describing how Latin American women take literature between their hands like mirrors. As Castillo argues in *Talking Back*, Castellanos does not describe criticism as *excavation* – a finding of hidden and forgotten women – but as an everyday activity of thinking (Castillo, 1992).

'Once Again Sor Juan' (Ahern, 1988) is, as its title implies, a revivication of the three key women figures of Mexican history. Castellanos treats history like literature and aims to put women from the past into a contemporary frame. She does this by means of intertextuality. By appropriating other genres (for example, the fairytale) Castellanos transforms patriarchal images such as 'the temptress' La Malinche (frequently portrayed as a giant in Indian festivals) into positive images. Sor Juana, the woman of the essay title, was a poet nun, often 'dissected' since her death by the 'instruments' of psychoanalysis: Castellanos argues, however, that Sor Juana had an 'intellectual vocation' (Ahern, 1988, p. 223). Castellanos subverts traditional representations of women in which 'fi fo fum our story be done', with a wider exploration of culture and gender (Ahern, 1988, p. 225). The fairy tale is an informing motif in much of her writing. Fairy tales are about power and the possession of children and women and reflect patriarchal myths of sexuality. They are frequently about a rural world and therefore match a Mexican landscape very well. By adopting the fairytale motif of magical change, Castellanos took the opportunity to liberate these literary women from the stereotypical gender roles of whore, virgin and spinster. The use of myth is characteristic of other Latin American criticism: for example the Argentinian writer Silvia Plager's *Prohibido despertar* (*Forbidden Awakening*) (1983).

The essay 'An Attempt At Self Criticism' (Ahern, 1988) reviews Castellanos's poetic career to date, and heralds a by now well-established feminist practice – the interweaving of critical and creative writing, a technique of which Irigaray and Cixous are well-known exponents. An 'Irigarayan' method marks Castellanos's 'Discrimination in the United States and in Chiapas' (Ahern, 1988). This essay opposes the voices of two men; one right-wing and the other left-wing in order to ironise the tension between language and politics. Castellanos's use of irony and her stress on the importance of speaking make her work seem very contemporary. 'Woman and Her Image' (Ahern, 1988) has a more conventional form. Here, as in her other essays, she takes issue with traditional constructions of woman as Other. She pursues the ideas of de Beauvoir and Virginia Woolf to argue against the masculine logic of a binary language which relies on oppositional terms – intelligent/stupid. Castellanos's principal technique in this essay is a skilful use of 'Woolfian' motifs such as irony, parenthesis, interrogatives, and 'mock' modesty – for example, 'it is not an easy task to explain, one laments' (Ahern, 1988, p. 242).

As a journalist Castellanos was particularly adept at creating dramatic visual episodes and two regular readers of her newspaper essays – the actress, Emma Teresa Armendáriz and her husband, the director Rafael López Mirnau – encouraged Castellanos to complete her brilliant farce, *The Eternal Feminine* (1975). 'Language as an Instrument of Domination' and 'If Not Poetry, Then What?' are two essays whose common strategy is discursive parody, a key feature of Third World testimonials. Both essays are autobiographies in which Castellanos reveals her fear that for her language is merely a way to appease 'the terror of the void'. She erupts into a Bakhtinian celebration of 'gregarious' languages. It was the Russian formalist, Bakhtin, who first argued that writing (and his examples are the novels of

Dostoevsky) progresses and regenerates itself through dialogue, through interaction with the Other, with multiple languages. Similarly Castellanos argues that 'the meaning of a word is its addressee: the other being who hears it . . . and that is only fruitful between those who wish each other to be free' (Ahern, 1988, p. 253).

Castellanos refused a kind of feminism which 'is a demand for equality' because such feminism is no more than 'an acknowledgement of a masculine life style and behaviour as the only feasible ones' (Ahern, 1988, p. 260). Rather, Castellanos prefers to focus on the *distinctive* features of women's lives and culture – the diversity of a 'sportswoman who water-skis at Acapulco' and a servant girl who has just discovered the 'miracle of the automatic blender' rather than to suggest literary universals. The relation between self and other, between rural/urban, educated/uneducated Mexicans informs all of her criticism, plays and poetry. Castellanos wrote criticism as a form of consciousness-raising to enable women to challenge machismo stereotypes of femininity.

GLORIA ANZALDÚA

Although Chicanos are the largest Latino population in the United States, twenty years ago Chicana feminism did not exist as a literary identity. In 1973 the Chicano press, Quinto Sol, devoted an issue of its journal *El Grito* to the work of Chicana writers but it was not until 1975 that the first novel by a Chicana appeared – Berta Ornelas's *Come Down From the Mound*. Gloria Anzaldúa could be said to have created Chicana feminist criticism, editing *This Bridge Called My Back*, the first multiracial and multigeneric collection of writing by women of colour, followed by *Making Face, Making Soul* (1990) and her fine autobiographical literary work, *Borderlands* (1987). Although in the early 1960s, Chicanos attacked the Women's Liberation Movement as a destabilising force in Chicano culture, the past twenty years have seen a flowering of Chicana feminist criticism, fiction and poetry. That there is now explicit attention to Chicana literature (journals such as *Comadre* have feminist issues) is due largely to Anzaldúa's pioneering work.

The study of Chicana culture is doubly difficult for feminist critics. White racist publishing interests combine with Chicano oppression. Chicanas are women in a macho culture and minority figures in a white culture. While Chicano writing is itself a border writing inevitably shaped by two cultures – its own history and that of contemporary society – Chicana critics cross another border, into a feminist culture.

The tension between these different identities 'Chicana', 'writer', 'woman', 'lesbian', 'feminist' is the subject matter of Anzaldúa's criticism. She explores the problems involved in maintaining these different identities in America, and she is also writing in tension with mainstream sources and with European theories. The contradictions and paradoxes created by these juxtapositions make her writing rich and diverse. In varying degrees all three of Anzaldúa's major texts deal with issues central to Third World feminist criticism. The collection *This Bridge Called My Back* has the distinctive features of Third World writing – a use of untranslated words, popular songs, myth and poetry and theoretical discussions. Many of the contributors, including Anzaldúa herself, make clear their disillusionment with white feminism and with any literary hierarchy of favoured genres. The book both confronts racism in the white women's movement, and rewrites the Chicana record by exploding tight disciplinary definitions of marginality. Anzaldúa's work is marked by bilingual heteroglossia, an interweaving of Spanish and English which has become a major feature of Chicana aesthetics. She refuses to be chopped into pieces of feminist, Marxist, intellectual (Anzaldúa, 1987). Instead, she places her multivoiced literary identity on the border of Mexico and Texas. Written in three languages, *Borderlands/La Frontera: the New Mestiza* is a rich exploration of Chicano history and myths, combined with the material lives of migrant farmworkers (her family) together with her lesbian feminist responses to that reality. Her title, like the title *SisterOutsider* by Audre Lorde, suggests that border crossing, or the experience of two cultures, is central to the feminist identities of women of colour and particularly of lesbian women of colour.

What startles the reader immediately in *Borderlands* are Anzaldúa's historical leaps, as she moves back in time to 3500 BC. Naming is a crucial part of this story. Anzaldúa takes her personal history to date from the 1930s, when 'we were jerked out by the roots', but also creates a diachronic history running from pre-Columbia to the United States Mexican war (Anzaldúa, 1987, p. 8). In both histories, Anzaldúa argues, women are especially at risk but women are also bearers of culture and myth. For example, in her history of Coatlalopeuh the serpent goddess (changed by Spain into the Virgin of Guadalupe), she makes the snake into a symbol of the psyche and of instinctual and dark feminine sexuality. Lesbian women have a special capacity here, *la facultad*. Anzaldúa defines *la facultad* as a survival skill, a consciousness or perceptivity, which enables lesbians to read below the surface of any culture. *La facultad* is a particularly appropriate term for all Third World feminist criticism, because as Sandoval argues, Third World criticism is 'capable of disrupting the dominations and subordinations that scar U.S. culture' (Sandoval, 1991, p. 23).

Each time Anzaldúa has to make sense of culture, she has to 'cross over', knocking a hole out of the old boundaries of the self and slipping under or over 'dragging the old skin along . . . a screaming birth' (Anzaldúa, 1987, p. 49). This is a writing obsessed with the substance of bodies. She conflates two separate metaphors: the body as Other, 'an old skin' and the body as a potential site for new ideas, new 'births'. The moment of 'collision' will be a mystical experience. That is to say, by radically refusing her subordinated minority body and constructing a different self beyond racism and sexism, Anzaldúa is involved in an intense inquiry into the characteristics of femininity.

Her work deliberately subverts particular examples of contemporary Western theory. For example, her mirror is a 'door to her soul' not a Lacanian metaphor of objectification and she describes how Mexican Indians made mirrors of obsidian (volcanic glass). In addition, she continually emphasises the importance of sightlessness at moments of key ecstasy – a refusal of the 'gaze'. The distinctive features of Chicana culture – its books, movies, music and food – all have equal space in her text. Each feature is itemised and celebrated, with its own special vocabulary. Like Virginia Woolf in *Three Guineas*, Anzaldúa immaculately footnotes her every claim about Mexican culture. She does not idealise Chicana history: for example, like

Castellanos, Anzaldúa demythologises the historical figures of La Malinche, the Virgin Guadalupe and La Llorona. The title *Borderlands*, then, refers both to the place and to the form of critical writing. Very few critics write so perceptively and so movingly about the *process* of criticism as part of the *content* of their work. What is interesting about Anzaldúa's writing is her ability to feature process syntactically. She divides her text into two halves. Part one is her autobiography interwoven with Chicana history and Part two contains her poetry. Yet the poems themselves become in their sequential linear development an emblematic history of the emerging Chicana writer.

Anzaldúa explores literary identity in a postmodern mixture of poetry, myth, critical catalogues and dramatised speeches. *Borderlands* resists genres in order to cross the boundaries between cultures by continually switching codes. Her autobiographical history comes to stand both for the historical experience of South West Chicano Texans colonised by the Anglos and that mestiza border culture. Her mixture of ethnicities, sexual preferences, and genres is an exciting new Third World feminist writing.

'How To Tame A Wild Tongue' focuses this theme. The essay demonstrates Anzaldúa's trilingualism yet simultaneously problematises the 'I' form because she talks about her entry into *la facultad* in the third person. There are no parenthetic translations and many untranslated words (Anzaldúa, 1987, p. 49). Adopting a Brechtian technique of distancing subtitles – for example 'The Loss of Balanced Opposition and the Change to Male Dominance' – Anzaldúa creates stories of Chicana culture about the dynamics of race, gender, class and lesbianism.

Her subsequent collection *Making Face, Making Soul* (a further anthology of writings by women of colour) makes a similar address to white readers. She aims to teach white critics to read in non-stereotypical ways by again aligning the personal with the theoretical. 'Making face' is Anzaldúa's term for self-construction, a process of stripping away a mask and 'facing' racism. The book is a collection of writings ranging from Audre Lorde's poems to the criticism of Barbara Christian and Trinh T. Minh-ha. In seven sections, it focuses on artists, on racism and on the importance of community alliances.

Anzaldúa's introductory essay focuses on the main themes: racism and resistance and the survival strategies of women of colour. Like her other writing, the essay is a hybrid mixture of academic theory and family stories. She takes us into a Foucault-like topography of the body. The essay is full of body images – the scars of racism and the maps and blueprints of sexual survival – a particularly apt choice since medical risk and injury is much greater for non-white women than for white women in the West today. The essay exemplifies many strategies of Third World feminist criticism: a use of myth, a refusal of literary hierarchy and Otherness. Anzaldúa achieves this mixture through montage, and through a fragmented discourse: all dialogue in *Making Face* is necessarily incomplete. As Anzaldúa argues, the 'listener/reader is forced into participating in the making of meaning – she is forced to connect the dots' (Anzaldúa, 1990, p. xviii).

REY CHOW

Rey Chow was born in Hong Kong and educated both in the East and in America. In Chow's work, the focus shifts markedly to major and innovative questions about theory and Third World representations. Her essay 'Mandarin Ducks and Butterflies' and subsequent essay 'Rereading Mandarin Ducks and Butterflies' (both collected in *Woman and Chinese Modernity: The Politics of Reading Between West and East* (1991)) are startling exposés of Western ethnocentrism.

The book's title flags its main themes. Chow argues that by viewing the Third World as an object – as a set of literary or cultural experiences to be studied – the West misreads Chinese modernism and more importantly misreads women. Western theory – and Chow's specific attack is on Fredric Jameson's 'appropriation' of Chinese culture – denies Eastern writing a complexity, a subjectivity, a modernity and its own cross-cultural appropriation of the West. Chow's reading of Chinese culture and Western appropriations is a strong, subtle analysis of a 'newer' form of Western imperialism, one in which the mappings of cultural theory have replaced earlier Western territorial acquisitions. In her first essay, 'Mandarin Ducks',

Chow describes Butterfly writings as the Mills and Boon, or Harlequin romances, of China: popular stories about love, sexuality and social status. Butterfly writings, Chow claims, act as the 'Other' to Chinese nationalist realism with its positive heroes and heroines. Yet Butterfly writings are themselves authored by writers influenced by the May Fourth Movement (named after a student-led demonstration against foreign occupation) a movement dedicated to a critique of Chinese culture.

Chow's point, and it is subtly put, is that to speak of Western modernity and postmodernity against the 'Other' of nationalistic literatures is absurd and ethnocentric because such a view ignores the way in which all Third World writing is itself continually in interaction with the West and is itself busily constructing a world of 'Others', here Butterfly writing. These Others, Chow argues, are frequently idealised and sensual images of women. The task facing Third World critics, Chow claims, is not to seek out a 'purer' ethnicity which is in any case, as her argument shows, fallacious, but to articulate the specific ways in which ethnicity functions, in terms of cultural predicaments and of possible formations of collective 'identities-in-resistance,' (Chow, 1991, p. xi). This is an unambiguous call to criticism to map the sociohistorical with the private and personal. It is crucial, following Chow, for white Western feminists to recognise a different Third World discourse – that of 'the non-Western, but Westernized, feminist subject' (Chow, 1991, p. 95). For example, Chow's dynamic mixture of psychoanalyis, film theory and literary analysis shows that such disciplines are not the prerogative of the West alone.

The perennial question here is one of gender: why are 'women' – or as Chow puts it when discussing the Chinese films of Bertolucci, 'images-as-feminized-spaces' – so constantly imagined and invoked? The answer, which Chow works towards in the pages of her densely and eclectically determined work, is a Freudian one. That is to say, Chow argues that images of masochistic women in literature and film often represent the threatened nation. In the West, colonised nations have often been mythologised as female in order to excuse the paternal order of a dominating power (see Nasta, 1991, p. xiii).

It is imperative, Chow argues, that critics look for a range of different forms of resistance in writings which we might not conventionally associate with the literary. Hence Chow makes brilliant use of film theory, cultural studies, poststructuralism and postmodernism, theories of ethnicity, Chinese history and literature. Only with multigeneric criticism can we, as Chow hopes, problematise 'the dichotomy between the "realpolitical" non-West and the "imaginative" West' (Chow, 1991, p. xiii). Otherwise the West will continue to associate Third World socioeconomic 'underdevelopment' with an imagined Third World literary underdevelopment, as does postmodernism.

If there is one thing that unifies traditional types of criticism, Chow argues, it is a simultaneous neglect of women and yet the constant invoking of 'woman', or the feminine, as a central object of attention. Chow's two main examples are Bertolucci's film *The Last Emperor* (with its feminisation of Chinese culture) and the critical attack on Butterfly literature.

By focusing on signifiers of 'woman', Chow is able to unsettle the binaries of tradition/modernity, Other/civilised. For example, Chow describes how Butterfly literature consists of sentimental love stories which centre on an unfulfilled love between scholars and beauties where both die of a broken heart. Yet the issues of tradition and subjectivity which the stories invoke cannot be read, Chow argues, either as mere entertainment (although their popularity suggests the issues do respond to unfulfilled personal demands) or obviously as replicas of reality. Such writing must be read as a contestation of language. The second strand of Chow's argument is about how images of the West and China are played out. Traditional criticism portrays the West as sophisticated, theoretical and as having a power and control over literary history and theory. It portrays the East as non-contradictory, as 'pure' ethnicity. The experience of this binary in the East is often gendered. That is to say, Chinese male writers, such as Ba Jin or Mao Dun, often couch their own uncertainties in terms of femininity; in, for example, sensual detail (Chow, 1991, p. 85). Chow instances the Western reception of the Chinese writer Ding Ling (1904–1986) as an example of Western essentialism. Western Chinese scholars, she argues, approve Ding Ling's move to social realism as an example of positive 'Chinese-ness'. The reality of Ling's writing,

Chow demonstrates, is more complex and cannot be evaluated 'teleologically, in terms of progress from "immaturity" to "maturity", from being "Westernised" to being "Chinese" ' (Chow, 1991, p. 97). The issues that surface in Chow's work, are clearly central to Third World criticism.

Although Chow focuses on China's interaction with the West, her analysis of theory's use of 'woman' is significant and of general importance. Chow's account of the feminisation of culture foregrounds questions about popular culture and critical institutions as well as questions about experience and the unconscious. Her work raises the knotty question of the relation between postmodernism and 'women' in the postcolonial context. Postmodernism, Linda Hutcheon argues, has none of the imperialistic imperatives of other schools of criticism because postmodernism pays close attention to differences. Third World writing and postmodernism share a number of characteristics. Both focus on themes of displacement, both interrogate history, both refuse literary hierarchies and binary structures such as subject/Other or negative/positive. Both use textual parody combined with a suspicion of realism. But even these similarities need to be qualified. The assumptions and methods informing postmodernism are rather different from those informing Third World feminist criticism. One major distinction, for example, is the way in which postmodernism constantly denies to Third World writing an unconscious and its literary representation. As Chow argues, postmodernist criticism about the Third World (and here she cites Kristeva's *About Chinese Women* and Fredric Jameson's essays in particular) makes no attempt to apply the techniques of psychoanalysis to Third World texts. Yet psychoanalysis has been a central method of inquiry in contemporary criticism about *Western* writing.

Chow attacks Fredric Jameson's essay 'Third World Literature in the Era of Multinational Capital', but not because Jameson's project is *consciously* ethnocentric. Indeed, Jameson addresses Third World writing in that essay precisely to question Western ethnocentrism and literary hierarchies. He asks criticism to think relationally about global cultures and to establish 'situational differences in cultural production and meanings' (Jameson, 1986, p.88). Yet his argument does not satisfy Chow. Why for example, she asks, should Jameson so sharply distinguish between Third World texts and those of the First World and claim that all Third World texts commonly create or represent national allegories? Why does Jameson ascribe expressiveness to Third World texts alone? Other critics have asked Jameson the same questions and share Chow's unease with the creeping co-options of Western theory: in his essay, 'Jameson's Rhetoric of Otherness and the "National Allegory"', Aijaz Ahmad looks at Jameson's political rather than his literary theories but quickly arrives at Chow's conclusion. Ahmad argues that Jameson is in danger of freezing and de-historicising political forms because he locates capitalism in the West and socialism in the Third World. The absolute of that binary (postmodernism/nationalism) does not permit any space for the idea that Third World writing is not unitary (Ahmad, 1987, p.8).

   Chow points out that Julia Kristeva takes a similar, though gender-specific, tack. In *About Chinese Women* Kristeva is intrigued by her own idea that the Chinese represent a people prior to consumerism, before Western capitalism (Kristeva, 1986, p.12). This delight, Chow argues, stems from Kristeva's need to catch her own favourite moment – the semiotic – on the wing of its formation. Kristeva refuses to see that China is marked by psychic complexities, or that China is marked by interrelation with the West. Kristeva places the semiotic in opposition to a Western symbolic order and 'outside', or repressed in, Western discourse. So that although Kristeva clearly admires China she analyses Chinese culture in terms of specifically feminine features such as footbinding. Kristeva places 'China' in an ideal time and place with its own unique logic in opposition to the sophisticated West. Chow pinpoints exactly how Kristeva 'Others' and feminises the Third World by limiting China to a time before psychoanalysis.

SUMMARY

The expansive critiques of Castellanos, Anzaldúa, Chow and others have developed in response to the West as well as being part of a process of cross-cultural theorising. By exposing how the Other is feminised and ethnicised by the West, denied a subjectivity and an imagination, Third World feminist criticism directly challenges the West. Third World feminist critics argue that it is impossible to classify Third World writing into traditional literary schools or movements isolated in some precise geographic and diachronic place. Third World feminist criticism draws from feminist theory, theories of ethnicity, poststructuralism, popular culture and autobiography in an eclectic trawl designed to map the socioeconomic with the literary. A crude binary opposition between capitalist First World and pre- or non-capitalist Third World tumbles down faced with political complexity. For example, Brazil is a post-colonial country with Third World inflation but shares many of the characteristics of a First World country, such as a sophistic-ated system of higher education. Brazilian feminism grew in close rapport with feminist movements in Paris and London sparked by the activism of returning émigrés and is today intensively reworking French feminist theory (see Humm, 1990). As Norma Alarcón points out in 'Chicana Feminism: In the Tracks of "the" Native Woman', the quest for a fixed identity – the initial aim of the Chicano movement in the 1960s and early 1970s – 'gave way to a realization that there is no fixed identity' (Alarcón, 1990, p. 250). The term 'Chicana' is itself not a name that women are born into but one which is consciously and critically chosen. The notion of a unitary cultural nationalism overlooks the ways in which Chicana working class and intellectuals, to take one obvious example of cultural difference, are differentially marked by multiple experiences of migration, regional variation and particularly by urban/rural communities.

We are at a particular stage in Third World criticism. Because fixed points of reference for all social identities have evaporated with, for example, women's entry into higher education, migration, and the changing pattern of global economics, questions of cultural identity are crucial. In the 1960s it was feminism which first put questions of subjectivity into the field of politics. The 1970s witnessed a shift in political thinking from the notion that a political group could simply mobilise existing identities to a notion that politics and culture involve a repositioning of subjects. This idea necessarily widens definitions of cultural identities and literatures to include the *process* of identification. No longer can we assume that literary history totally represents literary identity.

The reason why questions of identity and difference are so salient and so heterogeneous is that there is a Janus face in all contemporary societies, Third World and First World. We all share a global media network yet retain an attachment to the specifics of ethnicity and place. If there is one contribution which feminist criticism makes to this struggle over identities it is in pointing to positionality. Trinh T. Minh-ha, for example, describes Third World women not in 'mutual enslavement' to a concept of fixed identity but in negotiation with similarities and differences, as when a woman chooses to veil or unveil (see Minh-ha, 1990).

Because Third World writing so often responds to different social, regional, and national groups whose aesthetic interests are very diverse, Third World feminist criticism is necessarily eclectic. Traditional literary criticism offers only two models: a selective incorporation into the existing Western canon or the construction of a separate canon leaving intact the notion that the Western canon is the master. The large and dynamic theories of Third World critics such as Castellanos, Anzaldúa and Chow would make a more fundamental revision of literary studies. By using many disciplines, by iconoclastically attacking Western ethnocentricity, by restoring plural subjectivities to literary history, these critics have created the most provocative feminist criticism of recent years.

SELECTED READING

Basic texts

Ahern, M. (ed.) (1988) *A Rosario Castellanos Reader*, Austin: University of Texas Press

Allen, P. G. (1990) 'Interview', in L. Coltelli (ed.), *Words: American Indian writers speak*, Lincoln: University of Nebraska Press

Allgood, M. F. (ed.) (1990) *Another Way to Be: Selected writings of Rosario Castellanos*, Athens: University of Georgia Press

Anzaldúa, G. (1987) *Borderlands/La Frontera: The new mestiza*, San Francisco: Spinsters/Aunt Lute Book Company

Anzaldúa, G. (ed.) (1990) *Making Face, Making Soul/Haciendo Caras: Creative and critical perspectives by women of color*, San Francisco: Aunt Lute Foundation Books

Bell, D. (1983) *Daughters of the Dreaming*, Sydney: Allen & Unwin

Bell, D. (1991) 'Aboriginal women, separate spaces, and feminism', in S. Gunew (ed.), *A Reader in Feminist Knowledge*, London: Routledge

Chibber, R. S. (1990) 'Patriarchy and the Indian woman poet', *Indian Literature*, 139, xxxiii: 5, (Sept/Oct) pp. 165–79

Chow, R. (1990) *Woman and Chinese Modernity: The politics of reading between west and east*, Minneapolis: University of Minnesota Press

Chow, R. (1991) 'Violence in the other country: China as crisis, spectacle and woman' in Mohanty, C. T., Russo, A. and Torres, L. (eds) *Third World Women and the Politics of Feminism*, Bloomington: Indiana University Press

Coltelli, L. (ed.) (1990) *Words: American Indian writers speak* Lincoln: University of Nebraska Press

Dwivedi, A. N. (ed.) (1984) *Studies in Contemporary Indo-English Verse, Vol. I, A Collection of Critical Essays on Female Poets*, Bareilly: Prakesh Book Depot

Ferrier, C. (1988) 'On "Not Doing Much" on black women writers', *Hecate*, 14:2, pp. 107–9

Ferrier, C. (1990a) 'Resisting authority', *Hecate*, 16:1/2 pp. 102–10

Ferrier, C. (1990b) 'Interview with Pearlie McNeill', *Hecate*, 16:1/2, pp. 134–9

Grewel, S., Kay, J., Landon, L., Lewis, G. and Parmar, P. (eds) (1988) *Charting the Journey: Writings by black and Third World women*, London: Sheba

Gunew, S. (1988a) 'Home and away: nostalgia in Australian (migrant) writing' in P. Foss (ed.) *Island in the Stream: Myths of place in Australian culture*, Sydney: Pluto

Gunew, S. (1988b) 'Authenticity and the writing cure: reading some migrant women's writing', in S. Sheridan (ed.) *Grafts*, London: Verso

Hatzimanolis, E. (1990) 'The politics of nostalgia: community and difference in migrant writing' *Hecate*, 16:1/2, pp. 120–7

Huggins, J. (1991) 'Writing my mother's life', *Hecate*, 17:1, pp. 88–94

Minh-ha, T. (1988) 'Not you/like you: post-colonial women and the interlocking questions of identity and difference', *Inscriptions*, 3/4, pp. 71–9

Minh-ha, T. (1990) *Woman, Native, Other: Writing, post coloniality and feminism*, Bloomington: Indiana University Press

Minh-ha, T. (1992) *When the Moon Waxes Red: Representation, gender and cultural politics*, London: Routledge

Modjeska, D. (1987) *Exiles at Home: Australian women writers 1925–1945*, Sydney: Angus & Robertson

Mohanty, C. T. (1985) 'Under Western eyes: feminist scholarship and colonial discourses', *Boundary*, (12:3/13:1) (Spring/Fall) pp. 333–59

Mohanty, C. T., Russo, A. and Torres, L. (eds) (1991) *Third World Women and the Politics of Feminism*, Bloomington: Indiana University Press

Moraga, C. and Anzaldúa, G. (1981) *This Bridge Called My Back: Writings by radical women of color*, New York: Kitchen Table Press

Pathak, Z. (1992) 'A pedagogy for postcolonial feminists', in J. Butler and J. W. Scott (eds), *Feminists Theorize the Political*, London: Routledge

Pathak, Z. and Rajan, R. S. (1992) 'Shahbano', in J. Butler and J. W. Scott (eds), *Feminists Theorize the Political*, London: Routledge

Sandoval, C. (1982) *Feminism and Racism, the Struggle Within: A report on the 1981 National Women's Studies Association conference*, Oakland, Calif: Center for Third World Organizing

Sandoval, C. (1991) 'US Third World feminism: the theory and method of oppositional consciousness in the postmodern world', *Genders*, 10 (Spring) pp. 1–25

Saunders, J. (1990) 'A writer's friends and associates', *Hecate*, 16:1/2, pp. 90–6

Schipper, M. (ed.) (1985) *Unheard Words: Women and literature in Africa, the Arab world, Asia, the Caribbean and Latin America*, London: Allison & Busby

Sharkey, M. (1990) 'Zora Cross's entry into Australian literature', *Hecate*, 16:1/2, pp. 88–94

Spender, D. (ed.) (1988) *The Penguin Anthology of Australian Women's Writing*, Melbourne: Penguin

Spender, L. (ed.) (1988) *Her Selection: Writings by nineteenth-century Australian women*, Melbourne: Penguin

Wahini, M. (1993) *Ngahuia Te Awekotuku*, Otago, NZ: New Women's Press

Introductions

Ashcroft, B., Griffiths, G. and Tiffin, H. (eds) (1989) *The Empire Writes Back: Theory and practice in post-colonial literatures*, London: Routledge

Bassnett, S. (ed.) (1990) *Knives and Angels: Women writers in Latin America*, London: Zed Books

Chatterjee, L. (1986) *Woman/Image/Text: Feminist readings of literary texts*, New Delhi: Trianka

Chabram, A. and Fregoso, R. L. (eds) (1990) *Cultural Studies: Special issue Chicana/o cultural representations*, 4:3 (October)

Harlow, B. (1987) *Resistance Literature*, London: Methuen

Herrera-Sobek, M. (ed.) (1985) *Beyond Stereotypes: The critical analysis of Chicana literature*, Binghamton, NY: Bilingual Press

Horno-Delgado, A., Ortega, E., Scott, N. M. and Sternback, N. S. (eds) (1989) *Breaking Boundaries: Latina writing and critical readings*, Amherst: University of Massachusetts Press

Inscriptions (1988) *Special Issue: Feminism and the critique of colonial discourse*, 3/4

Nasta, S. (1991) *Motherlands: Black women's writing from Africa, the Caribbean and South Asia*, London: The Women's Press

Further reading

Ahmad, A. (1987) 'Jameson's rhetoric of otherness and the "National Allegory" ', *Social Text*, 17 (Fall), pp. 3–25

Aitken, S. H. (1986) 'Women and the question of canonicity', *College English*, 48, pp. 288–99

Alarcón, N. (1990) 'Chicana feminism: in the tracks of "the" Native Woman', *Cultural Studies: Special issue Chicana/o cultural representations*, pp, 248–57

Castillo, D. (1992) *Talking Back: Toward a Latin American feminist literary criticism*, Ithaca: Cornell University Press

Chowdury, S. (1990) 'An introduction to the women poets of Bangladesh', in *Contemporary Literature from Bangladesh*, London: The South Asian Literature Society

Davies, C. (1991) 'Writing off marginality, minoring and effacement', *Women's Studies International Forum*, 14:4, pp. 249–65

Deleuze, G. and Guattari, F. (1983) *Capitalism and Schizophrenia: Anti-Oedipus*, trans. R. Hurley, M. Seem and H.R. Lane, Minneapolis: University of Minnesota Press

Eisenstein, H. (1985) *The Future of Difference*, New Brunswick, NJ: Rutgers University Press

Gordimer, N. (1985) 'Preface', in E. Kuzweyo, *Call Me Woman*, London: The Women's Press

Head, B. (1985) 'Foreword', in E. Kuzweyo, *Call Me Woman*, London: The Women's Press

Humm, M. (1990) 'An experimental collage, an adventurous college: feminism in Brazil', *Fiction International: Special issue third world women writers*, 19:1 (Fall) pp. 64–72

Jagger, A. (1983) *Feminist Politics and Human Nature*, New York: Roawman and Allanheld

Jameson, F. (1986) 'Third World literature in the era of multinational capital', *Social Text*, 15 (Fall) pp. 65–88

Khan, N. (1992) 'Contemporary Asian women writers', *Daskhat*, 1 (Autumn/Winter) pp. 35–40

Kristeva, J. (1986) *About Chinese Women*, London: Marion Boyers

Menchú, R. (1984) *I, Rigoberta Menchú: An Indian woman in Guatemala*, edited and introduced by E. Burgos-Debray, trans. A. Wright, London: Verso

Mukherjee, M. (1985) *Realism and Reality: The novel and society in India*, Delhi: Oxford University Press

O'Hanlon, R. (1988) 'Recovering the subject: subaltern studies and histories of resistance in colonial South Asia', *Modern Asian Studies*, 22:1, pp. 189–224

Parry, B. (1987) 'Problems in current theories of colonial discourse', *Oxford Literary Review*, 9: 1/2, pp. 27–59

Plager, S. (1983) *Prohibido despertar*, Buenos Aires: Galena

Showalter, E. (1985) *The New Feminist Criticism*, New York: Pantheon

Spivak, G. (1987) *In Other Worlds*, London: Methuen

Uma, A. (1989) *Woman and Her Family: Indian and Afro-American: A literary perspective*, New Delhi: Sterling Publications

Valenzuela, L. (1986) 'The other face of the phallus', in B. G. Chevigny and G. LaGuardia (eds), *Reinventing the Americas: Comparative studies of literature of the United States and Spanish America*, Cambridge: Cambridge University Press

10 Feminist futures

Throughout Europe there is a marked discrepancy between the economic status and the educational status of women. During the last decades women's representation in education has grown enormously but so has our participation in low paid and part-time work. So that, for example, the percentage of women in German higher education has doubled yet the degree of confidence German women express for women in non-traditional jobs is one of the lowest in Europe (see Kaplan, 1992). This discrepancy is more deeply etched into Black and migrant women's lives. Fortress Europe offers few trellises for Black women. Similarly feminist literary criticism has created a lively and substantial body of work in the last decades but continues to exist in a hostile and often marginal academic place. At a time when nationalisms and right-wing politics are being energetically asserted it is even more crucial to assert with equal force a truly gendered, anti-racist reading of culture.

A Reader's Guide addresses a wide range of feminist criticism emerging from these decades of rapid change. It describes how feminist critiques brilliantly interrogate literary assumptions and tries to make clear how cultural politics shape literary conventions. What might be the future of feminist literary criticism seems to me to involve a gendered dynamic of race and scholarship which attends to all women as subjects of literature. Hence, making the subjectivity of the critic part of the subject of criticism has become an important aim for several reasons. First, feminist literary criticism has to be feminist as much as it is literary. It must continually expose the social agencies of literary construction, its own as well as those of traditional critics.

Second, while self-reflexivity cannot in itself become a radical politics, by declaring a 'politics of location' and the differences of race, age, sexuality and class critics can address a wider readership. Finally, and most important, by continually generating new paradigms, new ways of seeing, feminist literary criticism can suggest ideas for new social agencies. There are new and now major axes of explanation. First, there is the work within the African diaspora on matrilineal/matrophobic discourse, spirituality and differing cultural traditions (for example, *Wild Women in the Whirlwind*) as well as the 'creative and critical perspectives of women of color', the subtitle of Anzaldúa's *Making Face, Making Soul*. Second, there are the alliances and radical methodologies coming under the umbrella of queer theory and sexual/political criticism in general. Third, there is the 'decolonisation' of the subject in literary analysis which includes the subjectivity of the critic *textually* within positions of difference. Nor, of course, are these necessarily separate axes since, for example, the essays of Audre Lorde subtly and consistently interweave critical analysis, lesbian autobiography and spirituality within an African diaspora.

In addition, critics often turn the critical text into a battleground of representations by shifting between genres and between subjectivities. 'Representation wars' are not new, of course (see Virginia Woolf's famous battle with the work of her father, Leslie Stephen, in Humm, 1986), but rarely has the battle been so varied and so enjoyable. I should like to conclude by drawing attention to a few of the new weapons wielded by feminist critics; and I should like to suggest that feminist criticism is now much more able to help readers to shed conventional and set responses to literary texts. One reason for this is that contemporary feminist literary criticism itself negotiates between different sign systems – for example, media/ literature; postmodern/decolonial; author/autobiography – and different politics.

Feminist critical anthologies are good examples of the dialectic between political and critical thinking. Anthologies are crucial to a collective voice. Often the contributions to anthologies step outside the conventions of academic 'discourse', taking in autobiography and popular culture; in this way they share a

political collectivity. Writings from feminist anthologies challenge the individualistic author-focused norms of the academy
and often break down the hierarchical ordering of criticism
'above' creative writing (see Jay and Glasgow, 1990, in chapter 8
above, Lesbian feminist criticism). Many collections include the
work of students and can represent the first inklings of what will
become exciting and 'mainstream' feminist thinking in the
future.

Feminist anthologies have undergone a sea change since the
1980s. For example, two white feminist edited collections
published in 1985 are representative of the 1980s approach:
Elaine Showalter's *The New Feminist Criticism: Essays on Women,
Literature and Theory* and Gayle Greene and Coppélia Kahn's
Making a Difference: Feminist Literary Criticism. In these volumes
women's multiple differences of sexuality, race, class and age
were to some extent confined to a single Black feminist essay
and one lesbian feminist essay. By the 1990s the speculative
associations of white feminist critics with critics of Afra-
American and Third World literature (for example, Elly Bulkin,
Minnie Bruce Pratt and Barbara Smith's outstanding *Yours in
Struggle*) had forced feminist literary criticism to re-evaluate the
importance of the political.

What has happened in feminist literary criticism is, therefore,
a microcosm of what has happened to women more generally
outside the academy, in schools, in the media and in the wider
culture. There was a growing interest in feminist criticism from
the 1970s when it became clear that the *meanings* as well as the
causes of women's oppression were much more intransigent
than at first thought.

Like political feminism, critical feminism today is shaped by a
much richer understanding of difference. The recognition of
difference is now one of feminist criticism's major strengths and
has created a new future for critical and theoretical practice.
Theory can no longer be totalising or universal. Contemporary
writers' speculation about the collective differences of 'I' and
celebrations of divergent ethnicities shift the emphasis in
feminist criticism from a monolithic 'woman' to unfixed,
multiple and constantly changing experiences and literatures.
Diversity and deconstruction do not cancel out positives, or a

feminist politics; rather, together, they produce a broader change in knowledge about women.

Feminist politics has always been closely linked to feminist criticism. Campaigns about abortion and sexual violence as much as campaigns about media and cultural representations depend on feminist thinking about subjectivity, the male as cultural norm, and psychological and symbolic representations. Thus, campaigns against the Cruise missile base in Britain (Greenham Common) shared a growing critical concern about gender constructions in technology, the military and scientific language. Feminist criticism is a highly political activity in its belief that change in the cultural arena is a necessary part of any social change.

The work of several Asian and Black writers in Britain – the poets and non-fiction essayists, Grace Nichols, Debjani Chatterjee, Merle Collins and Valerie Bloom, among others – mark very powerful shifts in contemporary culture and criticism. In *Let It Be Told: Black Women Writers in Britain* (1988), Lauretta Ngcobo, Valerie Bloom and others aim to create a sense of culture and community in the face of British racism (see chapter 7, Black feminisms). This text is more distinctly political than traditional critiques and pursues a threefold goal: to range from Jamaican village life to burning issues of international concern, converting humour into protest; to celebrate the long tradition of 'talkers' with roots in African oral art and performance; and to have a clear-eyed and determined sense of women's collectivity particularly involving mothering and the family.

Valerie Bloom has written creatively for many years about traditional Jamaican customs and contemporary British sexual politics. She puts herself firmly into the camp of linguistic innovators arguing that patois touches deep nerve springs and has 'high' value. Bloom's own poetry is indicative of these concerns. Her approach, consolidated by her writing for children, consists in pursuing choral rhythms and musical clues while resisting the temptation to translate these into what Bloom calls 'sub Wordsworthian Romantic pastiche' (Bloom, 1988, p. 85).

Black British writing challenges both white racism and the aridity of much postmodern writing by insisting on the importance of dialect, rhyme and lyric. Black feminism's tement of communal purpose is more than a profession of aith. It is also a realistic evaluation of what is most needed by British Black feminists at this particular moment if Black writing is to validate what Edward Braithwaite calls a 'Nation Language' (Bloom, 1988, p. 87).

Here is a vision of criticism as a politics of identification, not singular identity, and as a sweeping sign of Black self-confidence. British Black feminists' continual double-edged and ironic interaction with Black culture is both feminist and broadly historical. Similarly the Asian writer Debjani Chatterjee gives attention to the multiple women 'victims' of history which include her mother as well as Medusa. These critics focus on matrifocal constants in women's lives and literature, often utilising mythical images and archetypes. In a companion piece in *Let It Be Told* the Guyanese writer Grace Nichols expresses concern about the destructive impact of white myths on the Black psyche and, in 'i is a long memoried woman', creates an alternative priestess figure of complex moods. All of this writing answers the key question – what *is* feminist criticism? – by undoing oppositions such as intellectual/rural, Black/white and the privileged binaries such oppositions carry with them. Other points of comparison among new critical writings devoted to ethnicities and scholarship are critiques in which the words 'feminism' and 'woman' are not flagged or even indexed but which address the uniqueness of gendered experience. A good example here is Shoshana Felman's *Testimony* (1992) a deeply moving account of Holocaust writing and memory co-written with Dori Laub, a psychiatric educator and co-founder of the Video Archive for Holocaust Testimonies at Yale. The book covers a whole spectrum from the literary to the autobiographical, from psychoanalysis to history, and describes the relation between memory/history and narrative/survival at crisis moments when the phenomenon of violence and the phenomenon of culture openly clash. The entire energy of the book is in debt to feminism, where the act of witnessing or writing the Holocaust can never be simply represented or reflected but is reinscribed by readers and witnesses in ways which are inevitably gendered.

Feminist criticism now resists any clean break between theory and practice and refuses to engage in a unitary and masterful deconstruction of texts, in favour of a plurality of readings and writing practices. What is at stake currently, it seems to me, is a complete 're-vision' of what it means to read, and how reading relates to critical understanding. Interesting examples of these innovative readings are those undertaken by the Milan Women's Bookstore Collective first translated as *Sexual Difference: A Theory of Social Symbolic Practice* (1991). The collective is a group of writers and teachers who founded the *Libreria delle Donne* in 1975 and have developed a number of projects. The group's resistance to traditional readings is clear in their practice of '*autocoscienza*', or self-consciousness, and in their intense concern with issues of authority and power. They place great stress on describing, while simultaneously *sharing in*, symbolic communities of women. These are communities which recognise the authority that mother-figures often carry in women's writing. Reading together and 'mothering' each other in the process enables members of the collective to acknowledge psychic roots in female sources of power.

A last example of discursive shifts is the work of Ailbhe Smyth, the Irish essayist and editor. Her 'The Floozie in the Jacuzzi' (1989) starts from the view that feminist criticism should represent no single female voice or female body since traditional Irish writing so frequently equates feminisation with colonisation. In traditional Irish literature women appear only as symbols of national identity. Smyth figures the myths of Mother Ireland and Irish women in the characters of the Floozie, 'The Whore in the Sewer', Bidet Mulligan, the Skivvy in the Sink, Anorexia and Anna Livia Plurability. The title plays off issues of naming and representation imaged by the stereotypical statue of Anna Livia Plurabelle (from Joyce) erected by the Dublin City Corporation in 1987.

Smyth draws a parallel between Joyce's patriarchal representations of women and the colonisation of Ireland which are recreated in metaphors and myths of mothering. Like DuPlessis's 'For the Etruscans' (see Postmodernism in chapter 6) but in a more overtly politicised gesture, Smyth uses a subversive epistemology. She slips between voices. One is autobiographical – the woman who struggles relentlessly with identity, Irishness and womanliness away from Ireland in Greece and France when 'exile' enabled her to 'see' the absence of real women in Irish literature and politics. Another voice is an 'academic' voice which utilises textual analysis and citations.

The double-voiced montage produces a multigeneric essay mixing poems, quotations and Irish history in order to disrupt traditional literary norms. Smyth writes in a form of *écriture féminine*, inviting into her essay a number of parallel voices of Irish women writers (Eavan Boland, Roz Cowman, Eithne Strong, Clare Boylan and many others) as well as the critics Julia Kristeva, Marina Warner and others. Smyth generously shares with her readers (who may not know those writers) some of their energy, historical knowledge and revisionary mythologising. The use of different voices opposes and ruptures traditional criticism and also challenges a traditional Irish aesthetic in which women are silent.

What is striking about all these critics is the element of danger. Their essays are intertextual, witty and daring. They all situate themselves against/within national/ethnic traditions yet all reveal a remarkable ability to illuminate new ways of thinking and writing. As a result literary criticism – the activity of textual *analysis* – and literary creativity – *the expression* of female experience come together. The 'body' of each essay acts as a container both for the critical practice and experiential testimony which erases the distinctions between fiction and criticism. Experimental writing is always a sign of impending cultural shifts. Feminist literary criticism is moving towards the year 2000 cutting a swathe through social history, psychoanalysis and popular culture as well as through the literary canon.

Feminist literary critics have confronted many issues in the last decades: how to celebrate the Mrs Browns as well as difficult theory; how to address racism and homophobia; how to gain a place in the academy without losing a place in women's worlds. The main theme is constant: how is women's literary subjectivity constructed stereotypically as well as positively and how can representations be deconstructed and reconstituted? Just as political groupings and nationalisms are changing rapidly in Europe and elsewhere, so the cultural and political alignments and agendas of feminist criticism are far more plural and open, potentially more creative, than any we have ever known.

SELECTED READING

Bloom, V. (1988) 'Valerie Bloom', in L. Ngcobo (ed.) *Let It Be Told*, London: Virago

Bulkin, E., Pratt Bruce, M., and Smith, B. (1984) *Yours in Struggle: Three feminist perspectives on anti-semitism and racism*, Brooklyn, NY: Long Haul Press

Cicogna, P. and de Lauretis, T. (eds) (1991) *Sexual Difference: A theory of social symbolic practice*, Bloomington: Indiana University Press

Felman, S. and Laub, D. (1992) *Testimony: Crises of witnessing in literature, psychoanalysis, and history*, London: Routledge

Greene, G. and Kahn, C. (eds) (1985) *Making a Difference: Feminist literary criticism*, New York: Methuen

Humm, M. (1986) *Feminist Criticism: Women as contemporary critics*, Hemel Hempstead: Harvester Wheatsheaf

Kaplan, C. (1992) *Contemporary Western European Feminism*, Sydney: Allen & Unwin

Showalter, E. (ed.) (1985) *The New Feminist Criticism: Essays on women, literature and theory*, New York: Pantheon

Smyth, A. (1989) 'The floozie in the jacuzzi', *Irish Review*, 6 (June) pp. 7–24.

Index

Notes: 1. References to women and critics are ubiquitous and have therefore largely been omitted; 2. Major references are indicated by emboldened page numbers

will, optimism of, 129
Williams, R., 83
Williamson, J., 40
Winnicot, D., 117, 126
Winterson, J., 216
witch-burning, 236
Wittig, M., **98–9**, 108, 114, 222–3, 225, 247
Wolff, C., 232
Wolff, J., 160
Wollstonecraft, M., 87–8, 221, 244
women, *see* preliminary note to index
Woolf, V., 2, 4, 5, 10, 12, 22, 109, 138, 291; Black feminism, 186, 193; deconstruction, 150–1; lesbians, 216, 226, 231, 239, 241; Marxist/

socialism, 78, 79, 82, 83; myth, 58, 59, 65, 68; postmodernism, 162–4; psychoanalysis, 124, 126, 127; second wave, 36, 38; Third World, 261, 274, 277
Worpole, K., 85
Wright, R., 184
Wycherley, W., 230
Wynter, S., 206

Yeats, W.B., 55, 151, 153
Yourcenar, M., 98

Zimmerman, B., 20, 25, 215–16, 217, 224, **227–9**, 230, 233, 247